In the Wake of the Sun

In the Wake of the Sun

Navigating the Southern Works of
Cormac McCarthy

Christopher J. Walsh

Newfound Press
THE UNIVERSITY OF TENNESSEE LIBRARIES, KNOXVILLE

In the Wake of the Sun: Navigating the Southern Works of Cormac McCarthy
© 2009 by Christopher J. Walsh

Digital version at www.newfoundpress.utk.edu/pubs/walsh

Newfound Press is a digital imprint of the University of Tennessee Libraries. Its publications are available for non-commercial and educational uses, such as research, teaching and private study. The author has licensed the work under the Creative Commons Attribution-Noncommercial 3.0 United States License. To view a copy of this license, visit <http://creativecommons.org/licenses/by-nc/3.0/us/>.

For all other uses, contact:

Newfound Press
University of Tennessee Libraries
1015 Volunteer Boulevard
Knoxville, TN 37996-1000
www.newfoundpress.utk.edu

ISBN-13: 978-0-9797292-7-0
ISBN-10: 0-9797292-7-0

Walsh, Christopher J., 1968-
    In the wake of the sun : navigating the southern works of Cormac McCarthy / by Christopher J. Walsh.
Knoxville, Tenn. : Newfound Press, University of Tennessee Libraries, c2009.
    xxiii, 376 p. : digital, PDF file.
    Includes bibliographical references (p. [357]-376).
    1. McCarthy, Cormac, 1933- -- Criticism and interpretation. I. Title.

PS3563.C337 Z943 2009

Book and cover design by Jayne Rogers
Cover image by Andi Pantz

I dedicate this book to my mother, Maureen Lillian Walsh, and to the memory of my father, Peter Anthony Walsh (1934-2000), as their hard work and innumerable sacrifices made all of this possible.

Contents

Foreword ix

Acknowledgments xix

Introduction xxi

Note on the Text xxv

Chapter 1: Contexts 1

Chapter 2: The Short Stories 27

Chapter 3: *The Orchard Keeper* 45

Chapter 4: *Outer Dark* 97

Chapter 5. *Child of God* 143

Chapter 6: *Suttree* 179

Chapter 7: *The Road* 253

Chapter 8: *The Stonemason* 295

Chapter 9: *The Gardener's Son* 323

Conclusion 353

Bibliography 357

Foreword

At the appearance of this addition to scholarship on Cormac McCarthy, the published contribution to American Literature by that writer runs to ten novels, a screenplay, a stage play, and his recent "novel in dramatic form," *The Sunset Limited*. Texas State University at San Marcos has archived a comprehensive collection of McCarthy's papers, including drafts of all these works, three unpublished screenplays, and at least early drafts of three novels as yet also unpublished. McCarthy's first fiction, set in the American South, earned him the Ingram-Merrill Award for 1959 and 1960. Over the intervening fifty years, he has been awarded a Rockefeller Foundation Grant (1966-68), a Guggenheim Fellowship (1969), a MacArthur Fellowship—the popularly-known "genius award" (1981), the National Book Award for *All the Pretty Horses* (1992), and the Pulitzer Prize for Fiction for his latest novel, *The Road* (2007). That last book's remarkable adaptation to film bears witness to many truths, both unsettling and reaffirming. Despite the filmmakers' intelligent use of several locales and the aid of computer-generated editing, one scene, uncannily echoing its source, reminds us of a basic truth in McCarthy's writing: however universal the range of his achievement, McCarthy began as, and in *The Road* became again, a Southern writer.

Christopher Walsh's organization of a conference centered on *The Road* made precisely this point. *The Road Home: McCarthy's Imaginative Return to the South* included a detailed tracing of the route of that novel's father and son by Walsh's colleague, Wes Morgan; it seems that walking the route of the novel in the real world would take one directly through the settings of McCarthy's first four novels. Before reaching the sea, one would have been able to pause and reach out and touch the home of the author, just across the river from most of Knoxville, Tennessee. Sadly, that home has since burned to the ground. The man in the novel, no less than his creator, needs to return to the site of his origins before moving on. Walsh's paper for that conference, "The Post-Southern Sense of Place in *The Road*," argued that McCarthy's work reaches an imaginative vision of the American South that enables a larger mythology of America, and even connects to America's troubled branching overseas.

The roots of McCarthy's American South, as our collective scholarship on this author began to realize through emerging details from McCarthy's life, seem to be more localized than we once thought. From the names of his characters to their relentless drive away from their homes, McCarthy's stories reflect, as if through a prism, an imaginative overlay, a vision drawn on top of places one might still walk, in the postage stamp of hills and flooded valleys in which the young Charles McCarthy Jr. (before he changed his name to that of the Irish king Cormac) grew up. Astonished by Walsh's ability to connect a deep theoretical and textual reading of the Southern novels to broader concerns of interest to McCarthy scholars, I was happy to hear that he was working on a book. Recognition of McCarthy's work finally grows apace with his production of it, and it becomes all the more important to revisit the earlier works, as well as to frame his later novels in terms of the region from which he, and those still-astonishing first four books, arose.

With the 2007 Knoxville conference, Walsh simultaneously accomplished a feat that might go unnoticed by a few readers of this book, but one of which we might take note for posterity. In the wake of devastated budgets for academic travel, and facing the sad fact that many conferences were attended only by specialized scholars whose

FOREWORD

papers were accepted for presentation, we had seen a troubling diminishment in the liveliness once afforded by academic conferences (particularly after September 11, 2001). Too often, conferences consist of insular panels, three or four people taking turns reading to each other but with little real interaction among participants, possibly no audience beyond presenters, and most distressing to some of us, likely no one from outside academia in attendance. Trends in scholarly publishing had meanwhile erected more formidable obstacles to scholarship finding the audience it deserves. The Newfound Press arose to meet these challenges, first by electronically publishing the proceedings of the 2007 conference, which they also videotaped and made available by streaming video. Walsh's conference not only drew many scholars beyond those reading, but also welcomed a remarkable number of lay people interested in McCarthy—Knoxville authors but also Knoxville area *readers*, and some from much farther away. His success organizing the Knoxville proceedings (one of the strongest collections of papers given at any of the roughly two dozen conferences at which I have heard offerings on McCarthy) was therefore extended virtually by Newfound Press to an even wider audience. Newfound's forward-thinking initiatives in electronic publishing, and in the asynchronous offering of proceedings to audiences unable to travel to particular conferences, have expanded the audience for scholarship on authors of interest to all serious readers. Walsh's earlier accomplishments therefore find a suitable culmination in the publication of this book by Newfound Press. When I had a chance to read his argument in full, I was delighted by the experience.

FOREWORD

In the Wake of the Sun: Navigating the Southern Works of Cormac McCarthy achieves a critical step in understanding this difficult contemporary writer's place in the literature and culture of the American South, as well as his place in post-WWII American fiction. Walsh's writing welcomes all those interested in this remarkable novelist and dramatist, from lay readers to high school teachers and students, undergraduates and their professors, and serious scholars of McCarthy from the graduate level up. As if following the model of his subject, Walsh may send some readers to the dictionary from time to time, but the trip proves worthwhile, and Walsh's language remains accessible to anyone already willing to take on the challenges posed by McCarthy's often disturbing subjects and sometimes difficult style.

Within McCarthy criticism, this book fills an obvious need: with the exception of the earliest journal articles and Vereen Bell's *The Achievement of Cormac McCarthy* (the first full-length study at that time), the Southwestern novels have received much more attention than have the Southern works. The major exceptions to this general situation were articles by Dianne Luce and Edwin Arnold; Luce's recent *Reading the World: Cormac McCarthy's Tennessee Period* could accompany this study well, though Arnold has not had time for a book-length work on McCarthy. At a time when some recent books on McCarthy (unnecessary to mention here) fail disturbingly even to suggest a passing familiarity with the half century of McCarthy scholarship that preceded them, Walsh admirably builds his argument without ignorance of the critical foundations laid by Bell, Arnold, Luce, and so many others. Walsh's wise attention to the writing of these scholars adds greatly to this volume, and yet he accomplishes a larger aim that runs far beyond a mere review of existing scholarship.

FOREWORD

That Walsh so fully realizes his own vision serves as proof that no matter the theoretical (or often merely political) aims of other critics, an open-minded reading of all the serious work on a subject need not impede one's desire to cover new territory. Lay readers should not be put off by Walsh's thoroughness; they will want to follow the paths he includes with his footnotes. Indeed, I wish I had done as good a job of referencing the many excellent writers on McCarthy everywhere that I might have, as this book regularly does. The inclusion of Peter Josyph especially redresses a regular absence of references to this perceptive McCarthy critic. Nonetheless, this is a good place to note that Walsh avoids the distractions of internecine tangles of counter-argument that plague criticism on some contemporary authors. Perhaps the hardest thing I teach students is how to engage other critics meaningfully and fairly—even the best scholars are vulnerable to the temptations simply inherent in grammatical constructions that lead to misreading and or misrepresenting the arguments of others. This book, by contrast, plays fair, and the argument achieved gains the power of the other voices allowed in conversation with Walsh's close reading as much as with his larger critical endeavor.

This book's attention to the haunting of *Suttree* by the historical realities of the Tennessee Valley Authority adds enormously to our knowledge, greatly extending William Prather's first work on it and my own slightly different attention to an overwhelming influence on McCarthy's fourth novel. Walsh in general handles historical evidence more expertly than many and in more depth than other arguments understandably can always allow. I can only assume that other McCarthy scholars will feel as I do: not only fairly represented but grateful. On more than one occasion, Walsh clarifies my argument more than I could. In all these matters of successful incorporation of secondary evidence for an argument aiming ultimately at a tertiary reading, this book's organization, where each "Overview of Critical Responses" stands apart from close readings, will of course be quite handy to undergraduates and beginning graduate students, and to other readers as introduction to the existing criticism.

At the tertiary level to which Walsh aims, this book explores the "hybridity" of McCarthy's work, and wrestles with other concepts generally identifiable under the rubric of postmodernism, particularly where we think we are when we refer to "the American South." Walsh nonetheless backs his argument with natural language, examples from the primary texts, or incorporation of a secondary or tertiary text's helpful change in voice. His use of theory (Lefebvre as a choice for discussions of space shows excellent judgment, for instance) helps, rather than hinders his argument. In general, the practical value of this work—as a guide to classrooms, but also as an entry in the under-appreciated form of practical criticism—runs side by side at ease with its more challenging points.

Work on McCarthy naturally poses several tough, though not insurmountable, problems in terms of genre and theory. Indeed, book-length studies of this author can fail to live up to their highest aspirations because one or another theoretical concern or overarching interpretive problem leads to misreading a particular passage or even an entire book. Instead, Walsh's aim to guide readers means attending to divisions of genre that are natural—or at least, unavoidable—in classrooms, and he is particularly good at placing McCarthy's work both in space and time in ways that will be helpful to undergraduates and teachers. Similarly, Walsh's negotiation of categories proved helpful to me, especially as my own ability to locate works in their historical and generic contexts remains a weakness among my critical abilities. Walsh's location of McCarthy's achievement within the context of Southern literature and culture helps me greatly, in my classrooms and outside them. A critical practice less carefully framed than this one of course runs the opposite risk (and this explains most of the failures in my own work on McCarthy) of trying to say too many things about the work in too many ways—the ever-present danger of interdisciplinarity. This book's focus remains one of its chief values, yet the author writes with a rhetorical ear to the variety of ways in which we read McCarthy. Walsh similarly and deftly anticipates the several common modes of resistance to McCarthy's work, as well as those readings that notably stretch a bit far from the novels in order to find home in more theoretical landscapes; he thereby moves to more nuanced, and therefore sounder, reading. That tactic should make the book again especially valuable to some undergraduates and most graduate students: the critical offerings otherwise plopped into their laps might lead them astray, as if squeezing novels through the sausage grinder of one or another fashionable trend in one's discourse community has much to do with understanding.

Walsh educated this reader more fully on Southern literature and culture in general without limiting his understanding of McCarthy to those terms which best serve that purpose. This seems to me a remarkable feat (I simply do not see it done very often.), as criticism—especially when attempting to avail itself of theory while remaining true to creative achievements—may also fall behind its subjects precisely because we critics must claim smaller postage stamps to examine than are allowed artists. As Richard Pevear and Larissa Volokhonsky remark in the introduction to their translation of *Crime and Punishment*, we regularly make the mistake, when speaking outside a novel of a novel, of speaking "monosemantically of the polysemous"* (viii).

This book rather accomplishes that most difficult and therefore honorable task of allowing the reader to see those parts of the evidence that might not most easily fit his thesis; he thereby proves more convincingly what does fit, and furthermore, that understanding McCarthy in terms of his locations and their histories need not be done at the expense of appreciating the universality of his work. Whether or not the early novels were meant to perform a critique of Agrarianism, I certainly learn more from Walsh about the differences between McCarthy's Southern works and those of many other Southern writers. Indeed, wherever I might focus on McCarthy as a Southern writer—and Walsh has me convinced to think more regularly of McCarthy in those terms—I will turn to this book first. Those programs that most regularly teach literature by period and place will benefit enormously from inclusion of this book on reading lists for undergraduate and graduate work. Scholars specializing in literature of the South will similarly benefit from those parts of the argument where McCarthy's works finally find their place alongside other—and often newer, not only older—novels already accepted through or beyond healthy revisions to the canon.

Walsh's readings at the sentence level are most persuasive, and they suitably join the already formidable amount of valuable work on McCarthy. His tertiary sources (his theoretical, generic, and historical texts) move back in where most helpful, in an argument blessedly free

---

* Dostoevsky, Fyodor. *Crime and Punishment: A Novel in Six Parts with Epilogue.* "Foreword." Trans. and annotated, Richard Pevear and Larissa Volokhonsky. New York: Knopf, 1992, vii-xx.

from jargon. Beyond studies of McCarthy and scholarship specific to the literature and culture of the American South, this work serves as a model for future critics, as the author does not back down from engaging philosophical problems in these primary works that cannot be fully treated in terms of region, history, or literary movement.

Ultimately, Walsh should serve as a model for students and scholars, and should help serious readers of McCarthy deepen their understanding of this difficult yet rewarding writer. From the ground beneath that novelist's feet to his remarkable sentences, to Walsh's rewarding close readings and his admirable inclusion of other scholars, to his larger regional and generic concerns and the broader scope of history, *In the Wake of the Sun* follows its subject well. It will reward anyone interested enough in McCarthy to follow the paths behind those of his restless characters.

Jay Ellis
Boulder, Colorado
December, 2009

Acknowledgments

I would like to express my gratitude to scholars such as Edwin Arnold, Rick Wallach, Dianne Luce, Jay Ellis, David Holloway, and Georg Guillemin whose insightful work on McCarthy has made this work possible. I am particularly grateful to Wes Morgan whose knowledge, friendship, and generosity have been invaluable, especially during my time at the University of Tennessee. My colleagues in the English Department at UT were a constant source of encouragement, and the members of staff of the John C. Hodges Library have been enormously helpful.

This project owes a particular debt of gratitude to the Newfound Press. I am especially grateful to Linda Phillips whose unflagging enthusiasm for Cormac McCarthy-related projects (including the 2007 conference hosted by the university) has been a constant source of inspiration. I would also like to acknowledge the excellent level of editorial support provided by Newfound Press, especially Casie Fedukovich and Marie Garrett.

I owe many things to many people, especially since returning to England from the states in the summer of 2008. I would especially like to thank Elizabeth Every, Lawrie Fogg, and Jane Jenkins for their hospitality, and my brother Peter for his support and encouragement. Thanks are also due to Edward Heneghan and Antony "Cheech" Prior. I would also like to thank former colleagues Dr. Alan Bilton, Dr. Duncan Campbell, Dr. Craig Phelan, and Dr. Richard Watermeyer for their advice and informed suggestions. I am also grateful to an extent that cannot be acknowledged enough here to my wife Nikki, especially for her characteristic kindness and optimism.

Introduction

This book is designed to be an introductory guide to Cormac McCarthy's Southern works for teachers, undergraduates, postgraduates, and serious lay readers. Each chapter will offer close readings of McCarthy's primary Southern texts including his two early short stories, the novels (*The Orchard Keeper, Outer Dark, Child of God, Suttree*, and his 2007 Pulitzer Prize winning novel *The Road*), the screenplay *The Gardener's Son* and his play *The Stonemason*. Each chapter will also provide an overview of the critical responses to the texts and appropriate cultural and historical contexts.

McCarthy's work has a reputation for being complex and at times seemingly opposed to any kind of interpretation, and whilst it is undoubtedly connected to place, it also resonates beyond place. Perhaps above anything else, McCarthy's texts are characterized by their hybridity, and they can be simultaneously funny, brutal, and gruesomely violent, often within the same novel, chapter, or passage. His work includes elements of conventional mimetic narratives, yet his use and subversion of mythic techniques consistently transcends his use of conventional realistic strategies, and this study will explore the tensions generated by this hybridity. When teaching or discussing his work with students and first-time readers a sense of bafflement and frustration is often paramount, and it is the intention of this study to attempt to ease such responses. His work invites and yet denies neatly packaged readings, and it remains nothing less than vibrant and engaging, even in the early stages of his artistic development; indeed, Georg Guillemin is one of many critics who has remarked upon this, noting that "there is no way to retell the novels

INTRODUCTION

of Cormac McCarthy in a way that would make them more accessible, less multifaceted."[1]

It is the multifaceted nature of his work that makes it so rewarding, and this study will discuss the major themes and questions that his Southern works explore; in no way does it claim to offer the definitive, all-encompassing readings of the texts under discussion. The opening chapter will provide an overview of the relevant aesthetic, cultural, and historical debates and contexts which allow us to better situate and understand these texts and it will also discuss McCarthy's relationship with Southern and Appalachian literary and cultural narratives. The artistic and intellectual culture of the mountain South is mired in paradox and contradiction and McCarthy's work exhibits a respect for this distinctive Southern culture. However, he is also acutely aware that the culture he is celebrating is also disappearing, a fact that often accounts for the profound sense of melancholy that operates in his work. The introductory chapter will also attempt to outline McCarthy's relationship to the novelistic tradition itself, a vitally important task that will help us to chart McCarthy's relationship to the genre and other important practitioners of it. Issues addressed here will include McCarthy's relationship to the Jamesian school (a tradition he expressed a disliking for in an interview from the early 1990s) and the repercussions this has in terms of his use of psychology and interiority. This chapter will also discuss McCarthy's use of allegory, a conventional—if highly ambiguous—narrative strategy that is entirely in keeping with his challenging and multifaceted aesthetic.

Each subsequent chapter will be organized around a close reading of the primary texts, including a consideration of their narrative

---

[1] Guillemin, *The Pastoral Vision*, 142.

design and structuring principles, along with offering an overview of the pertinent critical debates surrounding them. I will work though the texts according to genre and their chronological order in the hope that this will provide readers with an overview of McCarthy's developing style and concerns. One of my objectives here is to attempt to outline how these texts speak back to each other over the course of a career and, where necessary, allusions will also be made to McCarthy's Western and Southwestern works. The Southern themes to be discussed in relation to these works include McCarthy's treatment of foundational Southern and Appalachian myths, his critique of pastoral and Agrarian philosophy, his use of gothic and grotesque motifs and, specifically in *Suttree,* his depiction of the Southern urban and metropolitan experience.

From his early short stories and his debut novel onwards, McCarthy has been involved in a process which dissents, critiques, and records the complex interaction of myth and history in fictional form, and his interest in this relationship secures his place as one of the foremost contemporary American authors. As Kenneth Millard has observed, "the United States has a history in which myth and mediation were crucially involved right from the beginning, so that writing has a special place in the formation of a national identity that became American."[2] McCarthy's aesthetic—much like the region that inspired this collection of works—continues to be a complex, paradoxical, and yet ultimately rewarding cultural site, and these texts reveal how much these myths and cultural narratives have given McCarthy and, in turn, how much he has contributed to their continuing development and relevance.

---

[2] Millard, *Contemporary American Fiction,* 5.

Note on the Text

Footnotes are provided to guide readers to bibliographic information for the secondary sources used in this study. A complete bibliography is included at the end of the manuscript.

Primary sources are referenced using in-text citations. The list of abbreviations for the primary texts is as follows:

"Wake for Susan":	WFS
"A Drowning Incident":	ADI
The Orchard Keeper:	TOK
Outer Dark:	OD
Child of God:	COG
Suttree:	S
Blood Meridian:	BM
The Crossing:	TC
The Road:	TR
The Stonemason:	TS
The Gardener's Son:	TGS

CHAPTER 1

Contexts

Until mid-2007, Cormac McCarthy had a reputation for being a reclusive figure who didn't like to talk about writing anywhere or at any time; indeed, he was a shadowy, marginal figure who haunted the periphery of the literary scene, much like one of his characters who operate on the margins of their own culture. His work had been a critical if not commercial success until this point, as his novels prior to the National Book Award winning *All The Pretty Horses* sold poorly despite receiving plaudits from figures such as Saul Bellow, who praised McCarthy's use of language and his ability to write "life-giving and death-dealing sentences."[1]

Despite his reluctance to undertake book tours, grant interviews, and appear publicly to speak about his work, McCarthy has provided us with some vitally important clues as to how we might approach his fiction, and one of these appeared in the interview he granted to Richard Woodward in the *New York Times* in 1992. In this interview, McCarthy claimed that good writers (which according to his definition include Melville, Dostoevsky, and Faulkner) are those who "deal with issues of life and death," and their influence can be clearly seen in his work, where death itself at times seems to be the central theme or protagonist. Tellingly, McCarthy goes on to discuss some writers for whom he never quite garnered a similar appreciation, who never conformed to his stringent criteria of what literature is and what it

---

[1] Quoted in Jarrett, *Cormac McCarthy*, 5.

should do. Significantly Henry James is one of the writers who McCarthy has never quite been able to see what all the fuss is.[2]

McCarthy's stated dislike of James is worth considering as it represents a tradition of the novel which he writes against to an extent. At this juncture we encounter one of the many ironies and contradictions in McCarthy's work, as a dismissal such as this may suggest that McCarthy has no time for the novel in the grandly serious Jamesian mode, that he believes the form has exhausted itself, and all that is left for a contemporary novelist is perhaps the ironic and self-conscious modes afforded by postmodernism. This couldn't be further from the truth as McCarthy maintains a belief in the humanistic potential of the novel and in its ability to "encompass all the various disciplines and interests of humanity," even as his themes and form so often tend to undermine such a belief.[3] Therefore, whilst his belief in the novelistic form remains, his faith in its traditional ability to maintain any kind of representative authority is increasingly challenged as his aesthetic develops. Specifically, one of the novelistic traditions which McCarthy consistently subverts—and which causes a large amount of frustration amongst readers and students—is his apparent refusal to grant any sense of interiority to his characters, a refusal to provide any kind of psychological motivation or ordering principle. As Rick Wallach perceptively notes, McCarthy "rarely admits us into the sanctuaries of his character's minds," which may be for the best, given the monstrous nature of some of his protagonists.[4]

---

[2] Woodward, "Cormac McCarthy's Venomous Fiction," 5.
[3] Ibid., 3.
[4] Wallach, "The McCarthy Canon Reconsidered," xviii.

This is where perhaps McCarthy differs most significantly from the Jamesian mode. James had a very clear idea about a writer's responsibilities and the subsequent shape and form that a novel should take, and he articulates them most urgently in "The Art of Fiction." In this essay James argues that novelists should grant their readership interior psychological insight and that a chief objective of writers should be to provide "the very atmosphere of the mind" of their characters for their readers.[5] This is not to say that we are unable to read the psychology of McCarthy's characters or that his narratives are entirely free of revealing the anxieties, punctured hopes, and troubled motivations of his protagonists; rather, McCarthy reveals this sense of interiority primarily through his description of landscape and natural phenomena. Jay Ellis has made the following insightful comments about this foundational element of McCarthy's style:

> McCarthy relies more on setting than on plot, or even character ... It is in the 'high passages' of McCarthy's style, especially in his descriptions of outer weather—of setting—that we may extrapolate from the style some sense of a character's interiority. McCarthy's descriptive modes therefore enable the inference of psychology in a style that refuses (usually) to indulge in standard psychological techniques, such as first person, interior monologue, free indirect discourse, or even direct indications of psychology by a narrator.[6]

---

[5] James, "The Art of Fiction," 559.
[6] Ellis, *No Place for Home*, 1-2.

Another significant departure from the Jamesian technique of psychological realism which we find in McCarthy's work is with his use of allegory and mythic archetypes. John Cant has remarked upon this aspect of McCarthy's work by acknowledging that "mythic characters do not exist to be repositories for psychological motivation. They are representative of large generalized ideas, values, and aspects of culture."[7] East Tennessee has furnished McCarthy with a series of mythic and allegorical narratives to employ and manipulate in his fiction from his debut novel to his Pulitzer Prize winning *The Road*, and his use of mythic and allegorical tropes infuse his Southern work with a vision and pathos which is epic in scope. Like Faulkner and the very best regionalists McCarthy uses this "postage stamp of native soil" to inform an artistic vision which transcends the local or regional.[8]

But what of allegory in all of this? Moreover, what do we mean by allegory, and how does McCarthy employ this technique? Allegory is a traditional mode which, in some regards, is in line with the radical instability that postmodern or poststructuralist readings encourage us to undertake. In *Allegory: the Dynamics of an Ancient and Medieval Technique*, Jon Whitman claims that "allegory is the most elusive of techniques," as it is "always pointing toward a goal that lies beyond it, [it] is forever having to come to terms with its own provisionality."[9] In the conventional definition, allegory "provides an initiation into a mystery," and it is directly into such mysteries that McCarthy's fiction takes us, situating us as readers (especially in

---

[7] Cant, *Cormac McCarthy and the Myth of American Exceptionalism*, 11.

[8] William Faulkner, interview with Jean Stein Vanden Heuval, 1956, in Meriwether and Millgate, *Lion in the Garden*, 255.

[9] Whitman, *Allegory*, 13.

Outer Dark) in the gap or separation of the *fiction* of a text from the *truth* or concealed meaning of the text.[10]

At this juncture it is useful to remind ourselves of Georg Guillemin's comment that was cited in the Introduction: How do we "retell" a body of work as rich as McCarthy's without becoming crudely reductive? How do we do justice to an oeuvre that is so multifaceted? The works under consideration here fully reveal the stylistic and thematic range of McCarthy's aesthetic. His debut novel *The Orchard Keeper* announces the hybridity of his style that would characterize all of his work, even when he made the physical and imaginative move westward. *Outer Dark* almost entirely dispenses with mimetic techniques as McCarthy develops his gift for manipulating allegorical form, whereas *Child of God* is written in a stripped-down, economical style which hints at much of his later work, including *No Country for Old Men* and *The Road*. *Suttree*, for all of its existential angst and the death-haunted phantasmagoric ruminations of its eponymous protagonist, has moments of boisterous, subversive humor where one can see the influence of Southwestern humorists such as George Washington Harris. In comparison, *The Road* has a cinematic quality which brings a certain clarity to the novel which is at odds with the gray, ash-laden landscape traveled in the text itself.

We can begin to see, even without close analysis of the primary texts themselves, how complex McCarthy's aesthetic can be. In his refusal to allow his readers to view the psychological interiority of his characters in a conventional manner, instead preferring to transpose this onto his descriptions of landscape, place, and all kinds of natural phenomena, McCarthy establishes his preference for creating mythic and allegorical types rather than fully formed mimetic

---

[10] Ibid., 2.

protagonists. These techniques have contributed to a style that is complex, epic, and unsettling. Moreover, one of our main interests here is to explore how McCarthy's critique of the myths bestowed by Southern culture—but more specifically, Southern Appalachian culture, which is perhaps a somewhat self-evident but crucial distinction—accounts for the enduring power of his work inspired by that region.

McCarthy and the Southern Tradition: An Overview

Any attempt to contextualize a body of work as rich and varied as McCarthy's and relate it to an imaginative, intellectual, and cultural legacy as equally rich and varied as that bestowed by the South is problematic. Indeed, an investigation of this nature warrants a book-length study in its own right. Nevertheless, it is important that we address some fundamentally important questions at this stage. How are we defining what we regard as the South for our purposes here? What repercussions does (or should) the distinction between "Cotton" and Mountain South have for our discussion, and how does that distinction impact McCarthy's relationship to the region? We have already indicated that McCarthy's work has an aesthetic range that in many respects resembles that of the high modernists, so how do we relate that to the foundational concerns of Southern literature such as community, tradition, and a sense of place, which seem so un-modernistic? What of race and gender in McCarthy's work? His work is most definitely marked out by a post-Southern Renascence flavor, but does this automatically make him a postmodernist? What of his treatment of pastoral and Agrarian philosophy, concepts that dominate so many of the discussions concerning Southern literature throughout the period when McCarthy has been writing and publishing?

One of the most important contemporary developments in the study of Southern literature and culture (in keeping with other such movements in the humanities and cultural studies) has been an increase in skeptical inquiries into the historically constructed and seemingly regionally sanctioned notion of a settled, stable, and homogenous South. Such ideas were propagated by groups within and beyond the South, especially through a series of movies and television shows which reinforced ideas of a backward, benighted South and which associated the region with images of poverty and crudely reductive stereotypes.[11] Conversely, the settled, unchanging, and inherently noble myth of the Old South has been championed in the work of some of the genuine intellectual heavyweights of the twentieth-century South—such as the Nashville Agrarians, including Allen Tate, Donald Davison, John Crowe Ransom, et al.—who claimed that only a return to the mythically settled (and quixotically imagined) anti-acquisitive and anti-industrial agrarian way of life could reverse what they saw as the nation's inevitable move to some kind of cultural and economic apocalypse.[12]

The fragmentation and dissolution of traditional organizing principles is a theme which McCarthy explores repeatedly in his work, and Southern Appalachia and East Tennessee provide the geographic setting for his imaginative deconstruction of the gnostic idea of a hegemonic, settled, and stable South. A great deal of recent scholarship has drawn our attention to the inconsistencies and irregularities

---

[11] See Graham's "The South in Popular Culture" for an overview of this phenomenon.

[12] Some recent excellent scholarship has been devoted to show how the Agrarians—as polemical essayists, authors, and poets—shaped the imaginative and critical discussions of Southern literature. See Bone's *The Post-Southern Sense of Place in Contemporary Fiction* and Bingham and Underwood's *The Southern Agrarians and the New Deal: Essays after "I'll Take My Stand."*

within the Southern tradition, to the sub-cultures, geographies, and groups who are, according to Richard Gray, "the people of highland and hinterland, the mountain people who have their own special customs, folkways, and traditions" who "help to pluralize our idea of a regional culture and to see Southern mythmaking as a process, a developing series of discrete stories."[13] It is precisely these people of "highland and hinterland," these marginal cultures and characters overlooked by the Southern culture below and ridiculed by the culture outside of the South that McCarthy brings to center stage.

Southern Appalachia "has often held a stepchild relationship to the larger South and the accompanying field of Southern studies" as its literary, intellectual, and even physical terrain has been contested and proved to be somewhat hard to map.[14] Such indeterminacy is perfectly suited to McCarthy's fiction as his work is full of crossings, of failed yet somehow heroic quests, and the transgression of all manner of physical, sexual, social, and psychological frontiers. It is perhaps important that we outline the geographical area which Southern Appalachia covers and which is, therefore, home to McCarthy's Southern fiction. Linda Tate claims that the following areas constitute Southern Appalachia:

> Though the map edges for the region are fuzzy, Southern Appalachia can loosely be understood as the mountainous areas of the South—the highland regions of eastern Kentucky, eastern Tennessee, northern Alabama, northern Georgia, western North Carolina, western Virginia, western Maryland, all of West Virginia, and

---

[13] Gray, *Southern Aberrations*, xi-xii.
[14] Tate, "Southern Appalachia," 131.

even southeastern Ohio and parts of western South Carolina.[15]

It is highly symbolic that Southern Appalachia has proved to be a contested site as McCarthy's Southern work is full of cartographic metaphors that relate to geographic, material, and metaphysical mapping. McCarthy's Southern work is predominantly rooted in the physical terrain of East Tennessee. There are some notable exceptions, such as Suttree's mountain sojourn into western North Carolina before he ultimately, like McCarthy, heads out west, and the father and the son in *The Road* who begin their journey in Kentucky before moving through East Tennessee and on to South Carolina. Whilst the themes with which McCarthy deals are universal, his attention to capturing the physical, ecological, and mythic character of this corner of the South exhibits a complex relationship to place which so much of the region's literature exhibits. As we shall see, this complexity is due to McCarthy's depiction of how such places and organic folk cultures are dissolving into history, progress, and modernity (to borrow a phrase from Jay Ellis) as federal and modernistic regulating agencies transform the Southern Appalachian landscape.

We can begin to see that the Appalachian setting problematizes the idea of a solid, homogenous South. Quite simply, Appalachia just doesn't fit into prescribed notions of "Southernness," whilst popular culture has historically sought to portray it as beyond culture and civilization. The celebrated Appalachian historian Ronald Eller has noted that "no other region of the United States today plays the role of the 'other America' quite so persistently as Appalachia."[16] In other

---

[15] Ibid., 132.
[16] Eller, "Foreword," i.

words, if Southern literary culture prides itself on an attachment to and love of place, nobody really wanted (for a long time at least) to recognize Southern Appalachia as *their* place.

In terms of the intellectual history of the mountain South this is a consequence of the fact that some of the first literary depictions of Southern Appalachia were constructed by people who were not actually native to Appalachia itself, which resulted in depictions of the region that were often crude and reductive. Ronald Lewis is a scholar of Appalachian culture who contends that this tradition was initiated by local color writers of the nineteenth century, and Lewis traces its genesis to "Will Wallace Harney's 1873 travelogue, 'A Strange Land and Peculiar People,' published in *Lippincott's Magazine*. His [Haney's] emphasis on physical and cultural isolation was greatly magnified over the next two decades by subsequent writers."[17]

This historical phenomenon is vitally important to the development and reception of writers such as McCarthy, as remarked upon by Linda Tate:

> Where Southern writers have written with the anxiety of the William Faulkner influence, Appalachian writers have had, not one of their own as the major figure setting the tone for the region's writing, but instead an outsider who misunderstood and misrepresented mountain people [Mary Noailles Murfree] ... Appalachian writers have had to reclaim their regional literature from a faulty start, working carefully—and in some ways unsuccessfully—to establish a more accurate vision of their world.[18]

---

[17] Lewis, "Beyond Isolation," 21.
[18] Tate, "Southern Appalachia," 132-3.

McCarthy and other Appalachian writers have therefore had to work against the local colorists and, to an extent, the hegemonic idea of Southern literary identity. This discourse was promulgated by the writers and critics (many involved assumed a dual role in this respect) who were directly involved in or remained loyal to the Southern Renascence, which ran from the early 1920s until the late 1940s.

In our discussions of the novels we shall see how *The Orchard Keeper* and *Child of God* offer a scathing critique of Agrarian philosophy, and we will also see how McCarthy's Southern fiction critiques the pastoral sense of place that is privileged in a great deal of Southern literature. Much American and Southern fiction depicts a fallen world in which characters and perhaps narrators attempt to reclaim what has been lost, which can include a certain Edenesque quality or an especially harmonious relationship with the natural or divine world; however, it regularly seems like there is nothing to fall *from* in McCarthy's fiction. His characters are those no one wanted to acknowledge, poor whites who are pariahs in every imaginable category, an affront to the stereotypical (and perhaps entirely imagined) idea of a noble, chivalric South.

Perhaps more significantly, his narrative consciousness increasingly bestows a strange equanimity upon his characters and the natural world, upon human and non-human matter. In McCarthy's fiction we fail to find anyone who is master of his landscape, anyone who dwells in a pastoral refuge from the ills of society and civilization, anyone who is able to successfully resuscitate a Jeffersonian/Agrarian ideal of small tenant farmers saving the region from the ravages of finance capitalism. Neither do we find, however, the standardized American landscape that was always lurking as a jeremiad within the more dystopian examples of Southern philosophy, as nowhere do we find suburbs or Wal-Marts, landscapes that were to become non-places, to borrow Walker Percy's phrase; in other words, McCarthy's Southern places seem to be neither pastoral nor post-Southern.

A brief synopsis of the novels supports this assertion: Uncle Ather Ownby of *The Orchard Keeper* is a failed subsistence farmer who, nonetheless, clings to a distinctly Appalachian dream of an isolationist existence that will never be realized. In *Outer Dark*, Culla Holme wanders through a hellish netherworld where the natural environment threatens to ensnarl him at every turn. In *Child of God*, McCarthy develops his critique of agrarian philosophy through the serial-killing necrophiliac Lester Ballard, whose descent into madness is initiated by his displacement by the mechanisms of rampant finance capitalism and exacerbated by the community at large. *Suttree* presents a community of the displaced who live in squalid conditions in Knoxville beyond, at least for a while, the bourgeois, conformist impulse of 1950s America, whereas *The Road* offers an ecologically dystopian critique of these themes following an apocalyptic disaster on an unimaginable scale.

McCarthy was born too late to be considered a figure within the Southern Renascence, yet his novels critique many of the ideas and imaginative paradigms formulated by this important movement in Southern intellectual life. His work has also been championed by the key figures of what could be referred to as the Appalachian literary renascence, although he steadfastly refused to talk about his work in relation to this movement as some of his contemporaries, such as Fred Chappell, Robert Morgan, and Wendell Berry, have done. Indeed, appearances by McCarthy on the celebrity and literary circuit have been a recent phenomenon, including an interview on the Oprah Winfrey show in the summer of 2007 and an appearance at the 2008 Oscars where the Coen brothers' adaptation of his novel *No Country for Old Men* swept the board.

Despite his reluctance to publicly speak about his writing, McCarthy's novels have done much to legitimize Southern Appalachia within the Southern and national canon, revealing that "life in Appalachia is not static, as some have assumed. The Appalachian region's literature reveals a modern, rapidly changing world that retains many aspects of traditional rural life."[19] McCarthy situates much of his narrative action in the conflict that ensues when archaic ways of mountain life come up against the agencies of modernization, which include the emergence of a robust finance capitalism, industrialization (and the ecological disasters that follow), and large-scale intervention from state and federal government agencies. Whilst his narratives are steeped in such regional myths, they ultimately tell us much about the American historical and cultural experience, as seen through the eyes of one of its finest and most capable writers.

So a complex, contradictory region produced an author who produced complex and, at times, contradictory novels which incorporate a diverse range of styles and themes. The Southern Appalachian mindset accounts for much of this, but it is worth considering the personality and exceptional character of East Tennessee and Knoxville itself, where the fatalism so often associated with the region is exaggerated somewhat. This sub-region, according to noted historian Bruce Wheeler, traditionally engendered a "collective mentality [that] can be explained by its citizens' history of near-helplessness against the forces of isolation, poverty, and fear of change."[20] Of course, many other sub-regions within Southern Appalachia could claim that such a thesis explains their aberrant position within the South or their exceptional cultural experience. However, histori-

---

[19] Miller, *Hatfield, and Norman*, xv.
[20] Wheeler, *Knoxville, Tennessee: A Mountain City*, xv.

ans maintain that it is the city of Knoxville itself which makes East Tennessee's historical consciousness unique and which, therefore, accounts for its aberrant nature in terms of ideology, politics, and literature. In "Knoxville's History: An Interpretation," William MacArthur observes the following:

> What has made East Tennessee different from the rest of Appalachia has been Knoxville. Southwestern Virginia, southeastern Kentucky, western North Carolina, northern Georgia, and Alabama are much like East Tennessee, but none of these areas had a center, a capital, a city like Knoxville which typified the ethos of the mountain South. Political talent, intellectual ability, and capital resources clustered here, and the city's politicians, journalists, and industrialists articulated or demonstrated a doctrine which was hostile to the Old South.[21]

From its origins as a frontier outpost beyond which the knowable, controlled cartographic space of colonial maps was transformed into unknowable wilderness, to its staunchly unionist sympathies during the Civil War, to the distinctly pre-modern characteristics that the region exhibited whilst modernity, industrialization, and finance capitalism were rampant transformative agencies throughout the rest of the South and the nation, East Tennessee is a region which seems to be hostile to *any* kind of doctrine, not just to the one propagated by the Old South. It is into the ultimate dissolution of mythic resistance to "alien" controlling forces that McCarthy takes us too in much of his Southern fiction. His masterly depiction of the clash between tradition, myth (some of which pre-dates any notion of Ap-

---

[21] MacArthur, "Knoxville History: An Interpretation," 23.

palachian culture, as it reaches far back to the very origins of homosapiens), and modernity makes him an author of the highest standing in Southern and American letters.

Before we conclude our admittedly brief overview of the historical narratives which have informed McCarthy's fiction, it is perhaps important to bear in mind the example provided by William G. Brownlow. Brownlow, editor of the *Knoxville Whig* for many years during the nineteenth century, is a figure who embodies so much of the region's fiercely independent (and perhaps even isolationist) sensibility. Brownlow was famed as a skilled journalist and colorful public speaker, even if he often relied more on *ad hominem* attacks than informed and logical rhetoric. In his public exhortations and journalistic offerings he did much to articulate the exceptional quality of Knoxville and East Tennessee, especially in terms of its unionist sympathies. Stephen Ash's summary of Brownlow's public career reads like the brutalities experienced by a typical McCarthy protagonist, and his characters share with Brownlow the experience of being immersed in highly charged cultural and ideological moments:

> Brownlow's relentless assaults infuriated many of his victims. Few public figures of his era were more deeply loathed by their enemies. A number of the injured replied in kind, though few could trade insults with Brownlow and come out ahead. Some decided that verbal dueling was insufficient to redeem their honor. In the course of his long career the Parson was threatened, sued, beaten up, shot at (and hit once), hanged in effigy, indicted, imprisoned, and even exiled by his adversaries. But such reprisals did not silence him; they merely gave him more ammunition to fire off in his devastating broadsides … Though he switched sides on certain other issues over the

years, he never renounced his Unionism. His steadfast loyalty to the United States brought him in 1861 to the gravest crisis of his career, and his one moment of real greatness.[22]

Although frequently belligerent and bombastic, his editorials and speeches often display a deep hostility toward the confederacy and what he saw as the alien, controlling doctrine of the Old South. Indeed, in another echo of some of McCarthy's anti-authoritarian, anti-conformist protagonists, he claims that the leaders of the Southern Confederacy were no better than a "set of aristocrats and overbearing tyrants," whereas elsewhere he claims that to be a Unionist of East Tennessee had become a term "now significant of long suffering, of devotion to a principle, of faith in the triumph of right, and the people are astounded with the quick succession of outrages that have come upon them, and they stand horror-stricken, like men expecting ruin and annihilation."[23] The verbose tone is clearly evident here, but his jeremiad is one fulfilled and explored by many of McCarthy's characters as they fight against the various "succession of outrages" which afflict them.

It is also crucially important to acknowledge how issues of race and gender function in McCarthy's work. These two categories are ideologically charged, and the analytical traditions developed within postmodern and poststructuralist readings encourage us to look for what a text doesn't do, what it doesn't include, what is missing or absent, to look for who only appears on the margins of the action, perhaps in crude, reductive, and serviceable ways. From this viewpoint

---

[22] Ash, *Secessionists and Other Scoundrels*, 4.

[23] Patton, *Unionism and Reconstruction; Portrait and Biography of Parson Brownlow*, 16.

we undoubtedly encounter some problems with McCarthy, especially when racial and gender discourses of the Southern experience are taken into consideration. In turn, this also leads us into some fascinating, if complex, questions about the ideological function of literature within contemporary culture. Where and when do non-white characters appear in his work? Do they appear in favorable, sympathetic, or stereotypical ways? To what extent should a Southern or American writer necessarily *have* to engage with such issues?

Teaching McCarthy can be a rewarding experience, but it is quite common to encounter some reticence—if not outright repulsion—to his style, especially from female students and readers, and such a reaction is perfectly understandable. When discussing the depiction of female characters in *Blood Meridian* Jay Ellis points out that McCarthy usually refuses to describe women in any but three ways in the novel—head-shot victims, vatic soothsayers, or prostitutes—and aside from the brief vignette of Sarah Borginnis, the novel is utterly free of a "civilizing female influence."[24] Of course, it could be equally restrictive to demand that female characters should only appear within the culturally prescribed roles of civilizing influences (whatever that may represent) or as symbols of biologically regenerative potential.

Nevertheless, a cursory summary of the female characters from McCarthy's Southern texts which develops Ellis's review of McCarthy's treatment of female characters in *Blood Meridian* makes for uncomfortable reading. The leading female characters from *The Orchard Keeper* (if we can even really call them characters, as they appear in such marginal, peripheral ways, and they are never fully developed) include John Wesley Rattner's religiously deluded

---

[24] Ellis, *No Place for Home*, 9.

mother, Marion Sylder's partner who appears only in the most serviceable ways, and the exotically presented witch doctor who makes an appearance in one of Ownby's childhood recollections and who informs him of his occult or magical capabilities, powers that lay beyond the normative reach of American society. In *Outer Dark* we have Rinthy, mother of an incestuously conceived child, who wanders a terrifying landscape bereft of any kind of knowledge or sense of the world, with milk from her breasts seeping through her worn and tattered dress. As if this were not enough the novel is littered with several grotesquely deformed female characters Rinthy encounters during the course of her desolate journey. In *Child of God* we follow Lester Ballard as he fails to function in any kind of conventional sexual or domestic practice, and we follow him deeper underground in his deranged version of the domestic with his succession of corpse lovers. In *Suttree* the eponymous hero's mother appears as an impotent figure, seemingly emasculated by her husband's authority and superior social status and her son's intellectually cold and detached dismissal of her. Suttree does eventually embrace a version of the settled domestic life and, whilst it is not quite on a par with Lester, it is with a prostitute in a hotel and other indeterminate domestic arrangements; indeed, one feels that his father, wrapped up as he is in the thoroughly bourgeois world of commerce and the law courts, would strongly disapprove. Finally we have the absent mother in *The Road* who chooses suicide over the tortuous journey she believes lies ahead for father and son; is suicide a braver option here, or does it perhaps suggest that she lacks the stoic, "ardenthearted" vigor (even if it is completely misguided much of the time) of McCarthy's male characters?

After reviewing a list such as this it is tempting to agree with Nell Sullivan that women in McCarthy's work appear as nothing but abject, threatening, and wholly other to the male protagonists, and that he is an unredeemed male author who excludes women from his books; in short, he exhibits misogynistic tendencies.[25] The case against him appears strong here, and these are not easy charges to deny. However, we can perhaps find a solution to them if we once again turn to McCarthy's use of myth. It may be unfashionable to talk of such grand narratives or organizing principles—nor should we argue that McCarthy romantically presents such narratives as a nostalgic alternative to his political moment—but he continually situates his characters in ideological and cultural conflicts which are larger than they are. It should also be remembered that his other characters, including children, fare little better, and that death haunts everyone in McCarthy's world, often in the most gruesome fashion. No one really comes away in a good light in McCarthy's world, and we can once again return to Ellis here as he manages to astutely counter the misogynistic charges often leveled against McCarthy:

> The invisible dividing line between nations, social classes, and even the philosophical dividing line between determinism and free will all prove more interesting in these novels than those between the sexes ... The son and father trouble simply eclipses other psychological tensions, and the focus on traditionally male subjects displaces ... any focus on women at all.[26]

Another rider to this debate is added by John Cant in his masterful study *Cormac McCarthy and the Myth of American Exceptionalism*. Cant argues that McCarthy writes against the alluring yet

---

[25] See Ellis, *No Place for Home*, 9 & 94, for a treatment of these themes and for his engagement with Nell Sullivan's feminist critique of McCarthy's work.

[26] Ellis, *No Place for Home*, 23.

ultimately destructive myths inscribed in American culture, and his fictional terrain is characterized by his configuration of America as a cultural wasteland. Within this barren setting, though, Cant suggests that McCarthy "frequently associates the female with water and thus with fertility and the essentials of life itself [thus] giv[ing] the female a special mythic significance in his texts."[27] However, does his mythical or allegorical depiction of female characters get him off the hook? Does the mythic function of female characters in his texts outweigh the traces of misogyny we find in their portrayal?

McCarthy's depiction of non-white characters is also problematic, even if his narrative consciousness repeatedly informs us that we all exist in a cosmos that cares little for such socially or culturally constructed categories. In McCarthy's world we will all ultimately have to confront certain inescapable metaphysical questions, and it is significant that *all* of his characters, in material and mythic terms, experience the denial of foundational American myths of progress, prosperity, and mobility. Of course, the inescapable historical reality is that the denial of such dreams has been more acute and painful for some groups, including Native and African Americans. Native Americans, especially the Cherokee in Southern Appalachia, were the first to suffer overt hostility and displacement as British Colonial rule spread and more land was required, a process that was intensified during the early years of the republic and which reached its tragic dénouement with enforced Indian removal programs, culminating with the Trail of Tears.

Although Southern Appalachia was largely free of the plantation system, it would be foolish to assume that the area was free of the racial strife that blighted so much of the South. However, the absence

---

[27] Cant, *Cormac McCarthy and the Myth of American Exceptionalism*, 16.

of large-scale plantations does have repercussions for the version of Southern identity and history that McCarthy depicts for us. John Cimprich notes that East Tennessee was full of "small, diversified farms," not plantations, although 9% of the region's population in 1860 consisted of slaves. The dominant pattern was of small slaveholders, substantiated by the fact that "a mere 3% of all East Tennessee masters held twenty or more slaves," and the region could boast leading unionists such as Brownlow. However, Cimprich also notes that despite "slavery's limited significance in East Tennessee, its legacy of racial, class, and personal conflict did not die easily or quietly."[28]

The legacy of racial strife can also be clearly seen in the Great Depression where, according to Bruce Wheeler, "the economic suffering of whites was mitigated by their wholesale displacement of black workers." Wheeler also notes that even the sweeping changes ushered in by the New Deal "failed dismally to assist Knoxville's black population, men and women who had considerably more to fear than fear itself."[29] *Suttree* in particular details the economic hardships suffered by African Americans in Knoxville, along with a large number of displaced agricultural workers who came to the city in search of improved material conditions only to find shanty towns and living conditions even more deplorable than the ones they had fled from. We should therefore not overlook the fact that McCarthy's work is part of a broader Appalachian discourse which implores us to reconsider the region's relationship to America as a whole, especially those narratives about the disempowered and marginalized. Ronald Lewis raises this important point as he notes that

---

[28] Cimprich, "Slavery's End in East Tennessee," 189, 196.
[29] Wheeler, *Knoxville, Tennessee: A Mountain City*, 58-59.

"the economic stratification suggested in the new studies [which include conventional and fictional histories] underscores the dangers of facile generalizations" about the region's association with "the notion of Appalachia as a Jeffersonian Eden"; indeed, McCarthy's work sets about subverting such romantically constructed notions.[30]

Whilst such "local" historical narratives can indeed provide useful paradigms which help to illuminate the work of an author such as McCarthy, it is perhaps tempting to become too locked in with them. This opening chapter has attempted to stress the high artistry of McCarthy's work, his inversion of conventional novelistic techniques—especially in terms of the access he grants readers to the psychology and interiority of his characters—and his skilled use of myth, allegory, and depictions of space and landscape. We have also attempted to highlight the fascinating contribution to the debate surrounding Southern literary studies his work has made, especially in terms of how his fiction challenges traditional approaches to the region's literature and how it enriches the literary culture of Southern Appalachia. McCarthy is and never has been a provincial writer; rather, he is a writer who—in the best tradition of regionalist writing and in keeping with his own concept of the value and function of the novel—uses the aberrant mythos afforded by his corner of the South to write a series of texts which interrogate the inescapable sense of the unknown that constitutes the human condition.

As already outlined, biographical information about McCarthy is scarce and although some important parallels can be made between McCarthy's own life and his art, it is not our intention here to read his work according to biographical detail. However, we should acknowledge some pertinent biographical facts. We do know that

---

[30] Lewis, "Beyond Isolation," 29.

he was born in 1933 in Providence, Rhode Island, and that he was originally named Charles; he would rename himself Cormac some years later. His family moved to Knoxville when Cormac was four years old when his father took a senior position at the Tennessee Valley Authority. Cormac attended Catholic high school in Knoxville, and he had two stints at the University of Tennessee between 1951-52 and 1957-59 that were punctuated by a four-year spell in the air force, where he was stationed in Alaska. Like Suttree, McCarthy is a university dropout who never completed his degree. Although his academic career stalled, his spell at UT was not entirely fruitless as in 1959 and 1960 McCarthy published his two short stories ("Wake for Susan" and "A Drowning Incident") in the student literary magazine *The Phoenix* and married fellow student Lee Holleman in 1961 (the marriage would be relatively short-lived).

Although *The Orchard Keeper* was anything but a commercial success, it landed McCarthy the William Faulkner Foundation Award, a fellowship from the American Academy of Arts and Letters, and a grant from the Rockefeller Foundation. The money from this grant financed a trip to Europe where he met Anne De Lisle, and they were married in 1967. Perhaps the most prestigious of all the awards McCarthy was to receive prior to the Pulitzer came in 1981 with the award of the MacArthur Fellowship (the so-called "genius grant") that came with a check worth some $250,000. McCarthy moved to El Paso in the late 1970s, and he now resides in Santa Fe, where he is married for a third time. He also has a young son, to whom *The Road* is dedicated.[31]

---

[31] For an extended biography, see Cant, *Cormac McCarthy and the Myth of American Exceptionalism*, 19-43 and the "Biography" section of www.cormacmccarthy.com

John Cant makes the interesting point that McCarthy and Tennessee are made for each other as the state "finds it difficult to know quite how it should locate itself in American life" and that East Tennessee, even to an extent in McCarthy's childhood, was a culture "rooted in pre-enlightenment epistemology and continued to feature superstition, isolation, illiteracy, and the blood feud."[32] Cant is one of many commentators who explores the profound sense of the *unheimlich*, of homelessness, in McCarthy's fiction, and the reasons are plentiful. We have the paradoxical status of Tennessee itself, where McCarthy and his family were Northerners who moved to the South. They were Catholics in the Bible Belt. McCarthy himself was a lover of the natural world whose father worked for a modernizing agency that did so much to irrevocably change the local environment, and the son was enamored with mythic culture whilst his father stood for jurisprudence and coldly detached enlightenment rationality.[33] In short, it is little wonder that he writes about the restless and the misplaced as his family background, intellectual makeup, and even adopted state exhibit these characteristics.

His fiction critiques the mythic and cultural narratives deeply entrenched in the American and Southern cultural imagination to reveal how their power wanes in the face of the increasing pressure of standardization, commodification, militarization, and increased governmental influence. Although his fictional terrains may not represent tranquil Edenic or prelapsarian refuges, they retain a wilderness quality beyond the reach of the pressures of bourgeois society. As we shall discuss, this quality increasingly becomes an internalized imaginative and narrative geography or site

---

[32] Cant, *Cormac McCarthy and the Myth of American Exceptionalism*, 35-36.
[33] Ibid., 46.

of resistance as his aesthetic develops. Indeed, before we move on to our discussion of the texts themselves it would be wise to consider John Lang's comments about Fred Chappell, another Appalachian writer, as they are entirely appropriate for McCarthy as well: "Fred Chappell is an Appalachian writer, a Southern writer, a profoundly American writer ... an author whose work intersects powerfully with the western literary and philosophical and religious tradition while achieving an excellence uniquely its own."[34]

---

[34] Lang, *An Introduction to Fred Chappell*, 14.

CHAPTER 2

The Short Stories

Cormac McCarthy published two short stories—"Wake for Susan" and "A Drowning Incident"— in quick succession in 1959 and 1960 in *The Phoenix*, the literary supplement of the University of Tennessee's student newspaper *Orange and White*. The two stories landed the young author (who was published as C. J. McCarthy at this point) the university's Ingram-Merrill Award for Creative Writing. Despite his current status, readers can only access the stories by contacting the University of Tennessee's Special Collections library.[1]

McCarthy never returned to the short story form, and he even turned down a lucrative offer from the *Virginia Quarterly* to republish them, stating that he would have to be a long time dead before they saw the light of day.[2] The stories are fine early efforts by an author who would go on to develop a truly remarkable aesthetic, and there is certainly no need for McCarthy to feel embarrassment or to be so reticent about the re-publication of these two early efforts. However, we must remember that McCarthy was at an early stage of his artistic development when he produced these two stories, and he was certainly not fated to go on to become one of the South's leading practitioners of the short story form such as Eudora Welty

---

[1] See Wallach's "Prefiguring Cormac McCarthy: The Early Short Stories," 15.
[2] Ibid.

or his fellow Tennessean Peter Taylor. With this in mind, we could best be served by reading the two stories as announcing the arrival of a major talent, and we can read them as a commentary about the major themes and concerns that he would go on to explore in his novels. Specifically, "Wake for Susan" announces his concern with narrative and storytelling, with a focus on the interaction between myth and history, the illusory nature of memory, and the failure of cultural artifacts to truly capture the history of the person, time, or moment they purport to represent. "A Drowning Incident," on the other hand, is chiefly notable for its exploration of the oedipal theme. In both stories nature and landscape function as characters in their own right, revealing the early workings of his burgeoning ecological consciousness; both stories imbue natural phenomena with agency, and both stories follow characters who are far more comfortable out of doors than in the confines of the domestic home. Significantly, McCarthy refuses to reveal the interiority of his characters in a conventional manner, and the border between a character's consciousness and direct authorial input is often ambiguous.

Before we turn to our analysis of the stories themselves we should briefly consider how McCarthy's two efforts conform to traditional approaches to the genre. In his study of the form Ian Reid identifies a strong Romantic flavor operating in many short stories as the characters they focus on are often "seen as separated from their fellow men in some way, at odds with social norms, beyond the pale" and that short story plots often feature "wanderers, lonely dreamers, and outcast or scapegoat figures."[3] Wes from "Wake for Susan" and the unnamed protagonist from "A Drowning Incident" adhere to this descriptive paradigm, as would so many of the characters

---

[3] Reid, *The Short Story*, 27.

that McCarthy would create when he moved from short stories to novels.

Reid also maintains that a conventional trope frequently deployed by accomplished writers of short stories (especially as the twentieth century developed) was that of the epiphany which results in "some instant of perception."[4] Whilst the protagonists of the two stories under consideration here do have moments of insight, the neatly packaged, all encompassing epiphanal moment is denied them. As we shall see, McCarthy's oeuvre denies any such neat and tidy endings for his characters, nor does it allow readers to apply singular interpretive strategies. Instead, McCarthy's short stories are more in line with those that end with an air of ambiguity and uncertainty, where the knowledge gained by the characters is not fully reconciled and resolved within the story itself but is taken by them into the drama that ensues when the stories themselves come to a close. We know the characters have changed, but readers and characters alike are "left uncertain about the nature and extent of the revelation" that has been experienced and about whether "its significance may not yet have been fully apprehended by that character."[5] This is a characteristically elusive and complex strategy that McCarthy employs with his first published efforts, and his work would go on to exhibit a challenging complexity throughout his career.

Like much of McCarthy's work "Wake for Susan" is partly a story *about* stories and storytelling, about the important and potentially humanizing act of creating a narrative, of making sense of the world and our place in it through storytelling. It is also a meditation and reflection on the silence of historical artifacts, of their inability to

---

[4] Ibid., 28.
[5] Ibid., 58.

illuminate or tell about the very thing that they supposedly represent or commemorate. Wes is the story's main protagonist, and he is one of McCarthy's first unhoused heroes who we find out of doors, engaged in the mythic act of hunting (although he's not very good at it, a failing at pastoral activities he shares with other McCarthy characters), and who puts off returning home to complete his chores, preferring instead to go deeper into the woods with the specific purpose of finding a burial ground he has visited before. When he reaches his destination and sees the burial stone for one Susan Ledbetter, who died in 1834, Wes recreates and re-imagines the dead woman with his own alternative narrative about her life. Stylistically, we know this is an early effort as McCarthy even uses quotation marks to differentiate between dialogue and the inner thoughts of his characters. McCarthy dispenses with such conventional devices after this, and his refusal to punctuate his characters' dialogue, to clearly delineate who is speaking and in what order, is often a cause of frustration for readers.

The story is infused with a striking gothic sensibility where everything seems embroiled in an irreversible "state of decay" (WFS 2). Wes makes his way through a landscape that is enchanting and disquieting, a fabled dream realm on the brink of darkness filled with "wind-tortured trees," where "the rich and lonely haunted feeling thickened the air" as he enters the graveyard where Susan is laid to rest (WFS 3, 2). The text is haunted throughout by memory, history, and myth, embodied in the "ghosts of lean, rangy frontiersman" Wes thinks about as he makes his way through the text, symbolically moving away from society and the domestic and further into the landscape (WFS 1).

The story's central motif is concerned with how artifacts remind us of the past but also betray it somehow, frustrating our attempts to accurately recapture it. This theme is announced at an early stage in the story as Wes wanders through "time haunted woods" where he discovers the hog-rifle ball: "Wes wondered when it had been fired, who had fired it, and at what or whom? Perhaps some early settler or explorer had aimed it at a menacing Indian … Perhaps it had been fired only thirty or forty years ago" (WFS 2 & 1). Wes ponders, as so many other McCarthy characters do, how he can recapture the histories and myths of those forgotten people who had "in all probability, walked here even as he did now" (WFS 2).

The most significant artifact is of course Susan Ledbetter's gravestone. The ceremonial stone commemorates her passing, but it fails to capture anything about the essence of Susan as "the mute stone left no testimony," forcing Wes to create a narrative about her, to create what he sees as his own more authentic account of her existence (WFS 5). The gravestone tells Wes that she died in 1834, a year "one could remember," a time close to the mythic pioneer and settlement days of Appalachia, unlike the unreal, unknowable history-book and decidedly Old World dates of 1215 (the year the Magna Carta was issued) and 1066 (the year of the Norman Conquest of England) that Wes refers to, dates steeped in an inaccessible mythic consciousness (WFS 5). The narrative becomes more complex here, a story within a story, as Wes authors Susan's existence to his liking, conjuring up an alter ego that becomes Susan's lover (WFS 2). The historically imagined Wes and Susan then go on to have a conversation that only McCarthy characters could have, as it is about "death and bass-fishing" (WFS 3). Wes's Susan operates as a typically serviceable female McCarthy character, and her greatest accomplishment appears to be cooking a meal for her family, and she "swelled with pride" as she watched her brothers eat (WFS 2).

We can clearly see McCarthy's voice forming and emerging in this story, especially in the way that he grants agency to natural phenomena. An example of this occurs with the brief italicized passage in which the trees are imbued with agency as they provide a commentary upon Wes's progress through the landscape, although it is also one of the story's more sentimental moments: "*You walk here, as so many others have walked. The ancient oaks have seen them*" (WFS 3). The parable of the chase between the fox and the chipmunk (another tale within the tale) depicts nature as predatory and antagonistic, undermining any kind of pastoral bliss Wes hopes to achieve in the narrative (WFS 4).

Although infused with pathos and a touch of sentimentality, Wes's act of creating a narrative enables him to come to something of an epiphany, an understanding about his own mortality that he takes with him as the story closes. As he leaves the burial ground and returns home to his chores, Wes "wept for the lost Susan, for all the lost Susans, for all the people; so beautiful, so pathetic, so lost and wasted and ungrieved" (WFS 5). This is the first time in McCarthy where one of his characters is paradoxically liberated by acknowledging the sure fact of his own end, and Wes is also something of a Romantic figure, a lover "of old things" who tries to evoke a sense of the mythic culture that has been lost via artifacts that both evoke and elide the very past which they claim to represent (WFS 2).

Initially published in *The Phoenix* in March 1960, "A Drowning Incident" is a more economically controlled effort than "Wake for Susan." In this second story we follow an unnamed protagonist who is younger than Wes, but who also forsakes his domestic responsibilities (babysitting, in this instance) in order to head outdoors, getting further away from carefully demarcated space as he orients himself using an old wagon road (ADI 2). The story announces the oedipal theme as one central to McCarthy's aesthetic, and it can be read in part as a discovery of parental betrayal and deceit (the drowning incident of the title concerns puppies that have not been taken to a new home but drowned in the nearby creek), and it also concerns sibling rivalry, the ramifications for a family when a child's position is usurped. Furthermore, it also reveals how McCarthy often uses dogs and how people treat them, as a moral gauge in his fiction, as their treatment of dogs often reveals people's moral character or worth. Thus the drowning of the puppies is a clear violation of McCarthy's moral code, and it is one that Legwater, the ironically named County Humane Officer of *The Orchard Keeper*, will also transgress with his shooting of helpless dogs.

The story is structured around an initial flight from the domestic and an eventual return to the family home so that the boy can deposit his grim discovery in the bed of his newly arrived sibling. The boy's first act is to extricate himself from the domestic setting, first by going to the outhouse and then further out into the nearby countryside. Symbolically, every domestic structure appears to be decaying and rotting, with peeling paint and ruined doors, and man-made structures beyond the home appear as if they are being reclaimed by the natural world, as the fence is described as sagging and "honeysuckled" and the planks for the bridge are "curling" (ADI 2). Like so many characters to follow, the boy goes beyond the fenced-off landscape, and as he steps beyond demarcated and regulated space, he achieves a brief moment of warm pastoral bliss even if, also like many to follow him, this innocence will soon be punctured with his gruesome discovery. The boy stops where the creek is perfectly clear and where "the sun was warm and good on his back through the flannel shirt" before he spies one of the drowned puppies flowing by in its "attitude of perpetual resistance" (ADI 2 & 3). The corruption of innocence motif was prefigured to an extent with the story's earlier predatory metaphor of the spider ensnaring the cricket in its web, and the antagonistic relationship between species is underscored as the boy discovers a crawfish feeding on one of the dead puppies: "It [the bag containing the dead puppies] was rotten and foul. When he opened it there was only one puppy inside, the black one, curled beneath two bricks with a large crawfish tunneled half through the soft wet belly" (ADI 4).

The boy uncovers his father's carelessness in disposing of the puppies, thereby discovering that his parents lied and that the puppies did not "go to a new home last week" as he has been told (ADI 1). In the time between his discovery and his journey home to plant the sack containing the dead puppy in his new sibling's cot—thereby avenging the entire family—we see one of the first instances where McCarthy ambiguously alludes to the interiority of his characters. McCarthy identifies the boy's interior processes but refuses to develop or pursue them as we see that the boy "had no tears, only a great hollow feeling which even as he sat there gave way to a slow mounting sense of outrage" but that is all the audience gets in terms of the boy's mourning (ADI 3). We also see that the discovery of the puppies is the catalyst for the boy to strike out against his family in an act of grotesque revenge as we see the "green entrails oozing onto the sheet" as he places the sack next to his sibling, but we fail to see *exactly* what those injustices have been (ADI 4). In the following passage, we get only the most limited access to the "inner recesses" of his mind, and McCarthy's refusal to directly enter the consciousness of his characters would become one of the most important features of his work: "What prompted his next action was the culmination of all the schemes half formed not only walking from the creek but from the moment the baby arrived. Countless rejected, revised or denied thoughts moiling somewhere in the inner recesses of his mind struggled and merged" (ADI 4).

The boy's vengeful act underlines how central the oedipal motif would be to McCarthy's aesthetic; indeed, it is one of the most significant ironies of his complex body of work that fathers and families play a central role by their absence. The mother is not really given any agency or consciousness in the story as she is just alluded to as an irritable presence for the boy, a figure on the margins of the text who "was always coughing" (ADI 4). Rather ominously, we see the child sitting and waiting for his father to come home at the story's close, and he is the first of many McCarthy characters who find themselves anxious and distraught about their (absent) patriarchal figure (ADI 5). The conclusion of the story parallels the somewhat ambiguous and open-ended conclusion to "Wake for Susan" as both Wes's and the boy's drama of revelation or discovery is only truly beginning as the story itself comes to an end.

Although both stories are devoid of any concrete references to Knoxville and East Tennessee, the landscapes described in them clearly anticipate those McCarthy would create in his novels set in the region. Although both stories have problems with their execution—an element of sentimentalism can be detected in "Wake for Susan," whilst McCarthy doesn't quite get the distance right between the consciousness of the author and that of the character in "A Drowning Incident"—they do signal the arrival of some of his major themes, especially the problematic relationship between historical artifacts and individual and cultural memory and the conflicted oedipal theme that would play a central role in the work to follow.

Overview of Critical Responses

Despite having received relatively little critical attention, discussions about the short stories insightfully anticipate the questions and themes that would concern critics when discussing McCarthy's future works. Although he locates a number of positive elements in both stories, especially in regards to how they anticipate the emergence of McCarthy's mature voice, Rick Wallach reads them as the "products of an immature art."[6] For Wallach, "Wake for Susan" "blurs the line between nostalgia and sentimentality on several occasions" whereas "A Drowning Incident" suffers from "lapses in the design of what otherwise appears to be a thoughtful deployment of multiple tropes."[7] Wallach maintains that both stories give several hints about how powerful the later work will be, and he refers to the hybridity that would go on to be a commanding feature of his work: "McCarthy's amalgamation of the themes of prodigality, oedipal anxiety, craft, and inferences of *Bildungsroman* [would] shortly [achieve] more disciplined shape in *The Orchard Keeper*."[8] Wallach also makes the important, although somewhat playfully expressed, point that a "Cormac McCarthy novel is the last place you would want to turn up if you were a child," which refers to the frequently gruesome ends that children meet in his work, belying the supposed innocence of childhood.[9]

Wallach argues that "Wake for Susan" is a step too far for McCarthy, that it is an overly ambitious attempt for a writer whose thematic range was not matched by his powers of execution at this early

---

[6] Wallach, *Prefiguring Cormac McCarthy*, 15.
[7] Ibid.
[8] Ibid., 17.
[9] Ibid., 19.

stage of his career. Although Wes's "distaste for quotidian responsibility prefigures the restlessness of many of McCarthy's youthful protagonists," he "reaches for an epiphanous moment beyond his spiritual capabilities and beyond McCarthy's skills to illustrate convincingly," and Wallach notes that "an excessive emotional response to an inadequate stimulus" is "the most glaring flaw in the execution of the story."[10]

For Wallach, "A Drowning Incident" is more "successfully executed" than "Wake for Susan," specifically because it "lacks the excess of the first story."[11] It also anticipates one of McCarthy's most important themes in that it displays "acute Oedipal anxieties," whilst it also introduces the theme of sibling rivalry "which finds its most virulent and problematic expression in *Outer Dark*."[12] Wallach draws our attention to the fact that the boy consistently refers to the baby in an "annoyed and contemptuous tone" and that referring to the child merely as "it" represents a "calculated depersonalization."[13] Wallach also refers to the somewhat problematic manner in which McCarthy outlines the interiority of his characters, another problem of execution that would resolve itself as his aesthetic matured: "We see the *process* of the boy's thinking but we see very little about its *content*. This descriptive distance from the character's center of consciousness reaches its apogee in the mature works, whereupon it would become another key tenet of McCarthy's style."[14]

---

[10] Ibid., 18.
[11] Ibid., 18.
[12] Ibid., 19, 15.
[13] Ibid., 19, 20.
[14] Ibid., 20.

In "'They aint the thing': Artifact and Hallucinated Recollection in Cormac McCarthy's Early Frame-Works" Dianne Luce discusses "Wake for Susan" alongside *The Orchard Keeper* and *The Gardener's Son*. Luce is interested in how these three texts offer a meditation "on the value and difficulty of recapturing the past" and how McCarthy explores "the ambiguous function of the historical artifact in its capacity to evoke or to displace the thing of which it is a record."[15] In all three of these Appalachian texts (short story, novel and screenplay), "artifacts of the past—gravestones, ruins, photographs—both evoke the past and obscure memory, but the search to re-imagine the past is valorized."[16] This act of creative re-imagination is crucial as it liberates Wes, whereas Culla Holme's failure to accomplish the same thing in *Outer Dark* ensures that he remains on his own doom-laden path.

Luce points out that Wes manages to come to terms with "human mortality and natural transitoriness through his act of creative imagination," and she claims that the story can also be read as "a portrait of the artist's creative awakening."[17] The "mute gravestone" is the artifact in question, and it prompts Wes's creative act along with stirring his mythic and historical consciousness, focusing on 1834 (the year of Susan's death) as a more "retrievable" year for historical memory, as opposed to the years of the Magna Carta (1215) and the Norman Conquest (1066).[18] Wes can therefore be read as a prototypical character for McCarthy, a young man who seeks "beyond the artifacts and records of history to come to imaginative ap-

---

[15] Luce, "'They aint the thing,'" 21.
[16] Ibid., 21.
[17] Ibid., 21.
[18] Ibid., 22.

prehensions of the past" whilst also making us aware of the paradox that confronts Wes and the author who created him in Wes's quest "to bring the past to life through the narrative act while entertaining no illusion that his invention represents what actually happened."[19] The creative narrative act is therefore essential, perhaps even heroic, even though memory will always prove to be elusive and fragile.

Although Wallach and Luce acknowledge the flaws of the stories under discussion here, they encourage us to overlook them in favor of what they anticipate. Nell Sullivan also focuses on how "Wake for Susan" foregrounds McCarthy's mature work, but for her the story is far more problematic as it contains "the germ of all of his subsequent portrayals of women." Whereas the other critics saw hints of greatness in this early short story Sullivan locates overt misogyny, claiming that McCarthy's subsequent portrayals of women would never be able to break free from the patterns found in this early creation:

> Although the story only hints at the artistic mastery Cormac McCarthy would eventually achieve, it does contain the germ of all his subsequent portrayals of women. Susan Ledbetter, its female romantic lead, is a long-dead woman onto whom a young man at her graveside projects his fantasies. With their conflation of the bridal bed and the grave, the lines from Scott's "Proud Maisie" introduce a theme echoing throughout most of McCarthy's fiction: the theme of female sexuality inextricably bound up with death and, therefore, posed as a source of masculine dread. This insidious association leads inexorably

---

[19] Ibid., 25.

> to the narrative death sentence for young women in the McCarthy canon.[20]

Sullivan draws our attention to the missing article from the story's title, as she argues that it plays on "both the funeral and arousal connotations of *wake*," suggesting that Wes (and perhaps McCarthy) is more comfortable with a dead woman than a live one.[21] This anticipates the problematic depiction of women in the remainder of his work as Wes is imagining a life for Susan that grants her no agency, will, or consciousness of her own, and Sullivan suggests that she even suffers a fate worse than the pitiful Rinthy Holme from *Outer Dark* because "she is completely subject to the desire of a man since she can offer no resistance in death."[22] Another hint in the story of the horror rather than the artistry to come is the fact that Wes preempts Lester Ballard in that his constant companion in the short story is a rifle, therefore making him "another man who dreams of love with dead girls."[23]

In the excellent *Cormac McCarthy and the Myth of American Exceptionalism* John Cant configures the stories within his overarching critical paradigm of how McCarthy's work critiques and subverts the foundational myths of (Southern) and American culture. Even though these two stories may well be the product of an "immature art" Cant highlights how McCarthy sticks with the themes expressed in them throughout his career, noting how the stories reveal "the stamp of the gothic on his work [and that] death and madness take the place of beauty and love." The stories "derive mythoclastic

---

[20] N. Sullivan, "The Evolution of the Dead Girlfriend Motif," 68.
[21] Ibid., 73.
[22] Ibid.
[23] Ibid.

significance" by combining "lyrical and eidetic descriptions of the East Tennessee woodlands" with gothic intimations of conflict, violence, and death, "marking out their author as one of harshest critics[s] of American mythology."[24] For Cant the first story reveals "a modernist preoccupation with the very nature, significance, and limitations of narrative," whilst the second "seeks to express what is for McCarthy the inexpressible, the inner consciousness of the individual human being."[25] The refusal to enter his character's consciousness would become a hallmark of his fiction, as would repeated expressions of skepticism about systems of knowledge and belief.

Cant offers an alternative reading of the apparent sentimentality in "Wake for Susan" by suggesting that the sentimentality belongs not to the narrative voice but to Wes, which reveals the complex narrative structure, another key characteristic of McCarthy's mature works. The epigraph from Walter Scott at the opening of the story serves a dual function, aligning the text with the myths of the Old South (where Scott's works were popular) along with revealing the broad intertextuality of McCarthy's artistic consciousness.[26] The story also hints at McCarthy's thematic and linguistic range as Cant notes how he "punctures the gothic atmosphere with passages of lyrical prose," whilst the symbolic use of blood is "emblematic of the continuing dialectic of vitality and insignificance that is one of his fiction's defining characteristics."[27]

Cant aligns himself with other commentators by noting that the story is also partly about storytelling itself, another hint at defining

---

[24] Cant, *Cormac McCarthy and the Myth of American Exceptionalism*, 51, 58.
[25] Ibid, 57.
[26] Cant, *Cormac McCarthy and the Myth of American Exceptionalism*, 51.
[27] Ibid., 53, 54.

features to come. Perhaps the most significant element for Cant is how the story initiates McCarthy's critique of American mythologies, how he reveals myths to be concomitantly "beguiling and destructive," and how "it [is] clear that Wes is the first of those McCarthy heroes that America sends into life informed by a myth, a story rendered false by the elision of the true nature of the world and of the people in it."[28]

Whilst Cant acknowledges that "A Drowning Incident" establishes oedipal conflict as a major theme, he feels that "the complexity of structure and meaning of the first story is absent from the second."[29] The decision to make the central protagonist a child is a key one for Cant as it "removes the possibility of articulate self-consciousness from the subject of the text," although his "innocent destructiveness" will become another recurring theme.[30] Despite these structural flaws Cant does maintain that the story plays an important part in initiating McCarthy's critique of cultural myths as in it "the notion of the impossibility of innocence, even in a small child, contradicts the American optimism that believed in the new Adam and his place in the New World."[31]

Although the stories have received relatively little critical attention the critiques outlined above are challenging and insightful. None of the critics shy away from highlighting the structural flaws of the stories (they certainly do have about them a hint of artistic awkwardness, of a writer attempting to find his true voice and rhythm), but the stories nevertheless represent an important introduction

---

[28] Ibid., 51.
[29] Ibid., 55.
[30] Ibid., 57, 55.
[31] Ibid., 55-56.

to McCarthy's body of work. "Wake for Susan" and "A Drowning Incident" reveal McCarthy to be a writer who has an involved mythic and historical consciousness, who would return again and again to conflicted oedipal themes, and whose thematic and stylistic range challenges our interpretive abilities, our ways of knowing and seeing the world.

CHAPTER 3

The Orchard Keeper

Published in 1965, *The Orchard Keeper* is undoubtedly an impressive and ambitious debut novel; indeed, many readers find it perhaps a little *too* ambitious, as we see McCarthy attempting to find his aesthetic and stylistic identity. Set primarily in the inter-war years and with a focus on three main protagonists, the novel exhibits the hybridity that was to become a hallmark of McCarthy's work as it shifts from mimesis to myth and allegory throughout. Access to the interiority of his characters is limited, but we can read their psychological condition in descriptions of the landscape and animals (cats especially), and the frequent use of italicized passages blurs the boundary between past and present, interior and exterior. The novel can be read in part as a *bildungsroman* whilst it also critiques regionally enshrined myths of patriarchy, the pastoral, and national myths associated with mobility and prosperity. In *The Orchard Keeper* we see myths disappearing into history, and it should come as no surprise that the mythical and allegorical aspects override the conventionally mimetic ones.

Our three main protagonists are Ather Ownby, Marion Sylder, and John Wesley Rattner. In the opening part of the novel Sylder kills Kenneth Rattner, John Wesley's biological father, and dumps the body in the spray pit in the ruined orchard that Ownby oversees. Ownby and Sylder then act as surrogate fathers (and are more devoted to their task than Kenneth Rattner could ever have been) to the young John Wesley throughout the text before they are safely "placed" by regulatory institutions at the novel's close—Ownby in the asylum, Sylder in the penitentiary. This leaves John Wesley free to leave Red Branch (the fictional community south of Knoxville where the majority of the narrative is set) and head out west, like so many other McCarthy characters, before his return to visit his mother's grave at the conclusion of the novel. As we shall see, a case could be made that John Wesley narrates the novel throughout.

However, the narrative sleight of hand that McCarthy deploys in an ambitious move that adds to the complexity of the structure is that we as *readers* are aware of the connection between Ownby, Sylder, and John Wesley, yet the characters themselves never are. Ownby and Sylder are bound together by their physical proximity as neighbors, by Sylder's act of dumping Rattner's body in the spray pit of Ownby's orchard, by their stewardship of the boy, and by Sylder's knowledge of Ownby's shooting of the government-owned tank (which is possibly used as a storage facility for nuclear waste generated by the nearby plant at Oak Ridge) on Ownby's property. However, aside from Ownby watching Sylder drive by from his porch, these two characters who are so central to the novel's action never actually meet.

The Orchard Keeper also provides a concept from the omniscient narrator to explain one of Sylder's many nighttime wanderings that is one of the key motifs in all of McCarthy's work. We are told that, on a Sunday night drive to seek out any kind of bar or tavern that is open, Sylder "turned to the mountain to join what crowds marshaled there *beyond the dominion of laws either civil or spiritual*" (emphasis mine, TOK 16). A great deal of the novel's emotional power is derived from the fact that Sylder, Ownby, and even John Wesley will no longer be able to find this mythical space beyond the reach and regulation of modernity and the bureaucratic state. Many of McCarthy's characters undertake such quests, and many of them fail, be it in the South or West, town or city, in a pastoral or wilderness setting, urban or rural; yet it is these quests that imbue McCarthy's aesthetic with a powerful mythic and allegorical force. If the pastoral can be read as an escape from society, civilization, and history, then we see them catching up here, as conceptions of mythic space and mobility are eroded by the increasing influence of state and federal government agencies.

It should also be noted that a key feature of *The Orchard Keeper* is its setting and its representation of fictional space. As mentioned, much of the action is set in Red Branch, the town south of Knoxville that is modeled on McCarthy's childhood neighborhood, and the mountain communities that surround it. The novel therefore switches its action from the relatively settled community of Red Branch to the mountain communities beyond it, which have about them a primordial quality that evokes the "wilderness aesthetic" that Georg Guillemin sees emerging in the novels that follow this one. Crucially the text also contains several important scenes set in the city of Knoxville itself, which means that the novel has a range of spatial settings and patterns of representation which enable McCarthy to powerfully critique national and regional myths. One such body of myth that the novel specifically critiques is the version of Agrarian philosophy articulated in *I'll Take My Stand*, the group's influential manifesto published in 1930. The novel's ecological consciousness also has ideological repercussions, bearing in mind that the Wilderness Act was passed in September 1964, a key moment in the fascinating evolution of the relationship between American culture and wilderness.[1]

---

[1] For a discussion of the significance of this act see Nash, *Wilderness and the American Mind*, 226-27.

Part of the novel's hybrid nature can be attributed to the fact that McCarthy critiques various foundational myths encoded in Southern and American culture. The novel can also be read in part as a *bildungsroman*, a conventional narrative structure in which we follow a protagonist from innocence to maturity, from naiveté about the workings of the world to some kind of knowledge about them. We have acknowledged that McCarthy's work always resists and transcends singular readings, but John Wesley's story—as do many of McCarthy's texts—certainly adheres to elements of the *bildungsroman* pattern. Chris Baldick's definition of the genre is useful for our discussion here:

> *Bildungsroman* [bil-duungz-raw-mahn] (plural *-ane*), a kind of novel that follows the development of the hero or heroine from childhood or adolescence into adulthood, through a troubled quest for identity. The term ('formation-novel') comes from Germany, where Goethe's *Wilhelm Meisters Lehrjahre* (1795–6) set the pattern for later *Bildungsromane*. Many outstanding novels of the 19th and early 20th centuries follow this pattern of personal growth: Dickens's *David Copperfield* (1849–50), for example. When the novel describes the formation of a young artist, as in Joyce's *A Portrait of the Artist as a Young Man* (1916), it may also be called a Künstlerroman. For a fuller account, consult Franco Moretti, *The Way of the World* (1987).[2]

The *bildungsroman* provides a structuring principle, even if the remainder of the narrative is perhaps overly complex at times, and we can see traces of the stylistic flaws critics discussed in their analysis

---

[2] "Bildungsroman," *The Oxford Dictionary of Literary Terms*.

of McCarthy's early short stories. The novel opens with an italicized passage, a familiar modernist technique, which disorients the reader as it is somewhat hard to frame and place. The section concerns African American cemetery workers attempting to cut through a tree only to find that an iron fence has *"growed all through the tree"* (TOK 5). This is a highly symbolic moment as the passage is allegorical in nature and it represents a man-made object destroying the natural ecological balance, and this theme will play out in this and other McCarthy novels. After this cryptic opening passage the novel is divided into four parts and each part has a series of mini-sections to it. The first part mainly concerns itself with Rattner and Sylder, leading up to the latter killing the former in self defense, although Ownby is also introduced as he undertakes one of his many walks across the landscape. Significantly the whole atmosphere of the first part is one of rank decay.

The second part of the novel introduces us to John Wesley and his mother Mildred, and we learn that John Wesley buys his hunting traps on January 1, 1941. One should always pay attention to dates in McCarthy as they often help us in temporally ordering and historicizing his work, and they are often hidden away in relatively inconsequential scenes such as this; on this particular date British Air Force bombers destroyed large sections of the German city Bremen in a devastating raid. It adds to the anachronistic feel of the narrative as it is hard to reconcile the antiquated world of Red Branch with the image of a burning, war-ravaged Europe blighted by World War II, especially in a scene where a relatively innocent young man sets out to buy traps for his hunting, an action which evokes a more innocent mode of existence. Ownby shoots the hole in the tank in this section, and John Wesley is united with Sylder after he rescues him from his wrecked car.

Although Part III is relatively short it does make symbolic use of the date December 21st, the winter equinox and the shortest day of the year, and this community is itself enduring a darkening, almost an end-of-days experience. This part contains one of the few scenes in the novel where John Wesley socializes with something resembling his peer group, and he and his buddies pay a visit to Ownby, the novel's grand patriarch. The final part opens with an apocalyptic feel as "a final desolation seemed to come, as if on the tail of the earth's last winter" (TOK 179) as we see a culture taking its last stand. The cat, the objective correlative for Ownby's psychological condition, is swept away by a predatory creature, and Ownby and Sylder, viewed as dangerous figures by the emerging bourgeois society, are safely "placed" in the asylum and penitentiary respectively. During John Wesley's final melancholic visit to Ownby in the mental institution the old man informs his young protégé that there "ain't nobody around no more" (TOK 227), a reference to the fact that we have witnessed a world vanish that will never be restored again, that has become—to borrow from the novel's final sentence—nothing more than myth, legend, and dust.

The Orchard Keeper introduces readers to one of McCarthy's major themes, namely that of a patriarchal culture in crisis, and Kenneth Rattner is the first in a long line of troubling and absent father figures in McCarthy's work. Rattner can also be read as a version of a mythic character as he is a second-rate confidence man and trickster, a character who is not to be trusted, as evidenced by the succession of lies that he spins in his brief appearance in the text, lies that continue to haunt his wife and son after his murder. Rattner is no noble rogue, though, as he is all too willing to violate the bonds of generosity, loyalty, and companionship embodied by his Southern community, bonds that are stoically maintained by Ownby and Sylder and passed on to John Wesley. Indeed, one calls to mind the occasion where he steals from and physically assaults the stricken drinkers following the collapse of the veranda at the Green Fly Inn and when he spins a series of lies to get a ride from Rattner from Atlanta to Knoxville in the opening part of the novel. Like many mythical American literary characters Rattner is on the road when we meet him, but drivers wisely pass him by, and he is symbolically associated with trash and rubbish in one of his first scenes (TOK 8). In a typical narrative gesture McCarthy only reveals his name on the tenth page of the novel, and his shiftlessness is revealed by the narrator who informs us that "had he been asked his name he might have given any but Kenneth Rattner, which was his name" (TOK 10).

Grand patriarchal portraits have an iconic status in Southern culture, and McCarthy "frames" Rattner in a scene that subverts this striking image of patriarchal control and order. His portrait looks out over John Wesley and his mother, and Rattner is posing in his military uniform with a completely fraudulent grandness about him, confirmed when other characters reveal their skepticism about his military record. This is also another instance in McCarthy's work where a photograph—a supposedly neutral and objective artifact—is exposed as fraudulent, its objectivity offering no accurate representation of the subject it represents, which in this instance is John Wesley's father: "From out his scrolled and gilded frame Captain Kenneth Rattner, fleshly of face and rakish in an overseas cap abutting upon his right eyebrow, the double-barred insignia wreathed in light, soldier, father, ghost, eyed them" (TOK 61).

Following Sylder's killing of Rattner, Ownby is the other character who becomes a surrogate father figure to John Wesley, and he is much more suited to this fatherly role than Kenneth Rattner could ever have been. Ownby is a mythical figure, a keeper of the old ways that do not sit easily with the emerging bourgeois order, an anachronistic figure who walks everywhere in an age where mobility in American culture would soon be mythically associated with automobiles. Ownby doesn't live by conventionalized business time or calendars as he is a "watcher of the seasons and their work," a figure who grounds himself by sniffing "the rich earth odors, remembering other springs, other years" (TOK 90, 56).

McCarthy's depiction of one of the few African American characters in the text is perhaps a little stereotypical, not to mention crudely reductive, but Ownby vividly recalls meeting the "colored woman" who chanted over him and informed him that he had the vision which enables him to "read where common folks ain't able," ensuring that he is another character in McCarthy with a mystical ability to map or see beyond the ordinary (TOK 60). This ability appears to be with him throughout the novel, as evidenced in his final meeting with John Wesley in the asylum when he states, "I look for this to be a bad one. I look for real calamity afore this year is out" (TOK 225). The "calamity" that Ownby foresees here is realized with the attack on Pearl Harbor in December 1941, just before the year in question is out. His mystical nature is also underlined by the manner in which he transposes his fears upon cats as we learn that they "troubled the old man's dreams and he did not sleep well any more. He feared their coming in the night and sucking his meager breath," whilst his shaman-like qualities are represented by the fact that he carries a goat horn and a unique walking cane around with him: "He had cut a pole of hickory, hewed it octagonal and graced the upper half with hex-carvings—nosed moons, stars, fish of strange and pleistocene aspect" (TOK 59, 46).

Although Ownby is a failed farmer, which is a commentary perhaps on the Agrarians' idealized program of subsistence agriculture as a viable alternative to what they saw as dehumanizing industrialism and finance capitalism (but which are irresistible and inevitable forces in McCarthy), he is nonetheless a fiercely independent Appalachian citizen. Ownby does conform to some aspects of Agrarian philosophy in that he seems to be the unreconstructed Southerner that John Crowe Ransom speaks about in that he "persists in his regard for a certain terrain, a certain history, and a certain inherited way of living" and that he still manages to extract a "primary joy" out "of so simple a thing as respect for the physical earth."[3] Ownby's isolationist wish echoes the sentiments expressed by Parson Brownlow and other Appalachians in that independence and an ability to maintain autonomy is valued above all else, and it is his inability to fulfill his isolationist wish—coupled with Sylder's inability to find a space "beyond the dominion of laws either civil or spiritual"—from which much of the novel's tragic power is derived. Ownby's isolationist impulse is summarized in the following passage, and it parallels Sylder's contemporized quest to fulfill the same desires: "If I was a younger man, he told himself, I would move to them mountains. I would find me a clearwater branch and build me a log house with a fireplace. And my bees would make black mountain honey. And I wouldn't care for no man" (TOK 55).

Another contributory factor to Ownby's tragic nature is that he is unable to comprehend the strength of the forces he is up against, unable to recognize the epochal civil, social, and cultural changes that were taking place in Appalachia. In an act of what would prove to be futile defiance he shoots at the government tank (which could be some kind of storage facility for the nuclear experiments being carried out at nearby Oak Ridge during this time) close to his home, which is

---

[3] Ransom, "Reconstructed but Unregenerate," 1, 9.

described as follows: "And on the very promontory of this lunar scene the tank like a great silver ikon, fat and bald and sinister" (TOK 93). His shooting of the tank brings him to the attention of the authorities, and he makes a spirited stand against them when they attempt to arrest him, displaying a skill at marksmanship as he fends them off. Ownby flees before they try again, and on their second attempt the authorities use aggressive, uncalled for tactics to arrest him as they use tear gas to smoke him out of his dilapidated cabin, tactics which evoke a hunt for serious criminals rather than a bewildered old man.

It is important to note that in his escape from the authorities Ownby heads out in search for the "harrykin" (hurricane), one of the few remaining wilderness spaces where he thinks he can fulfill his isolationist dream of existence. In another moment which signifies the rising affluence of the community Ownby is invited in for breakfast in the home of some men who inquire about his well-being. Whilst they display old-fashioned communal values their residence evokes images of holiday brochure, mountain retreat domestic comfort, a discrepancy that shocks Ownby. Furthermore, the use of natural phenomena (rocks) for interior design is another instance in McCarthy where mankind's use of the natural world is called into question, suggesting a commodification and human mastery over nature which is always a very dangerous thing to assume in McCarthy: "The house the old man entered that morning was no shotgun shack but a mountain cabin of squared logs rent deeply with weather-checks and chinked with clay. It was ... divided into two rooms of equal size, and at the far end of one a fireplace of river rock, rocks tumbled smooth as eggs, more ancient that the river itself" (TOK 192-3).

He eventually takes his leave of this hospitable family and heads further into the "harrykin" wilderness, and whilst on his journey Ownby achieves an all-too-brief moment of pastoral bliss before his arrest; nature can still offer a sublime and transcendental moment in McCarthy, but not for long it seems. It is also important to note Ownby actually manages to sleep without any disturbance here, without dreaming of cats-as-death, the only time this happens in the entire novel, and it occurs when he appears to be in a harmonious (and isolationist) natural setting: "The old man drank and then leaned back against the sledge. The glade hummed softly. A woodhen called from the timber on the mountain and to that sound of all summer days of seclusion and peace the old man slept" (TOK 195).

Ownby's failure to sustain his isolationist dream, which to an extent can be viewed as his own gnostic pastoral desire, can be read as an allegory of the fate of Appalachia itself. It is significant that McCarthy sets his debut novel in a decade when the federally created Tennessee Valley Authority (TVA) and its affiliate agencies were implementing social, economic, and ideological changes that would change the region forever. Whilst it is hard to dispute that the material conditions improved the region, TVA ruptured bonds to mythic cultures and ways of life that would never be put right again, and McCarthy's debut novel therefore becomes an allegory about displacement, change, and loss in cultural, political, and ideological terms. Moreover, we have noted how the conservation movement was gathering momentum during the period of the novel's composition and publication (evidenced by the passing of the Wilderness Act in 1964), but there were also parallels with the federal government's attitude towards Appalachia during the time of the novel's composition and setting as the Johnson administration passed the Appalachian Regional Development Act in 1965, another indication that the region needed philanthropic help from outside.[4] Therefore, both the decade

---

[4] Branscome, *The Federal Government in Appalachia*, 8.

of the novel's publication (1960s) and the decade of the novel's *setting* (mostly the 1930s) witnessed epochal ideological developments in how the government and perhaps the rest of the nation viewed this "other America."

A fascinating account of these changes is provided in Michael McDonald's and John Muldowny's *TVA and the Dispossessed: The Resettlement of Population in the Norris Dam Area*, which refers to a community close to Knoxville. The authors point out that the resettlement of the population of Norris embodied the ideological conflict that was being played out across the region as a cutting edge "modernity and a virtually premodern rurality" clashed, with the federal agency undertaking "a course of action which transformed thousands of lives and effected multitudinous environmental and economic changes." The TVA was able to purchase thousands of acres of land "under eminent domain," which rendered the inhabitants powerless and frequently meant they were denied a fair price for their land, the oldest ownership of which dated "back to the immediate postrevolutionary period."[5]

The most intriguing aspect of their study comes in the form of a series of interviews the authors conducted with the displaced members of the community. The interviews provide an authentic primary account of the events, and they have about them a very McCarthyesque flavor as his fiction also seeks to give a voice to those excluded from official historical records, and Ownby is an allegorical expression of the historical experience of those displaced in Appalachia. Curtis Stiner offers one of the most memorable interviews, and his condemnation of what he refers to as the "pushbutton" culture alludes to the series of changes that displaced him and thousands of

---

[5] McDonald and Muldowny, *TVA and the Dispossessed*, 26, 3, 4.

others. These were changes, he asserts, which displaced families and ruptured bonds to mythic and antiquated ways of life:

> With all this pushbutton stuff. Well, it becomes a part of you. You can't cook a meal without it; you can't take a bath without it; you can't get a drink of water without it, and you can't do nothing without it ... There you are, you're hooked. If you had the old wood stove there in the kitchen, and a pitcher lift pump there on the porch run into the cistern ... and if the power goes you can still get a meal and get your water, and you had an Aladdin lamp you could light and have a good light and go right on about your business...[6]

Sylder is unable to find that dominion where he can be beyond the regulatory reach of law and society, and Ownby's pastoral bliss is all too brief as the more sinister elements of the "pushbutton" culture that Stiner outlines above close in on him. He is eventually apprehended by the faceless lawman in his bland uniform of "clean gray chinos," driving an anonymous "black gray Ford" who hunts for him at Huffaker's store (TOK 196). Huffaker informs the agent about Ownby's antiquated trading and purchasing practices that lay outside of the cash nexus, and he simply points to the mountains when asked where Ownby lives, indicating that Ownby is as much a part of the landscape as the mountainside flora and fauna (TOK 197). A sorrowful scene ensues where, ridiculously, Ownby is accused of "resistin arrest," and his pitiful-looking dog Scout looks after him as he is driven off "like some atavistic symbol or brute herald of all questions ever pressed upon humanity" (TOK 205). It is also significant that Ownby encounters trouble when he comes *down* from the

---

6 Quoted in McDonald & Muldowny, *TVA and the Dispossessed*, 30.

mountain, when he leaves the relative sanctuary of the wilderness and heads closer to society and civilization; other McCarthy characters will encounter similar problems when their wanderings cease. Ownby's capture can therefore be read as an allegorization of the death of a myth and of an archaic culture.

The scene in which Ownby is diagnosed as an "anomic" type by "a young social worker recently retained by the Knox County Welfare Bureau" is one infused with irony and pathos (TOK 218-222). Indeed, for all the melancholy we find in *The Orchard Keeper* and McCarthy's other Appalachian works, we should not forget that he is highly skilled at writing touchingly ironic and frequently humorous scenes. The exchange between Ownby and the welfare worker lacks the type of humor we find in the various tales concerning the ribald denizens of McAnally Flats in *Suttree*, but the irony of the exchange is obvious as the two are unable to comprehend each other to such an extent that Ownby accuses the welfare officer of "talking like a Goddamned yankee" (TOK 211). Ownby ends up interned in the asylum, safely placed and out of sight of the emerging bourgeois order represented by the welfare worker who, with his coldly theoretical rhetoric and bureaucratic mindset, simply cannot comprehend this watcher of the seasons, an old-world patriarch at odds with the culture emerging around him.

McCarthy characters who end up institutionalized, even Lester Ballard to an extent, are far from the crazed individuals that lurk in the collective imagination. Ownby is such a pariah, but when John Wesley pays a last visit to him in the asylum Ownby informs him that there are "things you have to do on account of the fact that nobody else wants to attend to them" (TOK 229). It is a piece of advice which resonates with a degree of quintessential East Tennessee anti-authoritarianism, and we at least see John Wesley fulfilling his *bildungsroman* after being tutored by this mythical figure who somehow seems to transcend his historical and cultural moment.

Marion Sylder can be read in part as a contemporized version of Ownby. He also represents a familiar McCarthy archetype, that of the good bad man who is guilty of breaking laws (with his moonshining, with his own extra-legal forms of justice and punishment), but who nevertheless seeks to uphold a clearly defined moral code. He can also be read as an allegorical figure as his fate at the hand of the authorities reveals an aggressive federally sanctioned campaign as "the government gave full blessing to the wholesale abuse of civil liberties—warrantless arrests, jailings, beatings, and even murder—in the war against mountain moonshiners."[7] He is both the old and new mountain man, the accomplished driver that calls to mind the speeding moonshiners from Robert Mitchum's *Thunder Road*, a character who seeks out his own "harrykin" space beyond the "dominion of laws either civil or spiritual," the entrepreneurial bootlegger who is made obsolete following the repeal of prohibition. One can imagine Sylder socializing with Suttree, as both characters seek out places on the periphery that are beyond the respectable, and both have penchants for frequenting taverns that "hung on the city's perimeter like lost waifs" (TOK 29).

There is also something of the returning prodigal son about Sylder, the man who "was gone for five years. Whatever trade he followed in his exile he wore no overalls, wielded no hammer" (TOK 12). It is significant that like many other McCarthy characters he can't follow the regular practices of normative bourgeois society. He tries to be respectable but finds that "he was hard-pressed now on eighteen dollars a week, who had spent that in an evening," and he

---

7 Branscome, *The Federal Government in Appalachia*, 10.

eventually gets into a fight at the fertilizer plant that costs him his job (TOK 30). Ownby shoots the tank whereas Sylder gets fired from the plant, and both gestures bristle against the synthetic, modernistic intrusions into this curiously untouched mountain community. We should also note that Sylder acts as another surrogate father to John Wesley and following the crash that leads to their meeting we see that he leans on the boy in "an attitude of fatherly counsel" (TOK 102). This is a role Sylder maintains throughout, taking the boy hunting and advising him about the hypocrisy of the community's law enforcement officers.

John Wesley is in desperate need of the "fatherly counsel" provided by Ownby and Sylder as his dastardly biological father is absent, and he maintains only illusory fragments of memory about him: "The boy thought he could remember his father. Or perhaps only his mother telling about him" (TOK 62). John Wesley is another archetypal McCarthy character, the young boy-man who, one thinks, should be at school but never does attend, and the only book he consults (with his friend Warn) is entitled *Trapping the Fur Bearers of North America*, which is borrowed from Ownby (TOK 208). Like Ownby, he orders his days according to more antiquated and mythical patterns as "weathers and seasons were his timepiece," and he always seems more at home in the landscape afforded by the mountains (TOK 65). Like many other McCarthy characters, the domestic is not for him as he is drawn or called by another kind of natural sanctuary; indeed, note how he places his bed in the porch, on the very edge of the house and as close to nature as possible. John Wesley walks the landscape at night, eschewing the comfort of the domestic for the adventure of the landscape:

> His bed was still on the porch. These nights he could not bear to be in the house. He would go out after dinner and

come back at bedtime—and then out again directly she was asleep, walking the dark roads, passing by the shacks and houses, the people illumined yellowly behind the windowlights in gestures mute and enigmatic. (TOK 66)

The theme of the *unheimlich* is underlined when he returns to Red Branch at the novel's close as he visits his mother's grave and returns to his childhood home, which is now ruined and deserted. He notes that "it was never his house anyway" (TOK 244). In a scene that parallels his doubt about the authenticity of the memory of his father from the opening section of the novel, John Wesley experiences a moment where the narrator reveals his skepticism about the illusory nature of memory, and it is a moment of doubt that many other McCarthy characters will also experience: "he no longer cared to tell which things were done and which dreamt" (TOK 245). Just after this, he waves to a couple in an automobile who have pulled up at the stoplight by the cemetery but his gesture is not reciprocated as the couple head out on the black top as "mute and enigmatic" (TOK 66) as those figures who were also sealed off in the confines of the domestic at an earlier stage in the novel.

The trinity of characters represented here by Ownby, Sylder, and John Wesley represent a force for good. They develop a sense of kinship even if not related by blood, and their quasi-patriarchal bond is predicated on loyalty and responsibility, which stands in stark contrast to the devilish triune, a grotesque parody of patriarchy, who appear in the novel that follows *The Orchard Keeper*. The three characters also engage in acts of civil disobedience that are quintessentially American, and they are acts of resisting an alien hegemonic presence that, one thinks, would have met with Brownlow's approval. Ownby shoots at the tank, Sylder administers a night-time beating to Gifford following his harassment of John Wesley, and the boy returns the hawk bounty—a sign of state-sponsored extermination of nature—which signals his burgeoning old-time mountain and ecological consciousness. Although all these acts may be ultimately futile, they embody the stoic "ardenthearted" nature that, as John Cant observes, is a defining characteristic of so many of McCarthy's heroes.

As in the work of some of the most notable American writers, space and landscape play an extremely important role in McCarthy's fiction. In his study of McCarthy's spatial representations in novels, Eric Bulson notes that "what happens depends a lot on *where* it happens."[8] *The Orchard Keeper* has three main zones of spatial representation (mountain wilderness, the community of Red Branch, and the city of Knoxville), and trouble invariably starts for the characters the further away they get from the mountains. One thinks of the conditions under which Ownby and Sylder are arrested for example. Representations of space, wilderness, and landscape are of vital importance in McCarthy's work as they enable him to critique the culture and ideology of his historical moment. Bulson also makes the following valuable observation about spatial representations in novels, and it is one that we should bear in mind when reading McCarthy: "Spatial representations in novels *are* ideological, they are influenced by the culture, history, economy and politics of a particular time and place, they reflect ways of seeing the world and the scores of individuals who live, and have lived, and will live in it."[9]

The most ideologically significant spatial representations in the novel are those of the community of Red Branch and the orchard as they subvert and undermine the notion of the South as a blissful pastoral sanctuary. In one of the opening descriptions of the landscape,

---

[8] Bulson, *Novels, Maps, Modernity*, 11.

[9] Ibid.

the narrator informs us that it has a "primordial quality" and that it is characterized by a "cynical fecundity," which is a striking image (TOK 11). Critics have noted how the concept of "optical democracy" characterizes much of McCarthy's western work where all natural *and* human phenomena are made equal, and the notion of an immanent "cynical fecundity" expresses the ecological consciousness of the Appalachian novels, where the environment seems to resist mankind's attempts to subdue and order it. One of the opening descriptions of the ruined orchard adheres to this concept, and it evokes an image of apocalyptic waste with the "red dust" and reference to the wind like a "rancid breath" with withered plants and rotting vegetation. Indeed, the landscape described below is another example of the wasteland motif:

> In the late summer the mountain bakes under a sky of pitiless blue. The red dust of the orchard road is like powder from a brick kiln. You can't hold a scoop of it in your hand. Hot winds come up the slope from the valley like a rancid breath, redolent of milkweed, hoglots, rotting vegetation. The red clay banks along the road are crested with withered honeysuckle, peavines dried and in dust. By late July the corn patches stand parched and sere, sheathed stalks askew in defeat. All greens pale and dry. (TOK 10-11)

The orchard itself is infused with great metaphoric import. It is ruined, seemingly beyond the chance of any kind of replenishment or cultivation, full of "gnarled and bitten trees" (trees are often gnarled in McCarthy), and the spray pit (another sign of the synthetic management of nature) has been used as a crypt for Rattner's corpse over which Ownby has maintained his "deathwatch" for several years (TOK 52). The apples grown in the orchard are in keeping with the decaying nature of the landscape as Sylder discovers, to his displeasure: "There were apples on the trees the size of a thumbnail and green with a lucent and fiery green, deathly green as the bellies of the bottleflies. He [Sylder] plucked one down in passing and bit into it … venomously bitter, drew his mouth like a persimmon." (TOK 182-3)

There are other signifiers of ecological devastation in the novel, other signs that the relationship between man and nature is far from harmonious. One of the most notable is Ownby's recollection of the panthers (or "painters" as he refers to them) that have disappeared, and he is able to recall that "they ain't painters round like they used to be. Back fifty, sixty years ago they'd sing back and forth till you got to where you couldn't sleep lessen you did hear em" (TOK 149). This anecdote is also significant because it is upon such "painters" that Ownby projects his own psychological fears, and both Ownby and the panthers are gone from the landscape at the novel's end. Ownby can at least serve as a link between the past and the present, but the ability to recall such times becomes increasingly hard as the novel progresses, and when we see a "young and swollen bird" drifting in the "thick brown liquid" of the river "like a slowly closing eye," it is an ocular motif that calls our attention to the devastation of the landscape, much like the parable of the trout at the close of *The Road* (TOK 149).

Ownby's anecdotes about the past, which are usually imparted to young John Wesley and his peers, should not make us think that the pasts of characters like Ownby were blissfully Arcadian. John Cant warns about suffering from a "pastoral delusion" when reading McCarthy, and this is especially embodied in what we learn about Ownby's past as he is in fact a failed farmer, which also adds to the novel's critique of Agrarian philosophy as a viable alternative to rampant industrialization and finance capitalism. Ownby is initially proud of his first small holding as "I never had nothin, ain't got nothin now, but I figured it was a start," but his Jeffersonian dream would not last long (TOK 152).

The elopement of his wife with a Bible salesman serves as a catalyst for the demise of his version of the Agrarian dream of self-sufficiency and, as elsewhere in McCarthy, the absence of the female results in a wasteland in sexual, social, and, in this example, agricultural terms. Furthermore, it also adds to the waste and decay associated with the concept of a "cynical fecundity" that infuses virtually every description of the land and man's interaction with it throughout the novel: *"While the chickens grew thin and the stock screamed for water, while the hogs perished to the last shoat. An outrageous stench settled over everything, a vile decay that hung in the air, filled the house"* (TOK 155).

The Agrarian dream has failed, the landscape bristles against mankind's attempted management of it, and the ruin of the orchard is paralleled with the death of a community ethos around it. As previously alluded to, the tank placed near the orchard grounds suggests that space is also being militarized and suspiciously fenced-off, perhaps to aid the nuclear plant at Oak Ridge or to provide extra resources to aid in the displacement of settled rural communities undertaken by the Tennessee Valley Authority. The presence of the tank is incongruous, more suited perhaps to science fiction, but the symbol of the machine in the orchard is a striking harbinger of the changes to landscape that were taking place:

> Where the trees had been plucked from the ground and not even a weed grew. A barren spot, bright in the moonwash, mercurial and luminescent as a sea, the pits from which the trees had been wrenched dark on the naked bulb of

> the mountain as moon craters. And on the very promontory of this lunar scene the tank like a great silver ikon, fat and bald and sinister ... The great dome stood complacent, huge, seeming older than the very dirt, the rocks, as if it had spawned them of itself and stood surveying the work, clean and coldly gleaming and capable of infinite contempt. (TOK 93)

There are also other hints within the novel of the epochal changes that were occurring in Red Branch and other Appalachian communities during this period, a subtext of displacement and economic hardship. A faceless and voiceless group haunts the periphery of the novel, "unencumbered as migratory birds, each succeeding family a replica of the one before and only the names on the mail boxes altered," which hints at the extent of these Appalachian narratives of displacement (TOK 12). These families are also the least successful in fending off the claims of nature as we learn that their houses "held such an affinity" for decay as "gangrenous molds took to the foundations before the roofs were fairly laid down ... Some terrible plague seemed to overtake them one by one" (TOK 11). Whilst the stories of Ownby, Sylder, and John Wesley evoke sympathy in the reader McCarthy reminds us of the socioeconomic context against which the action takes place, a period in which hundreds and thousands of Appalachian families experienced one grave misfortune after another.

Whilst the narrative evokes sympathy for the dispossessed and marginalized the depiction of those in authority is far from flattering. Legwater, the ironically titled County Humane Officer whose shooting of dogs ironically juxtaposes his official title, is one such character. He is something of a comedic fool who sets out on a ridiculous errand to recover the mythical platinum plate from Kenneth Rattner's skull, something that the entire community (including the children who tease him) know to be false. Another ironic portrayal of an authority figure is represented by the coldly functional social worker from the Knox County Welfare office whose bureaucratic rhetoric leaves Ownby entirely bemused.

Sheriff Gifford becomes entangled in one of the novel's more complex moral dilemmas, as played out in his relationship with John Wesley and Sylder. Gifford harasses the boy in an effort to extract information about who he rescued from Sylder's car crash so that he can arrest them for bootlegging unbranded whiskey. This vexes Sylder, and he tells John Wesley that Gifford is "a lowlife son of a bitch and a caird [coward] to boot" who victimizes John Wesley as he "knowed you didn't have no daddy, nobody to take up for you" (TOK 161). Fulfilling his role as a good surrogate father Sylder pays a night-time visit to Gifford and physically assaults him whilst he sleeps, the punch connecting with his face "with a pulpy sound like a thrown melon bursting" in a typically vivid depiction of a violent deed in McCarthy's work (TOK 166). This presents the reader with one of the text's more complex moral dilemmas as we are forced to ask who the biggest villain of the piece is here: Is it Gifford for his uncalled for harassment of the vulnerable John Wesley or Sylder for exacting his revenge upon Gifford when he is defenseless? Is Sylder's act perhaps *more* cowardly than Gifford's?

Sylder is ultimately arrested when caught with unbranded whiskey as his car breaks down on the Henley Street Bridge as he approaches Knoxville; much like Ownby, he is finally caught on his way down from the mountains and into more settled society. He then becomes the victim of police brutality following his arrest at the hands of "deacon Gifford. With two buddies to hold me. Wadn't even that spirited about it till I kicked him in the nuts" (TOK 211). Although they never meet in the novel Sylder and Ownby are both victims of over-zealous law enforcement agents, evidenced with the unnecessary use of tear gas to capture Ownby and the underhanded and cowardly beating Sylder receives from the police. He does perhaps redeem himself by advising John Wesley *not* to take revenge on his behalf against Gifford, and therefore potentially endanger himself, but his interiorized monologue reveals the extent of Gifford's treachery, the extent to which this representative of the new social order has violated the old-world mountain ethos of loyalty and companionship that he and Ownby embody and that has been passed on to John Wesley: "*He's a rogue and a outlaw hisself and you're welcome to shoot him, burn him down in his bed, any damn thing, because he's a traitor to boot and maybe a man steals from greed or murders in anger but he sells his own neighbors out for money and it's few lie that deep in the pit, that far beyond the pale*" (TOK 214-5).

The Orchard Keeper also presents female characters in an unflattering mode, something that many readers and critics would find problematic throughout McCarthy's career. Mildred Rattner is a pitiful character who is convinced by her husband's lies to such an extent that she implores John Wesley to "find the man that took away your daddy," claiming that he was too proud to take the "govmnint disability" following his alleged war injury (when the truth of the matter was that he would never have been eligible for it). She also saddles John Wesley with the entirely false and unfair patriarchal burden by telling him, whilst "eyeing him doubtfully," that "you make half the man he was an you'll be goin some" (TOK 66, 72-3). The manner in which the narrator describes her calls to mind a disquieting figure from a nightmarish fairytale as opposed to a fully formed and functioning mimetic character, as her eyelids are "wrinkled like walnut hulls," she swallows like a toad, and her hair is described as "grizzled" (TOK 61). And yet in other instances Mildred Rattner does evoke a level of sympathy in the reader as she appears as an archetypal figure of female suffering at the hands of male treachery and abandonment. One particularly memorable description portrays her in mythical terms, suggesting that Mildred Rattner represents an atavistic type of the suffering female: "Rocking quietly in her chair she had the appearance of one engaged in some grim and persevering endeavor in which hope was the only useful implement" (TOK 73).

Other female characters are presented in nothing more than fleeting, marginalized, and serviceable roles, such as Sylder's partner who doesn't eat with him and John Wesley but merely "hovered about the table resupplying eggs and biscuits" (TOK 111) as does the woman of the family Ownby breakfasts with on his way to the "harrykin." This is certainly one of the more problematic aspects of McCarthy's aesthetic, and it encourages us to ask whether his depiction of (or, more specifically, his *failure* to depict) female characters underpins his portrayal of Southern and American culture as a mythical wasteland (as John Cant argues) or, alternatively, does it perhaps represent that culture's (and perhaps the author's) misogyny, as critics such as Nell Sullivan has argued.

One area in which McCarthy's debut novel conforms to the Southernist literary tradition is in his use of the gothic and the grotesque as the lurking presence of death is never far away. Moreover, McCarthy's gothicism and grotesquery acts as a corollary to the concept of "cynical fecundity" as the atmosphere of the novel is infused with images of death and decay. The image of Sylder following his car crash "burned such an image of death into [John Wesley's] brain" (TOK 101), whilst during the fight between Sylder and Rattner, the narrator tells us that Sylder "saw terror carved and molded on that face like a physical deformity" (TOK 38), and John Wesley notices Sylder's disfigured toe that was "curious-looking sort of like a nose"

(TOK 111). Images of world's end become more prevalent as the novel progresses and the normative world of civilization closes in. John Wesley and Sylder are described as resembling "the last survivors of Armageddon" in one instance (TOK 104), whilst perhaps the most memorable grotesque image comes with Ownby's discovery of Rattner's corpse in an orchard where the only thing that is cared for is the decaying corpse itself: "*The thing seemed to leap at him, the green face leering and coming up through the lucent rotting water with eyeless sockets and green fleshless grin, the hair dark and ebbing like seaweed*" (TOK 54).

We have noted how the description of the "molderous" shacks inhabited by a seemingly endless succession of displaced Appalachian families hints at a subtext of socioeconomic upheaval, and McCarthy's skeptical and unflattering treatment of the domestic in *The Orchard Keeper* is another theme he would develop throughout his work. Ownby, Sylder, and John Wesley are always more comfortable outside, walking the mountain communities, hunting, gathering, trapping or, in Sylder's case, using his excellent driving skills to outwit the authorities whilst on his bootlegging runs. Ownby's residence is as pitiful as his dog as we learn that "the hillside in front of the house was littered with all manner of cast-off things," a range of "antiquated items impacted in the mud" (TOK 56). It is also interesting to note that John Wesley and his mother paid no tax on their house as "it did not exist in the county courthouse records, nor on the land, for they did not own it" (TOK 63), which contrasts with Lester Ballard's fate at the opening of *Child of God* as he is evicted for non-payment of taxes, suggesting that the regulatory order that is taking hold at the narrative's close is more firmly in place by the time of McCarthy's third novel.

The novel also contains reminders of human culture's insignificance on the earth, and of discarded artifacts and phenomena that are becoming ossified. The Green Fly Inn, the rambunctious communal gathering place, significantly catches fire on the winter equinox and burns to the ground where "it is there yet, the last remnant of that landmark, flowing down the sharp fold of the valley like some imponderable archaeological phenomenon" (TOK 48). On one of his many walks, Ownby, a relic of another age himself, walks past "trilobites and fishbones, shells of ossified crustaceans from an ancient sea, [where] a great stone tusk jutted" (TOK 88). The reference to the mountains as once being an ancient sea is another instance where McCarthy embarks on a process of mythic mapping that goes beyond standard cartography, a strategy that implores us to reconsider our relationship to landscape and the materiality of culture. McCarthy's narratives always remind us of the void that awaits us all, and his reference to "the dead sheathed in the earth's crust and turning the slow diurnal of the earth's wheel, at peace with eclipse, asteroid" relegates the human form to one more piece of matter (TOK 244).

Cats and panthers play an important role in McCarthy's strategy of mythic mapping in the novel. Ownby is specifically important with regard to this theme, as he is frequently described as feline, and cats stalk his dreams and play a central role in his anecdotes about ecological devastation. Ownby associates cats with a kind of mystical power, as he acknowledges that "cats is smart" and that it is not uncommon for a soul to "takes up in a cat for a spell. Specially somebody drowned or like that where they don't get buried proper," a mode of death that is all too common in McCarthy, as evidenced by the fate of Kenneth Rattner and others (TOK 227). Moreover, when the cat is finally captured by the predatory owl, the scene parallels

Ownby's capture by the authorities, ensuring that the cat and Ownby's fates are entwined throughout (TOK 217).

A key feature of the novel's ideology of spatial representation is the depiction of the city of Knoxville, which also has significant intertextual parallels for McCarthy's work as the descriptions of the city in his debut novel anticipate those in *Suttree*. Ownby never makes it to the city itself, and Sylder is finally captured on his way into it, but the descriptions provided by the narrator during John Wesley's trips to Knoxville capture an antiquated and anachronistic space. It is significant that italics are used in these descriptive passages, underlining once again the images of a place and time that now exists in narrative and memory alone, as in so much of McCarthy's work.

The Market Square scenes call to mind both *Suttree* and similar passages in James Agee's *A Death in the Family* when young Rufus spends time in the city with his father, and the narrators of both novels comment upon the *"brown country faces"* and the city spaces peopled by the grotesque such as the *"old women with faces like dried fruit"* (TOK 82). The economic activity taking place feels almost pre-capitalist and curiously antiquated, predicated on barter and exchange as the traders bring their *"bundles of roots and herbs from sassafras to boneset"* and a *"meat market where hams and ribcages dangled like gibbeted miscreants"* (TOK 82). As in *Suttree* the Market Square scenes are filled with a kind of vibrant, grotesque, and anarchic energy, a clash of noise and produce that perfectly captures this anachronistic urban locale: *"Among overalled men and blind men and amputees on roller carts or crutches, flour and feed bags piled on the walk and pencil pedlars holding out their tireless arms ... an effluvium of frying meat, an indistinguishable medley of smells"* (TOK 82-83).

This otherworldly quality, the image of a city recorded before it was changed forever, is also memorably evoked in a passage where the narrator draws our close attention to the architecture and design of the buildings. This is a rare move in McCarthy as buildings are usually only described in order to draw our attention to their dilapidated condition:

> He was still standing on the sidewalk and now he saw the city, steamed and weaving in the heat, and rising above the new facings of glass and tile the bare outlandish buildings, towering columns of brick adorned with fantastic motley; arches, lintels, fluted and arabesque, flowered columns and crowstepped gables, baywindows over corbels carved in shapes of feet, heads of nameless animals, Pompeian figures ... here and there, gargoyled and crocketed, wreathed dates commemorating the perpetration of the structure. (TOK 81)

The Orchard Keeper is a quite remarkable debut novel even if its narrative structure is perhaps slightly too ambitious, a little too complex. It introduces us to all of the major themes that McCarthy would develop throughout his novels (a critique of pastoral and patriarchal culture is especially pronounced), and it fuses conventionally mimetic styles alongside more elaborate mythic and allegorical techniques. Perhaps most significantly his aesthetic would eventually be devoted to capturing narratives, spaces, cultures, and histories that, like Red Branch, Ownby, and Sylder, were to become nothing more than "myth, legend, dust" (TOK 246).

Overview of Critical Responses

Initial reviews of *The Orchard Keeper* were for the most part very positive, and many early reviewers were perceptive enough to realize that a major new talent had emerged. However, it was also somewhat inevitable that McCarthy would be compared to Faulkner, and he would find that getting out of Faulkner's shadow would not be that easy, something that has been experienced by a great number of other Southern novelists. It is somewhat ironic, therefore, that *The Orchard Keeper* was awarded the William Faulkner Foundation Award.[10]

One generally positive, if qualified, review was provided by Orville Prescott in the *New York Times* in May 1965. Prescott actually entitled his review, "Still Another Disciple of William Faulkner," and although he praised the power of the story, he criticized McCarthy for submerging his "own talents beneath a flood of imitation."[11] Walter Sullivan, writing in the *Sewanee Review,* praised the novel and acclaimed the arrival of a significant new talent, but his position would become increasingly ambivalent and disdainful as McCarthy's critique of the central tenets of the Southern Renascence (which Sullivan held dear) intensified.[12] Conversely James G. Murray's review in *America* claimed that the novel "almost (but not entirely) rejects the influence, more bad than good, of the Southern *mystique*," and Granville Hicks's critique in the *Saturday Review* noted that the novel developed erratically but that McCarthy was blessed with a gift for "vivid description," for making his readers "see." This is a theme that would be developed in many scholarly reviews of McCarthy's work.[13]

As McCarthy scholarship has developed, critics have generally agreed that the novel is an ambitious one for a first effort and that this ambitious design makes it a challenging read. David Holloway has noted that the novel "actually undermines the reader's attempt to map the identity of characters in certain scenes," whereas John

---

[10] Arnold and Luce, "Introduction," 2.

[11] Quoted in Arnold and Luce, "Introduction," 2.

[12] See Jarrett, *Cormac McCarthy*, 8.

[13] Quoted in Arnold and Luce, "Introduction," 3.

Cant claims that McCarthy "has perhaps indulged his narrative intelligence to excess."[14] Vereen Bell remarks that we are constantly "displaced from our authority as readers," and "by Jamesian standards *The Orchard Keeper* is a shambles."[15] Given McCarthy's opinion of James, perhaps we shouldn't be too surprised that the novel fails to adhere to his aesthetic and structural standards.

Although not as refined as in the novels that follow, *The Orchard Keeper* succeeds in carefully orienting and disorienting the reader throughout the narrative. Despite the demands it places upon the reader we can establish its temporal setting, and Georg Guillemin suggests that "the four parts of the novel correspond to the passing of the seasons, from summer to spring" and that the "main plot covers a seven-year span from 1934 to 1941." In one of the novel's many subtle parallels, this complements Ownby's prophecies about man-made and natural events occurring in seven-year cycles.[16] Matthew Horton analyses the paradoxical structural techniques at play, and he claims that the novel is littered with examples of "spatial-temporal distortion," which include McCarthy's penchant for depicting "stationary objects on moving backgrounds or from the point of view of a character in motion."[17] However, arguably the greatest indulgence of his narrative intelligence is the fact that "the action of the first page of the text is in a place and time that only becomes apparent on the very last page," a strategy that does provide a certain degree of symmetry, even if it is somewhat overdetermined.[18]

---

[14] Holloway, *The Late Modernism*, 12; Cant, *Cormac McCarthy and the Myth of American Exceptionalism*, 61.

[15] Bell, *The Achievement of Cormac McCarthy*, 12, 11.

[16] Guillemin, *The Pastoral Vision*, 28.

[17] Horton, "'Hallucinated Recollections,'" 290.

[18] Cant, *Cormac McCarthy and the Myth of American Exceptionalism*, 59.

Although the novel is split into four parts that each begin with Roman numerals, which are then divided into unnumbered sub-chapters of varying lengths, Jay Ellis echoes the frustrations felt by many readers as he observes that the formal aspects of presentation don't necessarily guarantee formal moments of closure. Furthermore, Ellis expresses his frustration in another example of McCarthy over-indulging his narrative intelligence regarding his "sometimes frustratingly modernist suspension of clear relation of pronouns to names."[19] Ellis also claims that the use of the prologue is somewhat misleading as it resembles "a modernist enigma, an offering of symbolism where symbolism will not be allowed to fully develop."[20] In his engaging discussion of *Suttree*, Noel Polk talks about a writer's "visual vocabulary," the manner in which a writer uses hyphens, dashes, and quotation marks to guide us through a text, to show us the difference between the author's consciousness and that of one of his characters.[21] Any reader of McCarthy will know that his "visual vocabulary" isn't very well developed, and where he does employ italics, for example, they are "generally invocations of the modernist narrative techniques of Joyce, Aiken, Woolf, Eliot, and Pound" than a direct homage to a writer such as Faulkner.[22] Even our ability to navigate our way through the novel via attachment to a particular character is frustrated as Kenneth Rattner "dominates the opening thirty pages" but is then killed.[23] How can we make sense of a novel where even the characters' attempts to reassemble and make sense of the past seems

---

[19] Ellis, *No Place for Home*, 62, 66.
[20] Ibid., 43.
[21] Polk, "A Faulknerian Looks at *Suttree*," 7-29.
[22] Jarrett, *Cormac McCarthy*, 24.
[23] Bell, *The Achievement of Cormac McCarthy*, 11.

futile, where they get so little help from the authorial consciousness, and where "fragmentation overwhelms holistic perception?"[24]

Although *The Orchard Keeper* certainly contains elements of a conventionally executed mimetic novel, attempts to interpret it as such will ultimately be frustrated. We arrive at a much more involved understanding of this challenging debut novel (and McCarthy's oeuvre as a whole) if we acknowledge its hybridity and fusion of forms, a fact noted by Guillemin, who claims that one could misread the novel if we overlook that "McCarthy's figures are types more than realistically developed characters." Furthermore, Guillemin contends that the narrative organization relies on the interaction of analogy, type, and fable, and that "such an interaction results in cyclical rather than a linear development."[25] Guillemin and other critics argue convincingly that we could view the narrative as an allegory about the importance of taking charge of the narrative of our own lives, whilst the picaresque model somewhat paradoxically helps bring a degree of clarity to the novel, with its emphasis on constant movement and episodic and fragmented (rather than realistically sustained) narrative action.[26]

Although allegory is an unstable and ambiguous form, our reading of the novel can be enriched if we view it, like so much of McCarthy's work, as an allegory about the importance of narrative in ordering experience in a world where all other organizing principles no longer have much currency. Perhaps above all else the novel is about narrative and development, and some critics have argued that *The Orchard Keeper* is indeed John Wesley's narrative from beginning to end.

---

[24] Horton, "'Hallucinated Recollections,'" 286.

[25] Guillemin, *The Pastoral Vision*, 24, 25.

[26] For a discussion of picaresque motifs in the novel, see Jarrett, *Cormac McCarthy*, 140.

In "'They aint the thing': Artifact and Hallucinated Recollection in Cormac McCarthy's Early Frame-Works" Dianne Luce argues that John Wesley can be viewed as the narrator and inventor of the novel. Moreover, she claims that the novel carries on where "Wake for Susan" left off as John Wesley (so similar in name to Wes from "Wake for Susan") is attempting to formulate a coherent and accessible narrative about his past after viewing a gravestone (his mother's), which is suggestive yet ultimately silent on the true nature of his past.[27] Horton argues that there is enough evidence to support the case that John Wesley is the book's narrative consciousness simply because "some of the most extended episodes in the narrative describe events that heighten his mental awareness."[28] In another (intertextual) parallel to a thoroughly conventional form, William Spencer has convincingly argued that *The Orchard Keeper* and *All the Pretty Horses*, the first novel of the Border Trilogy, "qualify as *bildungsromans*" as they "both contain major characters who are heroes in training, innocents whose progress to manhood is most clearly marked by an act of civil disobedience or of civic repudiation."[29]

The Orchard Keeper also announces another of McCarthy's subversions (but not complete forsaking) of conventional techniques as he "does not afford us the possibility of psychological insight into the motivations of his characters."[30] Whilst he dispenses with traditional access to the interiority of his characters (which in this novel includes direct authorial commentary or free indirect discourse), we instead

---

[27] Luce, "'They aint the thing,'" 27.
[28] Horton, "'Hallucinated Recollections,'" 304.
[29] Spencer, "The Extremities of Cormac McCarthy," 102.
[30] Cant, *Cormac McCarthy and the Myth of American Exceptionalism*, 66.

"read the landscapes to infer the psychology of the characters."[31] In keeping with this theme, Natalie Grant argues that in McCarthy's novels "the natural world often provides what T. S. Eliot has called an 'objective correlative' for defining the most mysterious aspects of his characters' personalities," and Guillemin makes the important point that from his debut novel onwards McCarthy "foregrounds nature as a character in its own right," as it commands a central narrative presence, and it is often imbued with as much agency as animate phenomena.[32]

The Orchard Keeper also initiates McCarthy's ambivalent (and perhaps even mythoclastic, to borrow Matthew Guinn's phrase) relationship to the Southern pastoral tradition. John Grammer claims that the novel "is a more or less straightforward, elegiac celebration of a vanishing pastoral realm" and that it "offers a positive image of a pastoral order."[33] Grammer argues that, like many works in the conventional pastoral tradition, the novel centers upon "the fortunes not of a single protagonist but of a community," which in this instance is the isolated mountain hamlet of Red Branch.[34] For Grammer, one of the novel's central quests or struggles concerns the efforts of Red Branch and "its representative citizens" (Ownby, Sylder, and John Wesley) to deny the gnostic will to transform their community and to thereby "preserve something of their old-fashioned existence," as it is the "civilized" modernistic threat that "ultimately dooms the community."[35] Red Branch and its representative citizens are "finally defeated by the gnostic will

---

31 Ellis, *No Place for Home*, 55.
32 Grant, "The Landscape of the Soul," 60; Guillemin, *The Pastoral Vision*, 37.
33 Grammer, "A Thing Against Which," 32.
34 Ibid.
35 Ibid., 34-35.

to deny history" but, like many of McCarthy's most memorable characters, they go down fighting in their own gestures and attitudes of defiance, vanquished in a battle they are doomed to lose.[36]

Grammer's analysis is an informed, thoughtful, and insightful one, but *The Orchard Keeper* sits uneasily within conventional pastoral readings. McCarthy's fiction consistently documents that, as a species, our gnostic visions and dreams of improvement and perfection will always undermine our claims to stability and order, and *The Orchard Keeper* represents his first meditation on such themes. McCarthy's work also exposes as folly the idea that we can somehow manage and tame the natural world, to bend it to our will. There is nothing in his debut novel to suggest that the older way of life that has been lost was utopian, that it was a time when man lived in harmony with the natural world as nature forever threatens to destroy all of our claims to stewardship over it. This has led John Cant to warn critics not to suffer from a "pastoral delusion" when reading McCarthy as "the notion that the way of life that has been lost was in any way Edenic is dispelled by McCarthy," and Cant goes on to note that *The Orchard Keeper* is "the first sign of McCarthy's attempt to create a narrative that escapes the confines of anthropocentrism and makes the world of nature, animate and inanimate, an equal principle in his epistemology."[37] This is a persuasive argument, and there is a significant amount of textual evidence to support McCarthy's critique of pastoral ideology, as by "letting his stock starve Ather committed the farmer's cardinal sin," whereas Bell notes that the orchard itself plays a symbolic role in McCarthy's critique of the pastoral as what was "once a productive negotiation between man and nature, [is] now un-

---

[36] Ibid., 35.

[37] Cant, *Cormac McCarthy and the Myth of American Exceptionalism*, 64, 70.

tended, slowly falling back into ruin, going back."[38] The traditional pastoral order seems as much of a ruinous wasteland as the modernistic order, with all its standardization and bureaucracy, that is about to replace it, and the world that has been lost certainly did not exist in some kind of pristine condition. Ownby, this teller of myths who keeps the old ways alive in narrative, actually assisted in the destruction of them by working on the railroad, thereby embodying this "pastoral delusion" and ambiguity, and no one seems able (nor does it seem wise) to attempt to halt "time's relentless flow" that will swallow "the pastoral dream of containing history, the desire for stasis."[39]

Other strains of this "pastoral delusion" lie in McCarthy's depictions and prophetic warnings of ecological and environmental damage. K. Wesley Berry's "The Lay of the Land in Cormac McCarthy's *The Orchard Keeper* and *Child of God*" draws our attention to the "signals" of "abused and abandoned land" in the novel, especially to the effects that "industrial farming, coupled with other heavy industry" have had on the landscape, to such an extent that "destruction to life is overbearing."[40] Berry claims that we should play close attention to representations of ecological and vegetative damage in McCarthy's work as it informs his "eerie prophecy of the next great extinction," a prophetic strain that receives its most desolate eschatological approximation in *The Road*.[41]

In *Animals in the Fiction of Cormac McCarthy*, Wallis Sanborn illustrates how McCarthy's construction of a "feline hierarchy" in *The Orchard Keeper* plays an important part in the development of

---

[38] Ibid., 70; Bell, *The Achievement of Cormac McCarthy*, 11.
[39] Horton, "'Hallucinated Recollections,'" 287.
[40] Berry, "The Lay of the Land," 61-77.
[41] Ibid., 74.

the novel's ecological consciousness. Sanborn posits that McCarthy "depicts three types of felines—domestic, feral and wild" and that in his "biologically deterministic world, proximity to man can only spell trouble."[42] Ownby's recitations of the lore of the panthers and wampus cats assume an added symbolic import as the gnostic impulse to commodify nature intensifies. The wampus cat itself is another mythic entity on the brink of extinction, surviving only in an old man's narratives, and Sanborn outlines how the wampus cat is the product of Anglo and Indian lore and that it is a "legendary and supernatural feline, the product of feline and woman," existing on an exalted place in the feline hierarchy "because of its cunning and savage exploits."[43] The demise of the wampus cat signifies the extinction of a mythic attachment to nature, whilst for Berry the fate of the "hungry [and] solitary panther" is the novel's "most memorable symbol of ecological catastrophe."[44]

The fate of the wampus cat and the panther parallels the fate of the "representative citizens" of Red Branch, and it also offers an alternative paradigm to the conventional pastoral reading. From his debut novel onwards, McCarthy is perhaps more concerned with a certain isolationist and wilderness aesthetic than a pastoral one as his characters seek out rawer untouched spaces "beyond the dominion of laws either civil or spiritual," and the melancholic force of McCarthy's work derives in large part due to the denial of this wilderness/isolationist quest. Georg Guillemin has provided the most enlightening critique of this aspect of McCarthy's work, claiming that "land or wilderness are in fact the principal protagonists of

---

[42] Sanborn, *Animals in the Fiction*, 27, 29.
[43] Ibid., 28.
[44] Berry, "The Lay of the Land," 66.

McCarthy's first novel. Once we have established that the principal commitment of the narrative consciousness is to a certain wilderness perspective, many of the seemingly incompatible components begin to cohere."[45] He goes on to demonstrate that McCarthy achieves this effect by combining "parataxis, cycles and typology" to subvert "the anthropocentrism that is essential in pastoral fiction to create an ideal realm that is a compromise between urban civilization and undomesticated wilderness."[46] *The Orchard Keeper* thus contains the landmarks of McCarthy's mature style that would be lauded by critics as he made the move westward, and his debut novel manifests "the main components of his later, ecopastoral fiction, such as their melancholy mood, allegorical composition, and ecopastoral genre," whilst we can also locate evidence of the origins of the technique that Holloway calls "optical democracy" which entails "the reduction of all that is animate and inanimate to a dead level of equivalence."[47]

The Orchard Keeper also announces that McCarthy's work will have an involved, ambiguous, and at times contradictory relationship to culturally proscribed regional and national myths. According to Jarrett, McCarthy's Southern body of work unquestionably critiques the myth of Southern exceptionalism which celebrates "the South's regional, cultural, historical, and economic differences from mainstream American culture."[48] McCarthy's subversion of the pastoral motif and his wilderness aesthetic are, for John Cant, a commentary on America's mission to domesticate the wilderness, a fact revealed in the perhaps unwitting exploits of John Wesley and his buddies,

---

[45] Guillemin, *The Pastoral Vision*, 22-23.
[46] Ibid., 30.
[47] Ibid., 18; Holloway, 135.
[48] Jarrett, *Cormac McCarthy*, 65.

which suggests that they will be "another generation who will, in the manner of Thomas Sutpen in *Absalom, Absalom!*, rip violently from the earth whatever is needed for the building of empire."[49]

It was perhaps inevitable that, given the timing of the novel's publication (when the imaginative and critical paradigms of the Southern Renascence were still fresh in the minds of those active in the intellectual life of the region) and the nature of McCarthy's style that comparisons to Faulkner would be uppermost in the minds of early reviewers. McCarthy is not the first Southern writer to be subjected to such a phenomenon, but there is a very real danger of overdetermining the nature of this relationship and the depth of this anxiety of influence, as Jarrett indicates: "Overemphasizing Faulknerian similarities … often prevented reviewers from recognizing not only the uniqueness of the style but the repudiation of Faulkner's imaginative constructions of southern history and culture in McCarthy's early fiction.… McCarthy's South isn't a South defined by slavery or the civil war."[50] There is of course something of an irony as "in 'disposing' of Faulkner McCarthy draws attention to him," but the idea that Sevier County and East Tennessee could be compared to Faulkner's Yoknapatawpha, that these landscapes could be viewed as "McCarthy's Bakhtinian chronotope" is dispelled as his (Southern) aesthetic develops.[51]

McCarthy's relationship to the commanding motifs of the Southern Renascence, particularly to certain tenets of Agrarian philosophy, is characteristically iconoclastic. *The Orchard Keeper* is most definitely a post-renascence novel (its critique of renascence, especially

---

[49] Berry, "The Lay of the Land," 65.
[50] Jarrett, *Cormac McCarthy*, 24.
[51] Cant, *Cormac McCarthy and the Myth of American Exceptionalism*, 71.

Agrarian, philosophy is given greater import as the novel is set during the most fecund years of the renascence itself), but neither can McCarthy be situated as one of the "grit lit" generation of Southern writers whose work is characterized by journalistic minimalism and a healthy dose of self-reflexive postmodern irony. However, Matthew Guinn claims that the novel was approved by critics such as Walter Sullivan as it offered "the sort of certainty that critics such as Sullivan seek in fiction," especially as Ownby "moves through a rural world much like the one the Agrarians conceptualized."[52] As we have seen, McCarthy's wilderness aesthetic is incompatible with the settled nature of Southern society and the economic program of subsistence yeomanry championed by Agrarian philosophy as a viable alternative to the severe problems of Depression-era America. It becomes clear that *The Orchard Keeper* "critiques the Agrarians' and Faulkner's assumption of an essential and meaningful connection between Southern past and present" and that the novel is primarily about "disconnection, and hence a break from the Agrarian tradition."[53]

McCarthy's treatment of patriarchy, family, and a settled domestic existence fare little better, which is another direct rebuke to the foundational myths of Southern culture. John Wesley's repudiation of his father's shiftless legacy could be read as a metaphor for McCarthy throwing off the artistic shackles bestowed by the patriarchal figures of his own culture (and perhaps his own family), and unlike Mildred Rattner, McCarthy and John Wesley refuse to interpret their "situation in the light of the old patriarchal mythology."[54] His

---

[52] Guinn, *After Southern Modernism*, 95, 97.
[53] Jarrett, *Cormac McCarthy*, 11; Berry, "The Lay of the Land," 63.
[54] Cant, *Cormac McCarthy and the Myth of American Exceptionalism*, 70.

mother is the first in a long line of problematic female characters in McCarthy as she appears enough to warrant a fuller treatment, but she remains marginalized, haunting the text throughout. The narrative consciousness paints an unflattering picture of her as someone who is seduced by a myth that all of the male characters deny without a second thought, so she remains lost "in her pious, irrelevant dreams," consoling herself with the "gnostic desire to remake a terrifyingly fluid reality by imposing stable order upon it," and characters who attempt anything like this in McCarthy simply do not fare too well at all.[55]

The Orchard Keeper is structured around patriarchal conflict, and this theme would go on to dominate McCarthy's work; indeed, Cant claims that Kenneth Rattner is "probably the most lamentable of all McCarthy's failed patriarchs," which is quite a statement given the competition he faces.[56] For Ellis, John Wesley's fatherless status "indicate[s] early on that son and father trouble lies beneath much of the impetus to character flight in McCarthy's work," a compulsion to flight that is compounded by their sorry domestic circumstances which, beginning with John Wesley (who is hardly *ever* indoors) expresses "the particularly American mistrust in the social, the urban, in civilization, and an especially American male distrust of the domestic."[57] John Wesley is fortunate enough to find some pretty good surrogate father figures, and Ownby frees the boy "from being haunted all his life by a task he can never complete," something that assists him in his development and which "suggests that before a boy can become a man, his father must be cut down to size."[58]

---

[55] Bell, *The Achievement of Cormac McCarthy*, 25; Grammer, 34.
[56] Cant, *Cormac McCarthy and the Myth of American Exceptionalism*, 69.
[57] Ellis, 8, 28.
[58] Luce, "They aint the thing," 28.

It would be a grave mistake to assume that McCarthy's work is completely nihilistic, though. In "Imposition and Resistance in *The Orchard Keeper*," Barbara Brickman ably demonstrates this by arguing that "the novel's three main characters ... adhere to an older code or system of values that shares much with Gaelic traditions in Ireland."[59] Brickman contends that the narrative "re-dramatizes ... the near destruction of Gaelic culture at the hands of English colonizers," as Red Branch becomes representative (in a reading that parallels Grammer's pastoral reading) in that it "mirrors the Gaelic model in its reverence for family ties and in its attention to certain bonds to community beyond those of blood."[60] Clearly delineated communal and moral constructs such as the one offered by the Gaelic paradigm mean that those who violate the bonds are easily recognizable, such as the duplicitous Gifford who represents the "dominance of law, urbanization, and modernization of the New South."[61] Furthermore the hapless Legwater's attempts to find the mythical platinum plate that is supposedly held within Kenneth Rattner's skull evokes a similar episode in Faulkner's *The Hamlet*, and Cant notes that "such intertextuality would be entirely in keeping with McCarthy's literary method."[62]

David Paul Ragan suggests that "the crucial challenge in approaching Cormac McCarthy's demanding first novel ... lies in the reader's locating a center of value, a source of moral authority," and that "moral center" (although this undoubtedly is an ambiguous term) can be found in the characters of Arthur Ownby, Marion

---

[59] Brickman, "Imposition and Resistance," 55.
[60] Ibid., 55, 58.
[61] Jarrett, *Cormac McCarthy*, viii.
[62] Cant, *Cormac McCarthy and the Myth of American Exceptionalism*, 71.

Sylder, and John Wesley Rattner.⁶³ Although this triumvirate never actually becomes aware of their inter-connectedness in the novel, they are, somewhat ironically, linked by their alienation from "the values and lifestyles of a newly dominant urbanized South." Indeed, these three who represent the moral crux of the novel are linked by the fact that they "shun human society, rarely talk, and barely think." In short, they are so very un-bookish, so very much unlike the people we expect to inhabit novels, and yet they imbue McCarthy's debut with its emotional and allegorical force.⁶⁴ They also establish McCarthy's penchant for writing about characters who are clearly antinomians, ironically existing "in such stark opposition to the normative constraints of the dominant culture that they seem all the more dependent on conflict with that culture."⁶⁵

Thus McCarthy creates the "moral center" of the novel out of three characters who are partly realistic and partly mythical, knowable yet wholly unknowable at the same time. Vereen Bell acknowledges that Ownby and Sylder are "anomic types" but that "each is also scrupulously obedient to a responsible inner voice and an ordered inner world," and William Prather observes that all three "attempt to retain some sense of human worth."⁶⁶ In Prather's analysis this effort to retain some sense of human worth is all the more problematic as all three have come to acknowledge the existence of an absurd and existential universe, and their inner voice or narrative is the only thing left that gives them some coherence and grounding. In a thoughtful

---

⁶³ Ragan, "Values and Structure," 17.

⁶⁴ Jarrett, *Cormac McCarthy*, 14; Bell, *The Achievement of Cormac McCarthy*, 24.

⁶⁵ Ellis, 54.

⁶⁶ Bell, *The Achievement of Cormac McCarthy*, 24; Prather, "'Like Something Seen,'" 50.

reading that anticipates his analysis of *Suttree*, Prather analyses the novel via the theories of Albert Camus's philosophy of the absurd, which recognizes that some kind of deep, traditional bond between man and his world has been broken and will never be put right again. The three main characters in the novel have come to recognize these feelings, and this conscious recognition of the absurd "can fissure one's myths of human centeredness and provoke an apprehension of a primordial, existential world."[67]

In one of the most succinctly memorable summaries of the novel, Prather claims that it is both "elegy and eulogy," containing the implicit melancholy and hope that these two rhetorical strategies carry within them (it becomes an elegy for a lost way of life, but John Wesley also eulogizes about it and carries it within him, if we read the end of the novel optimistically).[68] The world will undo our claims to understanding it, but we remain compelled to try to figure it out, and the construction of narrative out of this paradoxical tension is a truly heroic act, and all three characters (and indeed Suttree) wrestle with this throughout *The Orchard Keeper* and *Suttree*. The elegiac aspect accounts for the novel's melancholic tone, the eulogy accounts for the hope we derive from it, however tenuous that may be, and the grotesque world the characters do battle with could be no other way, as Prather outlines: "the grotesque is the existential world itself, the universe suddenly revealed through the loss of anthropocentric illusions. It requires, first, a world perceived as normal and stable, and then a breakdown of the boundaries, categories, and myths constituting that world."[69]

---

[67] Prather, "'Like Something Seen,'" 37.
[68] Ibid.
[69] Ibid., 38.

Critics generally see Ownby, Sylder, and John Wesley not just as representative characters of Red Branch but of McCarthy's work in general. Ownby is relatively content in his isolated state; he has no heir, no family, no real social structure, and no real connection or allegiance to the myths of the Old South and the Civil War, all of which makes him McCarthy's first real anomic type.[70] Like any McCarthy character, however, he is not as straightforward as he initially appears, and Grammer locates a typical example of polyphonic literary allusion as his dream of isolation with his mountain bees echoes William Butler Yeats's "The Lake of Innisfree," an allusion which for Grammer represents "McCarthy's own powerful attraction to the pastoral [or isolationist/wilderness] impulse."[71]

Ownby's allegorical and mythical status is properly revealed in his associations with an epistemology and spirituality that significantly pre-dates his historical moment. Spencer describes Ownby as resembling "some primal Shepard or like some primeval priest in the religion of nature," whilst for Cant he represents "the mythic, pre-enlightenment epistemology of a people about to vanish from American life."[72] Brickman echoes these views as she sees Ownby as the "spiritual center of Red Branch" whose "particular faith pre-dates Christianity and incorporates many more functions within the community," such as his recitation of the lore of the wampus cat to John Wesley and his buddies which assumes a mythical, almost sacramental quality. Interestingly, Brickman notes that Ownby is always prepared to offer, and in turn receive, hospitality, which

---

[70] Jarrett, *Cormac McCarthy*, 12, 31.

[71] Grammer, "A Thing Against Which," 32.

[72] Spencer, "The Extremities of Cormac McCarthy," 107; Cant, *Cormac McCarthy and the Myth of American Exceptionalism*, 65.

means that he could well be one of the few "good guys" that appear so infrequently in *The Road*.[73]

His dialect also marks him as "other," especially in his tragic-comic exchange with the welfare officer, and "his idioms and archaisms now seem representative of a 'pure' dialect, a standard by which we judge all other dialects." Ownby is "imprisoned with his dialect" and as tragically "aware of the agent's victory as we are," but it does hint at the oppositional potential of archaic folk or street language, especially when compared to the cold bureaucratic rhetoric of the agent, and this is a theme that will be developed in later works, especially *Suttree*.[74]

Given Ownby's hybrid nature, which fuses allegorical, mythic, and mimetic elements, it should come as no surprise that he is a more complicated character than we may initially suspect. One of the novel's most notable ironies is that despite his isolationist impulse Ownby actually "furthered human encroachment upon wild nature in the past" when he worked for the railroad company, and it is apparent that he has "tried the conventional human way and failed at it." Could it possibly be that Ownby's social failings are entirely his, and not his culture's?[75] His act of civil disobedience, his grand shoot-out against law enforcement officers, perhaps isn't as heroic or uncomplicated as it initially appears, as Cant claims that his behavior "can be seen as a product of the American cultural [and republican] tradition in which the citizen bears arms in order to protect himself from the tyranny of government."[76] If, as some have claimed, Gene Harrogate is a knock on the head away from Lester

---

[73] Brickman, 61, 63, 55.

[74] Jarrett, *Cormac McCarthy*, 128-129.

[75] Guillemin, *The Pastoral Vision*, 31; Bell, 23.

[76] Cant, *Cormac McCarthy and the Myth of American Exceptionalism*, 68.

Ballard's perversions and madness, could Ownby be one step away from guerilla-style violence and conspiratorial anti-federal government rantings?

Aside from these ambiguous questions, critics agree that at the close of the novel Ownby is worthy of our compassion. He ends up in the asylum, his movement restricted and curtailed, seemingly there for the rest of his life, perhaps dying sometime between novel's end and John Wesley's return to Red Branch. Guillemin reads his sadness at the end as "allegorical of a deeper melancholia" over the loss of his connection with the natural world, whilst Prather claims that he acutely experiences an existential and absurdist epiphany as he becomes aware of "the gap between the world as it is and the world as it is wished."[77]

Critics, especially Jarrett, concur that Sylder can be read as another allegorical study of alienation, a character unsuited to either the emerging industrial lifestyle or to the archaic mode of living as practiced by Ownby.[78] Bell casts Sylder as a "swaggering renegade" who "thrives upon taunting and thwarting the law," an attitude which assumes a philosophical aspect for Prather who views Sylder as living "in revolt against conceptions of value inherent in the new order," which can be read as a gesture of Camusean (metaphysical) defiance.[79] Like Ownby, Sylder also acts as a surrogate father figure for John Wesley, and he even gives the boy a puppy, which is "McCarthy's talisman of true fatherhood."[80] Although he seems more

---

[77] Guillemin, *The Pastoral Vision*, 33; Bell, *The Achievement of Cormac McCarthy*, 43.

[78] Jarrett, *Cormac McCarthy*, 13.

[79] Bell, *The Achievement of Cormac McCarthy*, 22; Jarrett, *Cormac McCarthy*, 13.

[80] Cant, *Cormac McCarthy and the Myth of American Exceptionalism*, 70.

comfortable with losing himself in a metropolitan environment, Sylder is also associated with the novel's wilderness aesthetic as his retreat into the mountains fuses "the idea of nature with the possibility for lawlessness, or for the transgression and transcendence of the world as given."[81]

John Wesley is also cast as a hybrid of mimetic, mythical, and allegorical tropes. For Jarrett he is perhaps "the most powerful representation of the theme of disconnection" as he embodies the postmodern Southerner or the Southerner-as-exile, "uprooted and cut off from his genealogical past through the mysterious death of a father he has never known and trapped within a present with which he has no relation."[82] Like his two mentors, John Wesley has lost "the illusion of centeredness, of being at home in the world" which for Prather can be attributed to his "accumulated experience with the details of death" throughout the narrative.[83] Like many characters that are to follow in his footsteps he is a "picaresque character, a homeless and parentless figure whose inner life remains undisclosed," a figure who leads a "practically wordless life" and who seems "guided exclusively by the need to become subsumed into that mysterious and wordless world."[84] Although lacking the sophisticated consciousness of Suttree, we can see how the two characters are literary kin as they seek out ways of knowing the world that are non-logocentric, that are instead attuned to older truths and rhythms.

For all of the melancholia associated with the novel's conclusion, Ellis reminds us that John Wesley offers that "rare instance in

---

[81] Holloway, 151.

[82] Jarrett, *Cormac McCarthy*, 13, 12.

[83] Prather, "'Like Something Seen,'" 51, 41.

[84] Guillemin, *The Pastoral Vision*, 20; Bell, *The Achievement of Cormac McCarthy*, 15.

McCarthy," as he is a character who may well develop and go on to better things, and it is fitting that workmen (figures McCarthy consistently portrays in a favorable light) make the way for him, successfully mediating between man and nature.[85] We should also remember that his act of civil disobedience may well be futile, but his return of the hawk bounty "suggests that John Wesley has cultivated an ontological appreciation for wild nature, a change from his earlier utilitarian preoccupation," which lends hope to the idea that at least someone will develop his own wilderness aesthetic after the narrative itself concludes.[86] Finding linear traces of development in an allegorical and picaresque character can be difficult, but he seems to have learnt the "crucial distinction between revolt against unfair laws and the betrayal of one's friends and neighbors."[87]

Like his two mentors, John Wesley's true significance rests with his status as an allegorical figure. Specifically, he embodies the potential that narrative affords to structure one's existence where all other ordering principles seem obsolete. The act of narration therefore affords him an "opportunity to reorder his past, a chance to recontextualize fragments of memory," and his "narration is simultaneously an act of revolt and an act of creation."[88] Narrative consciousness becomes his transcendence, and in much the same way as narrative itself and McAnally Flats operate for Suttree, Red Branch becomes an internalized geography or cartography and site of resistance for him as he leaves, seemingly for good. Dianne Luce draws significant intertextual parallels between the conclusion of the novel and the

---

[85] Ellis, 61.
[86] Berry, "The Lay of the Land," 67.
[87] Prather, "'Like Something Seen,'" 51.
[88] Ibid., 40, 42.

end of "Wake for Susan" as "both protagonists walk away from cemeteries into their futures, leaving behind the artifacts of the past that have attended their healing hallucinated recollections."[89]

The Orchard Keeper also contains a number of themes that would be revisited throughout the rest of McCarthy's work. The narrative reveals the hubris and "the vanity of moral constructs," whilst it is littered with examples of "geological and scientific phenomena as images for the mutability of every form of life and culture."[90] The novel contains a "high level of unassimilated raw material," and whilst McCarthy has been rightly praised for his ability to "make us see," certain passages threaten to overwhelm the reader "by the sheer accumulation of sensory detail."[91] McCarthy documents the fact that there aren't many "vast, unimplicated space[s] left" and that the only permanence available to us is "one based upon an intense awareness of impermanence," that life is "possible only in a continual and more or less cordial dialog with death."[92] *The Orchard Keeper* "emphasizes the layeredness of reality and the nonlinear aspects of time," and it suggests—as practically all of McCarthy's work does—that everyone is alienated and that narrative offers the best hope for coherence in a world such as this.

---

[89] Luce, "They aint the thing," 29.

[90] Guillemin, *The Pastoral Vision*, 19; Cant, *Cormac McCarthy and the Myth of American Exceptionalism*, 66.

[91] Bell, *The Achievement of Cormac McCarthy*, 13; Holloway, 83.

[92] Bell, *The Achievement of Cormac McCarthy*, 30; Grammer, 33.

CHAPTER 4

Outer Dark

Published in 1968, McCarthy's second novel is undoubtedly difficult in terms of theme, style, subject, and design. A plot exists only in the most notional sense, and although characters overlap, the protagonists are never fully aware of their inter-connectedness, as is the case with *The Orchard Keeper*. There are several references in the text which go some way in helping us place the action both temporally and geographically, yet overall, the novel denies any attempt to read it within socially realistic terms; indeed, McCarthy seems to have dispensed with the mimetic elements that we identified in his debut novel. The overriding ordering principle seems to be an allegorical one, but can we speak of an ordering principle in a novel that is so relentlessly dark, so metaphysically ambiguous?

For many, a first reading of the novel results in confusion, bewilderment, and shock; it is the aim of this chapter to help ease some of that confusion and attempt to illuminate what is, arguably, McCarthy's most complex novel. At the most fundamental level, *Outer Dark* can be read within the mythical paradigm of the American road narrative, even if McCarthy makes it even more gothic and grotesque than Faulkner's *As I Lay Dying*. Like many of McCarthy's novels it can be read in part as a *bildungsroman*, although we fail to witness a fully conventional maturation of characters and resolution usually associated with that particular form. The novel opens and closes with dreamlike sequences infused with motifs of blindness and darkness which involve Culla Holme, one of our leading protagonists here, and these terrifying nightmare visions are filled with longings for clemency and salvation that will never be fulfilled. These passages also reveal a disquieting sense of evil that surrounds Culla, and he can never quite rid himself of it for the duration of the narrative. We soon learn that the reason for Culla's dream-world guilt (a guilt that he never displays or ponders upon in the "real" world, such as it exists in the novel) principally lies in the fact that he has violated a foundational social taboo by sleeping with and impregnating his sister Rinthy Holme. He and Rinthy live in total isolation from any kind of community or social network, even from their own family, and the two live out a wretched existence in a characteristically awful (for McCarthy) domestic setting. Furthermore, Culla fails to summon any kind of medical help to assist Rinthy during the torturous delivery of the child (not even a midwife, or the "midnight" woman as she is referred to in the text).

However, Culla is not done with violating taboos. Whilst Rinthy is recovering from the birth, he takes the unnamed child and leaves it for dead in the nearby woods, and upon his return to their cabin he tells Rinthy that the child has died. Quite naturally, she demands to see where the child has been buried, and Culla reluctantly takes her to the supposed burial scene. Rinthy, despite her fragile physical and mental state, uncovers Culla's lie, and this allows for the road narrative proper to begin. Rinthy heads out on a quest to find her child, and Culla heads out to find Rinthy. In the interlude between Culla hiding the child and Rinthy uncovering his lie, the child has been taken up by an itinerant tinker, a stereotypical homeless pariah in a novel littered with such figures. As their respective quests unfold, they meet a cast of characters who exhibit a range of grotesque characteristics, some of whom readily articulate their essentialist readings of the world, and we are privy to various kinds of grizzly violence and brutality—ranging from disembowelment and domestic violence to cannibalism—and, specifically with regard to the effect Culla elicits, varying degrees of class consciousness and social snobbery. Against this backdrop, the narrative consciousness asks a series of profound metaphysical questions, with the most pronounced exploring the consequences we face if, like Culla, we renounce our claims to self-authorship and the telling of our own story in the world. This seems to be the true allegorical import here, and the treatment of narrative as a potentially grounding agency in the world is a major theme of McCarthy's later work (especially *Blood Meridian* and the Border Trilogy). We have seen how this theme is also a pronounced one in *The Orchard Keeper*, and it is of central importance in the shadowy, unsettling pages of his second Appalachian novel.

Although unnumbered in the text itself there are six italicized passages which structure the novel. Each section details, or is a prelude to, a variety of brutal, extra-legal acts undertaken by the murderous triune that haunt the text. The journey and fate of the triune and Culla are inexorably bound together, and it is no coincidence that when they join the text "proper" it is Culla whom they meet. However, the trail of ruin they cause in the italicized passages is also referenced in the text, and the series of bodies and corpses that we see rotting, hanging, or swaying in all kinds of grotesque ways have met their end at the hands of this dastardly trio. Following each italicized passage there are a total of eighteen sections which vary in length from a single sub-section to as many as seven. Culla and Rinthy appear together for the first and only time in the opening section (after the first italicized passage) and, following this, the sub-sections alternate between them as the road narrative itself begins.

It is clear from this brief synopsis that the subject matter and structure of the novel are undeniably complex. In this second novel we see McCarthy developing his style and aesthetic, and in *Outer Dark* there are several features that McCarthy would go on to employ throughout his work which many readers find confusing, as they are authorial gestures that add another cryptic later of impenetrability to the text. A chief source of frustration arises from his refusal to punctuate, especially sections of dialog, which make it hard for many readers to keep abreast of the action. One of his greatest strengths is his ability to capture local vernacular and dialect, which is often stripped down and spoken by inarticulate characters who offer a stark contrast to the often profound and archaic voice provided by the authorial presence or narrative consciousness.

In his second novel, McCarthy pulls off this juggling act throughout. Many of the characters seem to barely possess only the most basic cognitive functions, and on the rare occasions they do speak, they often articulate essentialist and highly cryptic readings of the world. The following passage offers an example where McCarthy switches from the omniscient authorial voice to the voice of his character without any grammatical or linguistic break. The first two sentences can be attributed to the narrator, but the narrative then switches over to Culla, who does his best to explain his predicament to (in this instance) the leader of the triune in his usual awkward and bumbling manner. In a writer so renowned for his refusal to interiorize or psychologize his characters in a conventional manner, the smooth transition between authorial and character voice compensates for this somewhat, and dialog in McCarthy therefore becomes not just a triumph of capturing dialect but a vital component in capturing, at least in some way, the motivation, failings, and limitations of his characters, as evidenced in the following passage:

Holme's voice came out quavering and alien. He heard it with alarm. I was huntin my sister, he said. She run off and I been huntin her. I think she might of run off with this here tinker. Little old scrawny lookin kind of a feller. Herself she's just young. I been huntin her since early in the spring and I cain't have no luck about findin her. They ain't no tellin what all kind of mess she's got into. She was sick anyways. She was never a real stout person. (OD 177)

Georg Lukács's critique that the novelistic form captures a particular kind of "transcendental homelessness" can be successfully applied to McCarthy's novels.[1] Indeed, perhaps nowhere is this feeling of "transcendental homelessness" more acute than in *Outer Dark* where homelessness—in social, geographic, and metaphysical terms—is one of the most pronounced themes. The theme of homelessness also has repercussions in terms of how McCarthy critiques some of the foundational myths of the Southern literary imagination, especially the manner in which he depicts place and his characters' relationship to it, along with their relationship to community, family, and religion. Although we can locate a gothic sensibility at play in his other Southern novels, the mood dominates in *Outer Dark* and McCarthy's treatment of the gothic, along with his depiction of a series of grotesque characters, enables us to firmly place the text within the Southern gothic tradition. Indeed, any attempt to apply a strictly (socially) realistic paradigm to the novel will be frustrated, as the landscapes presented to us, these "spectral wastes," are more akin to a world plucked from a horrid nightmare than a settled, civically ordered pastoral society.

---

[1] Lukács, *The Theory of the Novel*, 41.

Terms like "gothic" and the "grotesque" are frequently used in discussions of Southern literature, but we should perhaps take a moment here to define exactly what we mean by them and establish how they play out in the novel itself. Irving Malin offers a conventional definition of the Gothic in the following quote from his study *New American Gothic*, and it captures the mysteriously charged atmosphere we encounter in the novel: "In Gothic, order breaks down: chronology is confused, identity is blurred, sex is twisted, the buried life erupts. The total effect is that of a dream."[2]

Gothic literary "space" is conventionally characterized by feelings of claustrophobia, fear, dread, and isolation elicited by a succession of enclosed spaces, all of which we encounter in *Outer Dark*. Although the conventional signifiers of gothic dread such as castles, cathedrals, and dungeons are not to be found here, they have been replaced by forests, swamps, and a succession of ghostly "spectral wastes." In her study of the function of gothic spaces in Eudora Welty's fiction, Ruth Weston provides the following definition which corresponds to McCarthy's use of gothic space in *Outer Dark*:

> The most basic element of Gothic is the gothic space, the definition of which proceeds from the earliest literary appropriations of labyrinthine enclosures, such as cathedral and castle dungeons, as well as from a general awareness of a psychological or parapsychological realm that impinges upon the everyday world of actuality. The gothic space is a difficult and unpredictable setting that surrounds a center of suspense and ... [is] often part of a bare-stage wasteland that heightens the exposed nature of the human being who is trapped there. It is always

---

[2] Malin, *New American Gothic*, 9.

> mysteriously charged with power. Gothic spaces ... engender anxiety, dread, and the sense that escape is not possible.³

Vereen Bell initiated a fascinating critical debate by claiming that *Outer Dark*, more than any other McCarthy novel, embodies the nihilism that Bell identifies as operating throughout his work; indeed, Bell goes so far as to claim that *Outer Dark* is as "brutally nihilistic as any serious novel written in this century in this unnihilistic country."⁴ The catalog of horrors that one finds upon reading the novel certainly seems to support Bell's reading, although the manner in which allegory functions in the text perhaps offers a persuasive counter-point. Arguably the most pronounced allegorical themes are those associated with ideas of judgment, punishment, and salvation, especially as they apply (or perhaps don't apply) to Culla. From the apocalyptic dream sequence which opens the novel Culla is subjected to a series of mock trials and judgments where his "worth"—in material, spiritual, moral or philosophical terms—is assessed. In each of these trials, conducted first by different squires who gauge his market worth according to their self-righteous Puritanical beliefs, then by the preacher following his supposed failure to stop a hog driver from falling to his death and, finally, from the triune who represent a "mindless jury," Culla fails to offer a version of events or a narrative of his own making. This ultimately results in the murder of his child and his subsequent wanderings which one imagines will continue long after the text concludes, as in McCarthy's early short stories. His failure to assume the responsibility of self-authorship, of somehow determining his own fate, is what ultimately condemns

---

3 Weston, *Gothic Traditions*, 18–19.
4 Bell, *The Achievement of Cormac McCarthy*, 34.

him, and this ensures that *Outer Dark* has a profound allegorical power to it, a warning issued by McCarthy of the horrors that befall his characters when they forsake the possibility of narrative in a world where, to borrow from *The Crossing*, "we can never be done with the telling. Of the telling there is no end" (TC 452).

The most familiar Southernist motif that McCarthy employs throughout the text is that of the gothic and grotesque. The novel is populated with a series of physically grotesque characters replete with all nature of deformities and disfigurements. The majority of such figures are women, and it is Rinthy who invariably encounters them, such as the "ancient crone without a nose" or the "stooped and hooded anthropoid that came muttering down the fence toward her" before she leads Rinthy up to her house that lies brooding "in a palpable miasma of rot" (OD 57, 108-9). Female characters in the novel are for the most part grotesquely disfigured or symbolically embroiled in hate-filled relationships and domestic arrangements that resemble a particular type of entrapment experienced by women in gothic fiction. Rinthy is the victim of sexual abuse and incest, and other women she meets whilst on the road are the victims of hideous misfortune and domestic violence. Such an example includes the woman Rinthy briefly stays with whose five children all died from cholera and whose husband calls her a "flaptongued old bat" (OD 107) in the prelude to a heated physical altercation; she also encounters a series of older women who appear curiously asexual and who are seemingly without any reproductive capability. The gothic and grotesque characters thus lend a feeling of fairytale-like entrapment to the novel, as embodied by the family who Rinthy undertakes part of her journey with: "On their chairs in such black immobility these travelers could have been stone figures quarried from the architecture of an older time" (OD 77).

We have noted how McCarthy is a writer who uses the novelistic form to give his readers a sense of grounding in the world through his depiction of place, as evidenced in descriptions of Knoxville in *The Orchard Keeper* and *Suttree* especially. However, his narrative consciousness is also one that makes us feel homeless in the world, as time and again he asks complex and ambiguous metaphysical questions that make us aware of our fundamental homelessness in the world, and nowhere is this disquieting feeling more acute than in *Outer Dark*. With his second novel McCarthy removes virtually of all the techniques that he used to ground and orientate our reading experience in his debut novel.

The gothic strangeness and grotesque characters in the novel tend to dominate our reading, and they certainly thwart any attempt to impose a realistic analysis upon it. There seems to be no sense of order or progression to the temporal development in the novel, and descriptions of the natural world do not help matters here, as the environment seems to engulf, dwarf, and overtly threaten the human form, and violence abounds everywhere. At various points in the text we witness alligators viciously peering out from uninviting swamplands, rivers hissing and boiling, and forests are described as gnarled and ready to ensnarl anyone who dares to enter.

And yet, somewhat incongruously perhaps, McCarthy includes several geographic references and suggestions that modernity is encroaching even upon this barren wasteland, and such references, no matter how cryptic, allow us to place the novel as Southern. The world depicted here is hardly an Edenic sanctuary or pastoral idyll, but what work is carried out seems agricultural in nature, and the text suggests that mill towns are appearing throughout the landscape. An early description of the landscape near Culla and Rinthy's cabin informs us that the country was "low and swampy" (OD 16), which suggests a possible setting in lower Appalachia. Place names mentioned include Preston Flats, Chicken River, and Walker Springs, which suggests that this territory has been mapped in some way, using the technique of naming habitats after significant local environmental features, a commonplace feature of Southern settlements and cartography. The mention of such place names go some way to orienting the reader and placing the action, although the narrative consciousness undermines such attempts with its impenetrable metaphysical questioning. Throughout the novel, Culla is consistently asked where he comes from (to which he answers Johnson County), and one critic maintains this could be the Johnson County in Tennessee, which is in the far northeastern corner of the state.[5]

Descriptions of other people and places alternate between the archaic and the unreal in a historical period that is barely decipherable. At different points, Culla encounters scenes that suggest both modernity and the pre-modern, pre-industrial South, as he converses with a teamster fixing a car in one instance and then, a little later, is caught up in the frenzied rush of hog drivers taking their livestock to market, which suggests a landscape untouched by usable roads or sound railway links. Ronald L. Lewis notes that "shipment by train took the place of driving" in the 1850s, which reveals how McCarthy anachronistically subverts temporal order in the novel.[6] The temporal ambiguity is only increased when we see Rinthy conversing with a doctor and a lawyer, a sure sign that a settled and stable civic order must be in place and that not all is unregulated here. Indeed, there are also some indications that, as in the close of *The Orchard Keeper*, some kind of civic authority is beginning to manage human use of

---

[5] Cant, *Cormac McCarthy and the Myth of American Exceptionalism*, 83.
[6] Lewis, "Beyond Isolation," 26.

the landscape and environment, suggesting that this is no uncharted wilderness and that a level of modernistic bureaucracy has asserted itself. Furthermore, one of the characters with whom Culla converses informs him that he used to hunt for geese for a living "afore it was outlawed" (OD 121), although he fails to clarify whether this act was outlawed by a legal or extra-legal agency.

Outer Dark also continues McCarthy's savage critique of pastoral/agrarian ideology. As we have noted, early favorable reviews by some of the old guard conservative critics of the Southern intelligentsia became increasingly less favorable as McCarthy intensified his critique of the values of the Southern Renascence, particularly those espoused by the Agrarians. The landscape in the novel is consistently portrayed as a barren wasteland, where nothing seems to cultivate, grow, or prosper. Not only does the natural world here seem stricken by some terrible plague, but nature itself is a threatening presence which seems to engulf and ensnarl the human form. McCarthy continues to use landscape to articulate or represent the interiority of his characters, which is a valuable technique in a novel where many protagonists do not possess the vocabulary, cognitive reasoning, or consciousness to accomplish such a task.

Examples of threatening, apocalyptic nature abound in the novel. "Swollen waters" contain a "bloodcolored spume" whilst viciously hissing (OD 15), and a "spectral quietude" permeates the country, "as if something were about that crickets and nightbirds held in dread" (OD 16). Such threatening and unwelcoming descriptions of the landscape predominantly express the turmoil in Culla's soul, and in one memorable instance it seems as if he is caught in an inescapable and nightmarish fairytale realm: "the trees beginning to close him in, malign and baleful shapes that reared like enormous androids provoked at the alien insubstantiality of this flesh colliding among them" (OD 17). It should be noted that this description comes as he is about to abandon his child in the woods in what is yet another violation of one of the most fundamental social taboos; indeed, it is as if the landscape is recognizing the horror within him—and among itself—and the inanimate world seems to possess a consciousness of his act that Culla himself is lacking. The situation doesn't improve for Culla, there is simply no progression or development whatsoever, and he is doomed to wander in a barren wasteland at the novel's end, amongst "naked trees in attitudes of agony and dimly hominoid like figures in a landscape of the damned. A faintly smoking garden of the dead" (OD 242). This most definitely is not one of the gardens of the world, nor has it been for the duration of the narrative.

Culla therefore finds himself in this "faintly smoking garden of the dead" at the end *and* the beginning of the novel. From the opening of the narrative proper (after the first italicized passage) we encounter Culla in a dream world amongst "a delegation of human ruin" watched over by a prophet of whom Culla asks, "Can I be cured?" (OD 5). Salvation is denied Culla due to the fact that, in material and metaphysical terms, he fails to own or acknowledge anything—his sin, his transgressions, his guilt, his son, even where he is from. By foregoing this he forsakes his own narrative and is therefore condemned to a sorry but deserving fate in the novel. He is constantly asked where he is from, where he is heading, and what his purpose is (a hugely symbolic question) to which he always replies, "I don't know" (OD 81).

Yet it is hard to feel any sympathy for Culla, as we do for Rinthy, especially as he is openly hostile, impatient, and misogynistic towards her, imploring her to "mend woman" following her pregnancy, and he completely ignores the trauma he has put her through (OD 30). A palpable sense of evil seems to follow Culla wherever he goes, and he embodies—or is never far away from—"disciples of darkness" and the "very shape of evil" itself (OD 218). There are also some significant occasions where Culla reveals his complete inability to operate with the "normative" (as far as one exists in this novel) realm of society and work, and he is unable to even spell his own name (OD 202). His failure to name or identify himself even in this most elementary fashion has serious implications for the fate of his child as he also fails to name and identify with him.

Culla is clearly a worthless soul in a metaphysical and material sense. Indeed, it is important to note how he elicits a feeling of utter contempt from the landed or propertied class in the novel, and they never fail to display a self-righteous and condescending attitude towards him. They claim to sympathize with his poverty-stricken state although they never miss an opportunity to preach to him about the Puritanical virtues of hard work, self-discipline, and thrift. Store owners and their clerks, squires, work supervisors, and preachers all partake in this acutely class-conscious ridiculing of Culla, ensuring that the "normative" embodiments of the American dream in the novel, of progress, order, and responsibility, judge and denounce him, as the triune do in mythic and allegorical terms.

An early example of this occurs when he makes the long trek from his deserted cabin to the general store only to find that it's Sunday and the store is therefore closed. This earns him an admonishment from the store owner that "we still Christians here" (OD 26) intimating that he is beyond the morally ordering principle of Christianity and also beyond something so simple as the temporal ordering structure of the days of the week and the calendar. Elsewhere a store clerk regards him with a contemptuous "malignant smile" when he purchases a pitiful amount of cheese and crackers, whilst he is implicated into a criminal act outside a store in Cheatham by a clerk who had previously served him (OD 39, 88). Innocent or not, Culla—by simply just being there—is always implicated in things he did not do, and he is always judged or charged with something. Culla also invokes the chagrin of members of the working community other than store clerks, as the foreman in charge of the gang of black workers shoots him "one half-contemptuous look," and another local businessman of some repute regards him with a kind of "arrogant curiosity" (OD 131, 141).

Perhaps the most significant example of such an exchange occurs when Culla asks a local squire for some work. The squire asks where Culla is from, and he goes on to preach to him that family is a "sacred obligation" and that "shiftlessness is a sin" (OD 47). The squire speaks for the larger social and materialistic culture here, and he unwittingly exposes two foundational bedrocks of this order—family and hard work—that Culla has violated. A figure as self-assured in his own values as the squire is bound to be undermined in a novel such as this, and when we initially see him standing in a "coffin-sized doorway," it foreshadows his murder at the hands of the triune (OD 45). Ironically, the trio uses a type of scythe to kill the squire, using as a weapon an agrarian tool which is generally used to cultivate the land, whereas in this instance they use it to bring an end to such enterprises.

Culla is also subjected to another judgment from an upstanding member of the business community in yet another scene where he is placed in a mock trial. After (illegally) spending the night in the cabin of a reputable local landholder, Culla is once again asked where he came from and how he "happened" to run off from there, his "shiftless" appearance once again eliciting such a response. Culla represents an unknowable quality in metaphysical *and* geographic terms, and this serves to undermine the stereotypical notion of the traditional closeness of Southern communities. The squire concludes by instructing Culla in the ways of self-determination and the importance of making your own luck, beliefs enshrined within the patriarchal nature of his family and American culture at large. Culla certainly has made his own luck, but in no way does it conform to the paradigm of moral righteousness and disciplined self-improvement as espoused by the squire in this scene (OD 21-08).

Such absurd mock trials and examples where Culla is judged are a mere prelude to the awful denouement that awaits him when he is finally reunited with his son, who is by now in the hands of the evil triune. After narrowly escaping from the disastrous ferry ride which seems to have claimed the lives of the operator and his fellow passenger, Culla reaches the shore only to find a worse fate awaiting him as he stumbles upon the evil triune. This is the first time that the group has joined the narrative outside of the italicized passages, and it is inevitable that they would meet Culla when they do. Symbolically, the sinister leader of the triune is linked to Culla via their shared philosophy and beliefs in the importance of naming.

The process of naming in McCarthy is always a problematic issue, as is his use and portrayal of maps, another means by which we ground ourselves in the world, a technique which allows us to supposedly recognize the world and our place in it. At their most fundamental level, names give an indication of what something or someone is, who they belong to, and perhaps even where they came from, so it is a highly symbolic moment when, following Rinthy's request, Culla refuses to name their child because "you don't name dead things" (OD 31). His failure to name the child confirms his moral shiftlessness and lack of worth, just as the squires and landed gentry have judged him according to his lack of *material* worth, and Culla's link to the bearded leader of the triune is clearly established when he says to the mute member of their terrible gang that "I wouldn't name him because if you cain't name somethin you cain't claim it" (OD 177). By not naming his son, and therefore his sin or his guilt, Culla has ensured that the infant will meet its gruesome end at the hands of this satanic trio. Culla has found an answer to his own question of salvation expressed in the dream at the start of the novel, and this "mindless jury" has mirrored the hog drivers' claim to the preacher they meet that Culla is indeed "too mean to be saved" (OD 231-33, 225). Culla has symbolically found the "nowheres" that he has been heading to throughout the novel, as the trio represents a place that can't be named, a place beyond every imaginable taboo or normative moral code.

Due to Rinthy's pitiful physical condition, which was of course caused by Culla, her alienation and isolation are even more acute than her brother's, although she manages to evoke sympathy in the reader rather than contempt. She is unable, and perhaps never even has, travelled the four miles to the general store despite being in her late teenage years. In her conversation with the doctor, we discover that the child was born some six months ago and that she has been on the road searching for him for the majority of that time (OD 153). These are rare historical or temporal insights into Rinthy's existence, and they remain all we get for a character who otherwise remains engaged in her stoic and melancholic attempt to find her child. We know nothing of her hopes, motivations, history, or anxieties other than those caused by Culla's dreadful actions, and throughout the entire novel, she is engaged in an attempt to somehow make them better.

Even when her road narrative begins, she declares that "they ain't a soul in this world but what is a stranger to me," whilst elsewhere she confirms her state of utter homelessness by stating rather awkwardly, "I ain't even got nowheres to run off from" (OD 29, 101). Road narratives in popular American culture are associated with the mythic dream of freedom, new beginnings, and the thrill of adventure, yet Rinthy finds none of these things during her sorry travels. Her isolated condition also forms another part of McCarthy's critique of the myth of Southern community and generosity; if a spirit of cooperation and neighborliness is supposedly paramount in such romanticized agrarian communities, how did she end up in such an awful condition? No legal, neighborly, or community agency comes to her aid whatsoever here. This is confirmed in a pitiful exchange she has with the father of the family that she will shortly spend several days with as he claims that it "must be a considerable piece for me not to know ye. You live towards town? / I don't know, she said. / Ha, the man said, don't know where ye live? / I mean I dint know where town's at" (OD 58). McCarthy continues his critique of the supposedly wholesome Southern ideal of family as the text intimates that the same man, along with his son, sexually abuse Rinthy whilst she stays with them:

> It was only a few minutes before they entered, stepping soft as thieves and whispering harshly to one another. She watched them with squint eyes, the man all but invisible standing not an arm's length from where she lay and going suddenly stark white against the darkness as he shed his overalls and posed in his underwear before mounting awkwardly bedward like a wounded ghost. When they were all turned in they lay in the hot silence and listened to one another breathing. She turned carefully on the rattling pallet. She listened for a bird or for a cricket. Something she might know in all that dark. (OD 65)

In other instances, Rinthy is cast as a fabled fairytale character that is oblivious to and ignorant of the evil that permeates the world she wanders through. Indeed, at times, she is ironically described in scenes reminiscent of pastoral tranquility such as the following: "Butterflies attended her and birds dusting the road did not fly up when she passed. She hummed to herself as she went some child's song from an old dead time" (OD 98). Culla is associated with images of perpetual darkness, and he embodies an atavistic sense of malice and evil, whereas Rinthy—despite her physical condition which evokes a great deal of sympathy—still manages to represent some kind of innocence.

The most ironic moment where McCarthy uses Rinthy to subvert the pastoral comes when she unknowingly stumbles upon the remains of her "chap," the child she has been searching for throughout the novel. We see that that child didn't even receive a proper burial (another mark against Culla's character, as it leaves us to assume that he once again left the child without a thought after his encounter with the triune), a final indignity not uncommon in McCarthy's fiction. The melancholy mood is heightened as Rinthy unwittingly fulfils her quest by stepping into the glade "delicate as any fallow doe," walking as she does over the ashes and remains of her child, "the chalk bones, the little calcined ribcage" (OD 237) as the tinker's corpse swings in a nearby tree, looking over this desolate scene. One of the grotesquely deformed characters she stays with for a short spell tells Rinthy that "it's a poor lot wanderin about thataway" (OD 115), and indeed it is, but what other choice does she have?

The tinker is another desperate pariah in the book, and his position as a culturally designated outsider allows him an oppositional space, so to speak, from where he can critique the world as he finds it. Yet his status as an outsider is no romantic one, and he exposes his bitterness in his exchange with Rinthy (for whom he certainly has little sympathy). His words echo the essentialist viewpoint of other characters when he states, "I give a lifetime wanderin in a country where I was despised" and further that he's "seen the meanness of humans till I don't know why God ain't put out the sun and gone away" (OD 192). Here the tinker echoes Culla's dream from the opening of the novel, and it certainly seems that God has looked down upon all of this and decided that he may well have seen enough. The tinker also plays the marginal character/prophet role that is so important to McCarthy, and the prophecy he offers certainly has repercussions for both Culla and Rinthy: "Them accounts is in blood and they ain't nothin in this world to pay em out with" (OD 193).

Such essentialist philosophies add another layer of complexity to McCarthy's aesthetic, and they seem to call into question the very validity or relevance of the act (his art) that he is engaged in; if the world is like this, and will forever be so, then why bother? One character boldly proclaims to Culla that if you "study long ... ye study wrong" (OD 125) and one of the hog drivers expresses a similar essentialist reading of the world, embodied in his analysis of hogs themselves, which metaphorically represents the larger epistemology of the novel and the culture that it springs from. Indeed, we could replace "hog" with human here and still get to the heart of things: "What can a feller know about one? Not a whole lot. I've run with hogs since I was just a shirttail and I ain't never come to no real understan of em" (OD 216). However, as Culla's fate reveals, it is *not* studying the world that is the fatal error in McCarthy, not undertaking the existential act of self-authorship that lies behind the power of the allegory at play in the novel. This may not entirely satisfy some readers, but it does perhaps go some way to refuting the idea that the novel is nothing but nihilistic or a sensationalist expose of the fact that there are "darksome ways afoot in this world," as the blind man identifies as operating at novel's close (OD 241).

The reason essentialist or nihilistic readings remain so persuasive is the continued presence of the grim triune, and they also underpin the allegorical themes explored in the narrative. They represent the most savage aspect of McCarthy's treatment of the foundational myths of Southern literary culture in the novel, incorporating a critique of agrarian or pastoral philosophy, community, and religion. They wander around the empty fields with their "crude agrarian weapons," using tools meant for cultivating the land for their own gory harvest (OD 35). Symbolically, one of their victims is the landed squire who had preached to Culla about his "shiftlessness." He meets a suitably gruesome end at the hands of these three who care little for his (or anyone else's) sermonizing or adherence to Puritanical doctrines: "the brush hook ... missed his neck and took him in the small of the back severing his spine and when he fell he fell unhinged sideways and without a cry" (OD 51). Like Anton Chigurh from *No Country for Old Men*, they display a kind of entrepreneurial genius when it comes to finding things to kill people with. They also serve as a perverse extra-legal agency, responsible for leaving a very tangible sense of death wherever they go: "In the cool and smoking dawn there hung from a blackhaw tree in a field on the edge of the village the bodies of two itinerant millhands" (OD 95).

In the fifth italicized passage they disembowel a man with whom Culla had conversed in the previous section and who had ironically claimed that he wouldn't turn away Satan for a drink (OD 117). His failure to do so results in his grizzly (yet vividly striking) murder, where he mistakes his assassins for his minister:

> *Minister? he said. Minister? His assassin smiled upon him with bright teeth, the faces of the other two peering from*

> *either shoulder in consubstantial monstrosity, a grim triune that watched wordless, affable ... The fist rose in an eruption of severed viscera until the blade seized in the junction of his breastbone and he stood disemboweled.* (OD 129)

It is important to note how they always seem to arrive at a place where Culla has just left, and it is inevitable that their paths will cross and that when they do it will not be pleasant. The tinker is one of their final victims, and he, like their other victims, "*could not account for them,*" as the narrator informs us (OD 229). It should also be noted that all of the italicized passages appear on odd numbered pages, as if the trio cannot even be accounted for or made "square" and neat by the most elemental mathematics.

The "grim triune" (OD 129) finally have their encounter with Culla following his involvement in the ferry crash, and he stumbles upon them as they are camping by the river. Their leader has a darkly menacing presence about him, and he warrants the disquieting feelings that he invokes in people he encounters. His textual presence, and his cryptic mocking of Culla, clearly preempts Judge Holden from *Blood Meridian*, as illustrated by the following example: "In the upslant of light his beard shone and his mouth was red, and his eyes were shadowed lunettes with nothing there at all" (OD 171). His devilish characteristics are further underlined as he "seemed to be seated in the fire itself, cradling the flames to his body as if there were something there beyond all warming" (OD 179). This trio, who refuse to fully name or identify themselves, ensure that Culla will remain on his path to nowhere, and they are indeed bound by nothing, no moral, ethical, or communal bond, as evidenced when the mute member of their gang gleefully devours Culla and Rinthy's child in one of the most viscerally shocking scenes in all of McCarthy's work: "The mute one knelt forward. He was drooling and making little whimpering noises in his throat ... The man handed him the child and he seized it up, looked once at Holme with witless eyes, and buried his moaning face in its throat" (OD 236).

It is perhaps hard to reconcile the trio to any kind of code, so steeped are they in myth and allegory. It could perhaps be argued that they do serve some kind of moral purpose here as they do punish Culla for his prior transgressions, although cannibalizing his innocent child makes this a hard argument to support, as not even Culla—let alone the child—deserves to meet such an end (although "fairly" administered justice is another extremely problematic concept in McCarthy's work). Interestingly, we can find a potential historical antecedent for them in the murderous Harpe brothers, an evil group who roamed parts of Appalachia in the late 1700s. We know that McCarthy thoroughly researches his novels, so it is possible that he came across stories of these mythical badmen as they committed a series of gruesome murders throughout Appalachia that resemble those committed by the group in *Outer Dark*. The following example, summarized here by Knoxville historian William MacArthur, has all the hallmarks of the group from McCarthy's second novel:

> Knoxville had its share of drunkards, thieves, and murderers. Among the most notorious of the latter were the Harpe brothers who settled eight miles west of town in 1797. They stole hogs and horses in the neighborhood and finally committed murder upon one Johnson whose body they cut open and filled with stones before dumping it in the river.[7]

---

[7] MacArthur, "Knoxville History: An Interpretation," 12.

Outer Dark is undoubtedly a complex novel in theme, subject matter, and structure. I hope that this section has gone some way to clarifying a work which is as dark and unsettling as any in McCarthy's body of work. The novel critiques foundational myths of the Southern literary imagination, most notably agrarian philosophy and the region's religious sensibility, whilst its sophisticated use of allegory guarantees that it simply isn't a sensationalist piece of gothic local-color fiction (although a case could be made that it parodies exotically imagined and falsely constructed local color depictions of Appalachia). The second part of this chapter will be devoted to reviewing the critical responses to the novel.

Overview of Critical Responses

Our textual overview of *Outer Dark* made it clear that it is a dark and unsettling work which, like so much of McCarthy's work, invites yet frustrates interpretation. For this reader at least *Outer Dark* is the most complex of McCarthy's entire oeuvre, and we find it difficult to historicize the novel within broader cultural or mythic narratives as we can do with *Blood Meridian*, a work that is perhaps even more allegorically complex. *Outer Dark* is a historical novel set in a loosely defined historical period; it functions as allegory even if the deeper, second meaning is somewhat hard to identify, and what resolution there is often leaves readers frustrated.

It should come as no surprise that such a complex work has generated a healthy amount of critical discourse. A central feature of many critical discussions refer to the difficulty of analyzing the novel, and Vereen Bell observes that McCarthy's work has an "uncatergorizable quality" which is only accentuated in a work that denies "the grids of understanding we habitually impose" upon the world, be they ethical, psychoanalytical or cultural.[8] Teri Witek echoes Bell's observations when she states that there is plot resolution but that it is "strangely qualified."[9] Rinthy does fulfill her quest by eventually finding her child, but what kind of meaning can we glean from the novel when she does?

Outer Dark functions as a mythical and allegorical novel rather than a socially realistic one, stylistic modes which more often than not frustrate attempts to neatly package it. In *The Late Modernism of Cormac McCarthy*, David Holloway provides a sophisticated theoretical reading which encourages us to rethink the relationship between fiction, aesthetics, and ideology. Holloway claims that the narrative is sealed in a place that is "cognitively inaccessible" to us as readers, and that although the timescale covered in the narrative is brief, "our ability to keep pace with its passing is consistently challenged by what is left out of the story."[10] Holloway goes on to state that "as readers of *Outer Dark* we loom alternately large and small, powerful and powerless, as participative cognitive presences liminal to the narrative itself." Further, there is an "overpowering sense of narrative lack or of missing content built into the fictive 'history' told by *Outer Dark*, abstracting the story as mappable totality."[11]

We highlighted how *The Orchard Keeper* (and all of McCarthy's work for that matter) manages to simultaneously ground and disorient readers. He frequently (and lovingly) describes place and landscape in his work, whilst the narrative consciousness leaves us metaphysically disorientated. In his debut novel, McCarthy pro-

---

[8] Bell, *The Achievement of Cormac McCarthy*, 38.
[9] Witek, "'He's Hell when he's Well,'" 83.
[10] Holloway, *The Late Modernism*, 88.
[11] Ibid., 90, 88.

vided incredibly vivid descriptions of Red Branch, the mountains, and even Knoxville, yet in *Outer Dark* he has dispensed with this strategy entirely, leaving us completely stranded in terms of temporal ordering and geography. This technique leaves the novel "cognitively inaccessible" for us as readers but, as Holloway claims, this is a central part of McCarthy's aesthetic which strives for "an objective critical distance ... between culture and the world upon which culture reports."[12] Although Holloway stops short of identifying this particular ideology, we shall see how many critics maintain that *Outer Dark* reports back on (and savagely critiques) the ideology and foundational myths of Southern culture and literature. In other words, McCarthy adopts an oppositional stance to the hegemonic narratives afforded by Southern culture, especially those crystallized in the Southern Renascence.

Many of the artists and critics who were directly involved or heavily influenced by the Southern Renascence propagated a myth of the South as a settled and stable society which embodied some of the more noble tenets of humanistic philosophy. This is why a critic such as Walter Sullivan could find words of praise for *The Orchard Keeper* but, as McCarthy's critique of renascence principles intensified, so did the chagrin of the more conservative body of critics affiliated with that seminal cultural movement. Indeed, Sullivan's disdain becomes evident when he discusses *Outer Dark*, which he regards as a "weird, almost gothic tale of incest," and he claims that *Outer Dark* and *Child of God* represent a "portent of barbarism" which offers "the best example of [the] destructive impulse in contemporary art. McCarthy is the artist not merely bereft of community and myth: he has declared war against these ancient repositories of order and

---

[12] Ibid., 93.

truth."[13] Another less than glowing critique is provided by Duane Carr, who accuses McCarthy of producing "some of the most blatant stereotypes of Southern 'rednecks' in contemporary American fiction."[14] Carr is also unimpressed with the multifaceted nature of McCarthy's style, and he claims that McCarthy can't quite pull off using realistic and allegorical techniques in the same novel, as "his capacity for rendering vivid realistic detail tends to pull his characters out of allegory, where they might safely be seen as archetypes, to the realm of realistic fiction, where they become stereotypes."[15]

Although Bell's readings are never anything less than thought provoking and illuminating we can also see traces of such conservatism in his critique of the novel. For Bell, McCarthy fills the "objective critical distance" that Holloway identifies with a nihilistic sensibility with the result that all "we are left with is the poignant sense that all human connections to a world of form, even the most basic, are illusory."[16] Bell goes on to offer a critique that would initiate a series of fascinating debates about the novel by claiming that *"Outer Dark*, in short, is as brutally nihilistic as any serious novel written in this century in this unnihilistic country."[17] As a result of this pervasive nihilism, Bell claims that "homeless wandering in *Outer Dark* is a metaphor for everyone's state," and that it is a "disturbing, powerful representation of not being at home in the world, of the perceived, scary disconnection of the human from the not-human that both Freud and Heidegger called the *unheimlich*."[18] By drawing some in-

---

[13] Sullivan, *A Requiem for the Renascence*, 70-72.

[14] Carr, "The Dispossessed White," 2.

[15] Ibid., 3.

[16] Bell, *The Achievement of Cormac McCarthy*, 83.

[17] Ibid., 34.

[18] Bell, *The Achievement of Cormac McCarthy*, 35, 32.

sightful parallels to Freud and Heidegger, Bell manages to show us how the novel's concerns transcend the regional and wrestle with some of the foundational meta-narratives of western civilization, and the novel's relationship with Freudian philosophy—especially the oedipal complex—will receive extended treatment here. However, his claim that the novel is "brutally nihilistic" is a viewpoint that many McCarthy scholars have disputed.

Before we move on to such critiques, we should consider Bell's assessment of Rinthy, as to an extent it arguably counters his nihilistic analysis of the novel. Bell claims that "her pain is *caused* by her choice to love and need, by her willingness to be less than human," and it is this quality in Rinthy, her epic stoicism, which adds another layer of complexity to the narrative.[19] Bell goes on to state that in a novel infused with images of homelessness, her "only true home is in words," a narrative "home" that is denied Culla due to his failure to recognize his guilt and shape his own tale.[20] A problematic resolution is offered, even if it does frustrate many readers, and one thing that is maintained to novel's end is the "medieval aura of allegory" to the narrative that "we find to be so successfully encoded that our approach to meaning is at once invited and thwarted."[21]

A number of critics have proposed readings which counter the one offered by Bell. In "Naming, Knowing and Nothingness: McCarthy's Moral Parables," Edwin Arnold refutes Bell's claim by stating that "in McCarthy's highly moralistic world, sins must be named and owned before they can be forgiven; and those characters who most insist on the "nothingness" of existence, who at-

---

[19] Ibid., 50.
[20] Ibid., 51-2.
[21] Ibid., 33.

tempt to remain "neutral," are those most in need of grace."[22] In this succinct quote Arnold gets to the heart of how allegory functions in the novel; by not "owning" or recognizing his sin, by not undertaking the self-renewing (albeit secular) act of staying true to his consciousness and narrating his tale, Culla is doomed. Thus the novel assumes a parable-like quality, a warning of what awaits us if we fail to do the same. McCarthy's vision is not one which generally suggests that our species can be improved or perfected, but the moralistic allegory at play within *Outer Dark* makes us aware of the perils of failing to narrate our own tale, which always amounts to a forsaking of moral responsibility in McCarthy's world.[23]

According to Arnold, Culla's increasingly desolate state can be attributed to the fact that "he creates a lie."[24] This lie puts him on his sorry quest and draws all kinds of trouble to him, including the grim triune and "it is as if his own guilt—or his denial of his own guilt—has called these figures forth."[25] Arnold's critique allows us to see that whilst the surface narrative of *Outer Dark* is one where the protagonists undertake a horrendous road journey in a gothic landscape with little hope of conventional novelistic resolution, the concealed narrative is about sin, guilt, and punishment. Perhaps McCarthy is too ambitious in the novel, perhaps he buries or obfuscates this too much, but informed readings such as the one Arnold provides help us get to the bottom of what is at stake here, and it is anything but nihilistic. Arnold makes a number of intertexutal parallels in his ar-

---

[22] Arnold, "Naming, Knowing and Nothingness," 54.

[23] It should be noted that the title of the novel is taken from the gospel of St. Matthew. For a discussion of how this pertains to the novel see William J. Schafer's insightful article, "Cormac McCarthy: The Hard Wages of Original Sin."

[24] Arnold, "Naming, Knowing, and Nothingness," 47.

[25] Ibid., 49.

ticle, and it is useful to consider one here before we move on. Arnold sees the kid in *Blood Meridian* as another Culla Holme, specifically as he fails to "examine his own heart, to name and face the judge, to acknowledge responsibility."[26] Indeed, when the terrifying Judge Holden (himself an updated and more sophisticated version of the leader of the triune) foresees the kid's fate when he says "there's a flawed place in your heart" (BM 299) he could quite as easily be talking about Culla. The geographic setting changes, but the existential perils his characters face when they fail to author the terms of their own existence remain the same.

William Spencer advances the moralistic critique posited by Arnold by considering the novel's relationship to Judeo-Christian theology in another reading that counters Bell's. Spencer identifies the perils we face when we fail to undertake a creative act of will, meaning that the novel allegorically warns that "ignorance is a key element" in Culla's doom-laden fate.[27] Culla obviously displays a quite unbelievable level of ignorance throughout, but so do characters who proclaim essentialist and dismissive readings of the world (such as the man who mistakes the leader of the triune for his minister and the hog driver who falls from the bluff), and it is no coincidence that characters who have such a myopic worldview meet suitably grizzly ends. Spencer maintains that ignorance invites and calls forth evil (or at least makes it permissible), and this adds another layer to the complex allegory at play within *Outer Dark*. Indeed, even the novel's structure contributes to underlining this important theme, as Spencer outlines:

> Early on, the effect of this pattern of interwoven chapters and the changes in typography is to imply the

---

[26] Ibid., 65.
[27] Spencer, "Cormac McCarthy's Unholy Trinity," 69.

> separateness of evil, to posit evil as a nightmarish force outside of humanity—but as the italics are dropped, so is the illusion of the separateness of evil. The novel makes it increasingly clear that these evil raiders are not so different from Culla Holme ... readers are subtly encouraged to see evil as a tendency *within* human beings, perhaps even as the *essence* of human beings. The dramatic decrease in italics further reinforces the sense that the nightmare has become a reality.[28]

Spencer acknowledges that it was inevitable that Culla would meet the trio as he starts out on a path of evil when the novel opens, and he never manages to leave it. Spencer also sees the leader of the triune as a darkly authoritarian parody of the God of the Old Testament who accordingly hands out his own version of justice, and he argues that Culla even becomes an apprentice in their grim trade.[29] Themes of judgment and punishment were identified in our overview of the text, and Spencer offers a further analysis of these important themes that reveals just how closely Culla is aligned with the monstrous leader: "When Culla decides to leave his baby to die and then lies about it to Rinthy, he is guilty of the same abuse of authority, malevolence, deception, violence, and destruction that are embodied in McCarthy's parodic trinity."[30]

Our overview of the critical responses to the novel has, for the most part, focused on how different critics have attempted to refute Bell's nihilistic critique by drawing our attention to how moral and ethical issues allegorically play out in the text. Our next selection of

---

[28] Ibid., 71-73.
[29] Ibid., 74, 72.
[30] Ibid., 76.

responses will return to answering Holloway's questions about how we can make the novel more cognitively accessible and what kind of world and ideology the novel reports back on. The work of Matthew Guinn, Robert Jarrett, and John Grammer (amongst others) help us see how McCarthy reports back on—and savagely critiques—some of the most foundational myths, ideologies, and cultural, historical, and imaginative narratives of the South.

Matthew Guinn does an excellent job in identifying McCarthy as a mythoclastic writer who critiques the dominant ideological narratives of Southern culture. Guinn sees a subversive pattern at play in all of McCarthy's work as he employs foundational Southern narratives, including representations of pastoral and Agrarian philosophy, religion, community, attachment to place, and so on, but Guinn persuasively argues that McCarthy savagely critiques them rather than offering them as viable organizing principles. Because of this he has invoked the chagrin of conservative critics such as Walter Sullivan who look for Southern fiction to reinforce a sense of regional "moral certitude." Not only does McCarthy ruthlessly deconstruct such a belief, but he asks us to consider that any kind of certitude was always illusory.[31] Guinn was writing prior to the publication of *The Road*, but he sees this mythoclasm operating throughout all of McCarthy's Southern works, and he encourages us to see *Outer Dark* as McCarthy's "farewell to the southern pastoral."[32]

John Grammer is a critic who would concur with Guinn's analysis, and his "A Thing Against Which Time Will Not Prevail: Pastoral and History in Cormac McCarthy's South" is one of the most intelligent and significant pieces of scholarship available on McCarthy's

---

[31] Guinn, *After Southern Modernism*, 109.
[32] Ibid., 99.

Southern fiction. The term "pastoral" is frequently used in discussions of the region's literature and, like the conventional, blissfully sheltered Arcadian image it evokes, it often gets away with remaining neutral, stable, and unchanging when in fact it is an incredibly contested ideology. The myth of the South representing a pastoral haven against the horrors of the modern world was outmoded as soon as it was conceived, and McCarthy's fiction (especially *Outer Dark*) sets about exposing this fallacy. This is a complex part of McCarthy's aesthetic, and his examination of the dangerous repercussions the false conceptions of myth and history can have is also explored in his [South]western work where, due mainly to cinematic depictions, the cultural iconography is more recognizable to the popular imagination.

We identified how Ownby's quasi-pastoral and isolationist dream was denied in *The Orchard Keeper*, and Grammer identifies how this process is intensified in the second novel. According to Grammer, McCarthy "wants to question the old southern dream of escape from history ... [he reminds] us of the wildness at the heart of nature, despite pastoral efforts to domesticate it."[33] The novel therefore reports back on the moment when a myth that informed so much of the region's literature is no longer valid, and the drama that unfolds is epic in nature as we witness "the moment when a community organized as a refuge from history is forced to confront it."[34]

The reference to community is a crucial one, as the community in the novel is one governed by "near-total estrangement," although Grammer suggests it was "presumably once unified and solid, [but is now] shattered to atoms; such cohesion as remains becomes a

---

[33] Grammer, "A Thing Against Which," 31.
[34] Ibid., 37.

destructive centripetal force."[35] Even the notional stability or sanctity offered by the conventional community is shown to be nothing but another illusion in the lie the South has told itself and the world. The antisocial and psychopathic triune do their best to disrupt any kind of communal harmony, and Grammer maintains that they can be read as embodying the "deadly threat which history poses to the pastoral realm ... they are that community's nightmare, the seed of destruction which lurks within the pastoral realm."[36] Grammer reads them as parodic figures as they roam the landscapes of the novel using tools generally used to farm and cultivate the land for their own bloody purposes. Perhaps we could also read them as harbingers of a new kind of ruthlessly acquisitive finance or industrial capitalism that was about to change the South forever and which cared only for personal gain, not communal well-being.

If the triune can be read as representative or archetypal figures (of impending pastoral doom in their case, much like the trio of more noble characters from *The Orchard Keeper* were representative figures of a certain type of pastoral hope), then Culla and Rinthy are equally archetypal. Grammer maintains that they are "in a sense the first citizens of their dying pastoral world," which could account for why everybody seems to know Rinthy and why Culla, one of the chief architects here in undermining the pastoral, is always suspected of "some dire crime."[37] Whilst he condemns Culla, Grammer's reading of Rinthy is consistent with other critics in that he sees her as a sympathetic character who represents something of a corrective—at least on a mythic level—to the catalog of horrors committed in the novel.

---

[35] Ibid.
[36] Grammer, "A Thing Against Which," 35-6.
[37] Ibid., 37-8.

Grammer claims that "Rinthy is of course a figure of great natural fecundity, the earth-as-mother who lies at the heart of the pastoral myth."[38] As we shall see, readings structured around feminist paradigms expose some problems with such critiques, but Grammer is not alone in identifying Rinthy's narrative experience as an archetypal treatment of gendered myths relating to the pastoral, as opposed to a character who reveals the writer's misogynistic sensibilities.

Georg Guillemin's *The Pastoral Vision of Cormac McCarthy* echoes the readings provided by Guinn and Grammer, as Guillemin also proclaims that in *Outer Dark* "the death of Southern pastoralism itself is dramatized."[39] As a result of this, Guillemin identifies the novel as expressing what he terms as McCarthy's emerging "wilderness aesthetic," a style that would find its most sophisticated expression in *Blood Meridian* and the Border Trilogy. However, Guillemin does not dismiss the novel as an overly ambitious and unnecessarily complex work of a young author, and he notes how McCarthy pulls off the difficult narrative task of constructing "a sinister parable on the demise of a myth out of the very iconography of the myth itself."[40] This conforms to Guinn's reading of McCarthy as a mythoclast, a writer whose work has a complex relationship to myth and who employs myths to ultimately subvert them; as we shall see, such a reading also anticipates John Cant's assessment of the novel. Guillemin also claims that the novel is a "pastoral parable from cover to cover," which means that landscape and supposedly inanimate matter are imbued with a consciousness, which means

---

38 Ibid., 38.
39 Guillemin, *The Pastoral Vision*," 71.
40 Ibid., 68.

that "the representation of landscape in much of *Outer Dark* [can be read as] an obvious representation of the inscape of Culla's psyche."[41]

Guinn, Grammer, and Guillemin therefore frame the novel as a work in which the myth of the pastoral is savagely critiqued, parodied, and erased. As the pastoral has been such a central component to the Southern literary imagination the novel assumes an allegorical import that goes beyond the realm of socially realistic or conventionally mimetic fiction. However, the novel is a characteristically multifaceted McCarthy text, so it does much more than allegorize the death of the pastoral. Other critics, such as Robert Jarrett and John Cant, maintain that the novel can be read as a critique of the myth of patriarchy and the role that religion (especially a type of doctrinarian Protestantism) plays in Southern culture.

Jarrett offers an insightful analysis of how the oedipal drama in *Outer Dark* critiques the myth of patriarchy in the South, especially as it is encoded in the region's literary genealogy. This oedipal conflict plays a significant role in all of McCarthy's work, and Jarrett is quite correct when he states that "from the early Southern novels to those set in the Southwest, McCarthy's fiction enacts the death, absence, or denial of the father."[42] On the most literal level Culla exemplifies a denying and absent father, and Jarrett's reading can be aligned with Arnold's when he claims that he "repudiates his own fatherhood" and that it is his "inability to recognize his own sin in the form of his child" that ultimately condemns him to his endlessly dark wandering and his son to his ghastly end.[43]

---

[41] Ibid, 57-58.
[42] Jarrett, *Cormac McCarthy*, 21.
[43] Ibid., 21, 16.

Such weak patriarchal figures suggest that McCarthy is directly challenging the traditional patriarchal image associated with Southern culture *and* the influence of Faulkner himself. Jarrett maintains that every father figure in the novel (Culla, the leader of the triune, and the tinker) are flawed characters and that their combined influence is another example of McCarthy writing against one of the foundational myths of his regional culture. Jarrett makes the following important observations on this matter:

> The weak, dead, absent, or denying fathers of McCarthy's fiction point toward an imaginative repudiation of the central importance of patriarchal father and family in Southern culture and the South's heroic myth of its history figured in the revered patriarch—Robert E. Lee or Colonel Sartoris—of the Confederate Lost Cause.[44]

It was perhaps inevitable that writers of McCarthy's generation would be venerated or condemned according to their similarity to, or difference from, Faulkner's aesthetic. It is not the intention of this study to provide a detailed comparative study of the two authors, but it is important that we acknowledge a significant observation that Jarrett makes in this respect that allows us to see how McCarthy moves away from this overbearing literary father. Jarrett observes that "Faulkner's fiction often relies on *askesis*, a sudden revelation of historical insight to such Faulkner heroes as Quentin Compson or Ike McCaslin. But a historical awareness that takes the form of *askesis* is denied to virtually all of McCarthy's main characters."[45] This is especially the case in *Outer Dark*, as even

---

[44] Ibid., 23.
[45] Ibid., 29.

the use of italicized passages are reserved for the grim triune who are entirely bereft of any such historical consciousness. This is a significant departure from the Faulknerian model, and it reveals how *Outer Dark* is also concerned with the "problem" of history and memory, a thread that runs through all of McCarthy's work.

The novel's vague and anachronistic setting and prevailing gothic mood critiques the mythically held connection to place, but *Outer Dark* also challenges ideas of social hierarchy and class in Southern society. Jarrett also comments on this important aspect of the novel, noting that although these characters are free of modern lifestyles "based on consumption and excess," in no way can their existence be read as pastorally romantic or rustically charming.[46] Some characters have been absorbed into a cash-exchange economy yet, as we have seen, even their middle-class smugness does not save them from meeting grim ends, as evidenced by the fate of the squire and auctioneer. Indeed, Jarrett suggests that the murders carried out by the outlaws could "function as a type of revenge against the ideology of the propertied classes, who associate wealth with morality and ignore their own exploitation of the lower class."[47]

Although hard to specifically place, many critics have persuasively argued that the novel is set in Appalachia, thereby accounting for the lack of references or evidence of the plantation system that was so prevalent in other areas of the South. However it would be foolish to suggest that Appalachia, although not heavily reliant on slavery, would be free of racial bigotry and prejudice. Examples of such bigotry can be found throughout McCarthy's Southern novels—*Outer Dark* is no exception—and Jarrett identifies that the squire harbors

---

[46] Jarrett, *Cormac McCarthy*, 27.
[47] Ibid., 28.

such prejudices that are evidence of his class consciousness, social superiority, and racial bigotry. Therefore, the question of race "is seen through the crippled black liveryman working for a country squire who verbally abuses those whom he considers his inferiors."[48]

Jarrett's sympathetic analysis of Rinthy also aligns him with the other critics discussed thus far. Jarrett claims that Rinthy embodies an innate and elemental fecundity and innocence that we ignore at our peril (remembering of course that Rinthy is an allegorical representation of certain feminine characteristics that our culture seeks to silence or deny). Culla evokes the fury of the natural world whereas "by the novel's end, Rinthy's consciousness of the distinction between herself and the natural has so nearly disintegrated that it has become absorbed by the natural; here she, dehumanized, *is* the landscape."[49] She appears to maintain a harmony with the landscape that has been distorted by social and cultural constructions of the feminine.

John Cant also acknowledges McCarthy's critique of the Southern patriarchal myth, and he goes so far as to claim that "Culla Holme is the most extreme of the failed fathers of all McCarthy" texts.[50] Cant also argues that the novel critiques another of the foundational myths of Southern society by proposing that *Outer Dark* can be read as "a deconstruction of Southern Protestant fundamentalism."[51] The critique reaches its most gruesome working out with the drinking of the child's blood, which parodies the mass and, according to Cant, represents McCarthy's rejection of religious mythology.

---

[48] Ibid., 25.
[49] Ibid., 136.
[50] Cant, *Cormac McCarthy and the Myth of American Exceptionalism*, 87.
[51] Ibid., 15.

However, this subversion of religious mythology does not result in nihilism, and Cant argues that his mythic interpretation "deals with McCarthy's nihilism by pointing out that the moral grounding of myth is strictly implicit."[52] Specifically, Cant sees Rinthy as playing an integral role in informing this mythic interpretation as "McCarthy remains true to the full extent of his mythic form by representing cyclical, holistic, natural, matriarchal time in the person of Rinthy" who is a loving mother on an "unceasing quest to find her child, her lactating breasts symbols of her maternal pride."[53] Culla's tale can be read as an allegorical warning of the perils that may confront us if we fail to undertake the creative act of self-authorship, whereas Rinthy's fate can also be read allegorically in that she represents "a growing need to recognize the importance of the natural world to our chances of survival and our need to emancipate the female in both political and cultural terms."[54]

For the most part, Jay Ellis is a critic who outlines the potential dangers of adhering to close biographical readings, especially when presented with works as complex as McCarthy's. However, in *No Place for Home: Spatial Constraint and Character Flight in the Novels of Cormac McCarthy*, Ellis asks if the significance of the oedipal narrative within *Outer Dark* can be attributed to the fact that it parallels McCarthy's own experience as a first-time father, just as *The Road* optimistically revises these themes as McCarthy once again became a father at a much later stage in his life. Ellis acknowledges that the novel "remains more mythic and archetypal" than most of his novels, and it therefore explores the deep-rooted

---

[52] Ibid., 78.
[53] Ibid., 82.
[54] Ibid., 88.

patriarchal fear (via the novel's assortment of failed fathers) that "the son's existence will eclipse his [the father's] own."[55] Ellis continues to make the following connection between the novel and significant events in McCarthy's own life during the novel's composition:

> The names "Culla" and "Holme" echo the names of McCarthy's immediate family during the likely composition of *Outer Dark*—too closely not to invite some speculation on how this author's remarkable imagination might have transmogrified into extreme fiction the mild—but exhausting—problems of responsibility for a small child ... A first son, however, named Cullen, was born in the early sixties to McCarthy and his first wife, Lee Holleman. *Outer Dark* was published in 1968, four years after McCarthy's marriage to Holleman. The family name in *Outer Dark* of "Holme" includes several resonances. The first leads us into biographical onomastics. "Holme" suggests a reduction and slight transliteration of "Holleman," the family name of McCarthy's first wife.[56]

Ellis also reads Rinthy in a sympathetic light, claiming that "her pain ... serves as a reminder of the pain suffered by women abused by men: their bodies bear visual witness to the abuse."[57] If nothing else Rinthy survives in the novel, and its conclusion gives every indication that she will continue to survive after we leave her, just as Culla will continue with his perpetual blind wandering. Ellis notes that in McCarthy's other novels female characters simply don't last the

---

[55] Ellis, *No Place for Home*, 114-15.
[56] Ibid., 121.
[57] Ibid., 94.

pace, but in *Outer Dark* Rinthy is imbued with an understated heroic quality as she is charged with "a relentless drive to find and reclaim her son."[58]

So far the critical responses to Rinthy have been sympathetic and positive, and the majority of them attempt to understand what she embodies (and perhaps warns against) in mythical and allegorical terms. However, one does encounter some problems when she is viewed through approaches offered by feminist theory, and this is what Nell Sullivan and Ann Fisher-Wirth attempt to do. Indeed Fisher-Wirth states that "from a certain kind of feminist point of view, in which male authors are judged for their ability to create female characters, which are then judged for their independence and autonomy, Rinthy—and McCarthy—would be abysmal failures."[59] So does the mythic/allegorical reading satisfy, or does Rinthy betray McCarthy's (and perhaps his culture's) latent misogyny?

Sullivan contends that from "Wake for Susan" onwards, the theme of sexuality in McCarthy's work is "inextricably bound up with death" and is therefore "posed as a source of masculine dread."[60] Sullivan draws on the work of Gail Kern Paster who claims that, in the Western canon, the female body is perceived as "naturally grotesque ... which is to say open, permeable, effluent, and leaky."[61]

Conditions such as this make Rinthy's characterization problematic, as Sullivan outlines: "The fact that she is 'open' and 'permeable'—that is, pregnable—has rendered her an outcast ... and determined for her the life of misery that the novel details. After her water

---

[58] Ibid., 265.
[59] Fisher-Wirth, "Abjection and 'the feminine,'" 132.
[60] N. Sullivan, "The Evolution of the Dead Girlfriend Motif," 68.
[61] Quoted in N. Sullivan, "The Evolution of the Dead Girlfriend Motif," 69.

breaks, she leaks constantly for the rest of the novel—tears, blood, and milk, the three often combined and conflated."[62]

At this point we should clarify the meaning of "abject" and abjection in this context, as it helps us to understand the theoretical implications of Sullivan's and Fisher-Wirth's arguments. Both critics have derived the term from the theorist Julia Kristeva, who identified it as a central component operating within horror or gothic narratives. *The Oxford Dictionary of Literary Terms* defines abjection as follows:

> A psychological process of "casting off," identified and theorized by the Bulgarian French psychoanalytic philosopher Julia Kristeva as the basis of horror and revulsion, and so subsequently adopted by literary critics in attempted explanation of the imaginative effects of horror stories, Gothic fiction, and narratives of monstrosity. In her book *Pouvoirs de l'horreur* (1980; translated as *Powers of Horror*, 1982), Kristeva proposes that we are especially disgusted by anything that is ambiguously located at the physical boundaries of the self, neither clearly inside nor outside us: thus bodily excretions and secretions excite nausea, and so too, in this theory, do babies and indeed mothers. Such unsettling items are described as *abject* or *abjected* insofar as we attempt to maintain our stable sense of self by imaginatively expelling them or projecting them in the form of monstrous aliens, ghosts, or bogeys.[63]

---

[62] Ibid.

[63] "Abjection" *The Oxford Dictionary of Literary Terms*. Chris Baldick. New York: Oxford University Press, 2008. *Oxford Reference Online*. New York: Oxford University Press. University of Tennessee-Knoxville. 13 August 2008. Kristeva's philosophy of abjection receives extended treatment in the chapter devoted to *Suttree*.

Rinthy challenges our stable sense of self by lactating throughout, distorting the boundaries between the feminine and the culture she finds herself in. According to such a reading, she cuts a distressed and isolated figure throughout the novel as she is "frequently described in terms of what would deny her agency or even anima at all," and Sullivan notes that the "metaphor of choice for Rinthy seems to be the lifeless doll."[64] In this respect, Sullivan maintains that Rinthy becomes a template for many of McCarthy's other female characters as "the image of the female body prone and racked with pain is so powerful that it survived virtually unchanged" in McCarthy's work, as Sullivan identifies this image running from *Outer Dark* through to *Cities of the Plain*.[65]

There are a couple of moments within Sullivan's essay where she seems to conform to the critical consensus that has developed about Rinthy. She notes that Rinthy retains "the power of *yes* and *no* throughout the novel," suggesting that she has a surprising degree of autonomy and power and that the desire for her dead child drives rather than absents her from the text. Indeed, McCarthy seems to have bestowed a particular kind of "narrative kindness" upon Rinthy that he has denied many of his other female characters.[66] However, this "narrative kindness" is tempered with the image of the mire from the end of the novel, which once again links the feminine with a powerful and disturbing metaphor: "Metaphor works reciprocally, so if the mire that threatens to swallow Culla and the blind man resembles female genitalia, then obviously female geni-

---

[64] N. Sullivan, "Evolution of the Dead Girlfriend Motif," 68-69.
[65] Ibid., 70.
[66] Ibid., 71, 72.

talia must resemble the deadly mire. The sexual woman's threat can be diminished only by avoidance or neutralized by annihilation."[67]

In "Abjection and 'the feminine' in *Outer Dark*," Fisher-Wirth's thesis is heavily indebted to Kristeva's theory of abjection, even more so than Sullivan's. She opens her article by acknowledging the difficulty of bringing "psychoanalytic theory to bear on a nonpsychological novel," although she contends that such an analysis is made possible as the "imagery of landscape is so rich, so saturated with dreamlike excesses of beauty, terror, violence, [that] it serves as a projection of its subjects psyches."[68] Rinthy's condition could therefore be read as an allegorical exploration of the theme of abjection. According to this reading, Rinthy shares an unlikely intertextual literary kinship with Lester Ballard, as he too (albeit for different reasons) is "ritualistically repudiated" so that the community can maintain its order and stability:

> The abject then becomes those things—among them blood, pus, sweat, snot, unclean breasts, corpses, or the physicality of women—that stand in for the repudiated mother, and that the self and the community continually and ritualistically reject anew in order to maintain "identity, system, order"… the abject is not merely cast off but also ambivalently desired, for its sheer existence reveals "inaugural loss"—the loss of union with the mother—"that laid the foundations of its own being."[69]

For Fisher-Wirth, the novel becomes "one long series of outrages against the feminine," especially in those sorrowful scenes where

---

[67] Ibid., 73.
[68] Fisher-Wirth, "Abjection and 'the feminine,'" 128.
[69] Ibid., 126.

we see Rinthy at her most abject: lactating, stained with her own breast milk, traversing this horrorscape in search of her "chap."[70] As with all things ghastly in the novel, Culla is also implicated, and this theme reaches its fullest metaphoric approximation (as Sullivan identified) with the image of the "mire" at the novel's conclusion. By breaking the taboo against incest, by repudiating his fatherhood and his responsibilities towards his son and his sister, and "by fleeing his knowledge of the mother," Culla ironically "flees farther into the realm of the maternal" everywhere he goes in the novel.[71]

As these critical responses testify, *Outer Dark* is a challenging, disturbing, and disquieting novel; indeed, this reader would argue that it is perhaps the most complex in McCarthy's oeuvre. However, once we negotiate our way through the gothic landscape of the text, it becomes clear that McCarthy has created a powerful mythical and allegorical narrative which critiques some of the most foundational tenets of Southern identity. The charges of nihilism are countered by his use of myth and allegory, through which narrative modes McCarthy explores themes about sin, guilt, redemption, punishment, and justice. Placing Rinthy within the conceptual framework afforded by the theory of abjection certainly reveals some problems with McCarthy's aesthetic, but the allegorical force of the novel implores us to examine the relationship between myth and history and to undertake the task of self-authorship that could perhaps save us from heading down the road bound for the metaphysical nowhere space from which Culla is never able to free himself.

---

[70] Ibid., 128.
[71] Ibid., 130.

CHAPTER 5

Child of God

The most striking difference between McCarthy's third novel, published in 1973, and *Outer Dark* is one of style. His second novel is a dark and impenetrable one, and it calls into question the validity of any kind of interpretation and critique, reaching as it does into the darkest corners of the imagination. Whilst the subject matter of *Child of God* is equally as bleak, focusing on various stages of emasculation which eventually lead Lester Ballard, the novel's chief protagonist, into cave-dwelling, serial killing, and necrophilia, the style of the novel is stripped down, economic, eidetic, and minimalist, perhaps even picaresque. Indeed, we can see the genesis of the late "McCarthy" aesthetic here, which is so successfully executed in *No Country for Old Men* and *The Road*. We see McCarthy shifting artistic gears, but the novel maintains his interest in critiquing the myth and history of the South and East Tennessee, a critique which (despite the novel's gruesome subject matter) transcends the regional and sensational, telling us much in the process about our own culture and the way we construct and talk about figures like Lester Ballard.

The novel has a three-part structure which, in keeping with McCarthy's style, has several polyphonic narrative zones. The omniscient narrator maintains a dispassionate position throughout, guiding us through Lester's miserable existence, inviting us to assess and perhaps pass judgment on him, although the narrative consciousness itself never does. In the first part of the novel, we have a group of unidentified narrators from Sevierville who retrospectively tell us about and frame Lester within that community's mythology and historical consciousness. The second and third parts of the novel increasingly leave culture and community behind as Lester goes from squatter to cave-dweller to serial killer and necrophile, and they reveal the increasing influence of what Guillemin has called McCarthy's "wilderness aesthetic," as Lester becomes increasingly associated with pre-modern and inanimate phenomena. The third section returns to the framing of Lester via the historical narratives offered by Old Man Wade, stories that reveal McCarthy's essentialist and atavistic sensibility. We even get glimpses of Lester's own tortured interiority, moments when his old "shed shelf" comes back to console him. Such glimpses—and they are, admittedly, few and far between—reveal the subtle complexity of the novel's design, as McCarthy manages to evoke some sympathy for Lester's plight, whilst encouraging readers to examine why he came down a road such as this in the first place.

What cannot be ignored (especially because such themes open the novel) is how *Child of God* continues McCarthy's critique of some of the foundational myths of Southern culture. With his third novel, McCarthy continues his deconstruction of the myth of the pastoral, especially with how it relates to Agrarian philosophy. The Agrarians, who gravitated to Vanderbilt University in Nashville (only a couple of hundred miles down the road from Knoxville and East Tennessee), were a group of writers and intellectuals who, perhaps more than any other group, helped to develop a powerful body of myth that Southern writers have subsequently endorsed or critiqued. The influence of the group cannot be overstated as in their dual role as writers *and* critics they succeeded in constructing a suitably quixotic model for Southern society. This model was predicated on how independent land-holding subsistence farmers could potentially counter what they saw as the destructive influence of aggressive finance capitalism, embodied in absentee ownership and the embourgiosement of the South, which was eroding what they saw as the traditional humanizing modes of Southern existence.

In his study *The Post-Southern Sense of Place in Contemporary Fiction*, Martyn Bone skillfully delineates the influence of the Agrarians. Their construction of a very particular type of Southern identity was not easy to shake off and, initially at least, Lester Ballard's tale of dispossession by forces that the Agrarians identified as anathema to the traditional Southern mindset allows us to historicize the novel and acknowledge the complexity of McCarthy's task here. Bone claims that "even now, the standard literary-critical conception of 'place' derives substantially from the Agrarians' idealized version of a rural, agricultural society," and *Child of God* takes us to a moment where this idealized version breaks down, serving in part at least as the catalyst for Lester's descent into madness and murder.[1] Bone goes on to outline that the Agrarian sense of place was a "rural, self-sufficient and nigh-on precapitalist locus focused upon the small farm, operating largely outside the cash nexus, and absent large-scale land speculation," and McCarthy takes us to the moment in the South's history where this locus is no longer viable.[2] This raises one of the most significant thematic issues of the novel: what happens when Lester, a "child of God much like yourself perhaps" (COG 4), is denied this cultural and mythic identity? What are the consequences for Southern communities when they forsake these traditional attachments? Jay Ellis has insightfully remarked

---

[1] Bone, *The Post-Southern Sense of Place*, vii.
[2] Ibid., 5.

that in *Blood Meridian* and the Border Trilogy we are witnessing the myth of the frontier dissolving into history, and in *Child of God* we see the same thing happening to a version of the Southern pastoral that is represented in Agrarian philosophy.

Let us remind ourselves of two of the most notable contributions to *I'll Take My Stand*, the seminal Agrarian manifesto published in 1930, especially as they pertain to *Child of God*. John Crowe Ransom speaks of the "unreconstructed Southerner who persists in his regard for a certain terrain," a regard that is shared by Arthur Ownby from *The Orchard Keeper* and by Lester Ballard in *Child of God*.[3] In "The Hand Tit," Andrew Nelson Lytle asks what if in "exchange for the bric-á-brac culture of progress he [the unreconstructed Southerner] stands to lose his land, and losing that, his independence."[4] Although Ballard doesn't exactly embrace "cultural progress"—indeed at times he is even shunned by some of the most traditional institutions of Southern culture—McCarthy shows us the most extreme scenario of a Southerner denied this most traditional of bonds, whilst concomitantly also exposing the naiveté of Agrarian thought. The economic program advocated by the Agrarians, structured around a quixotic model of Jeffersonian subsistence farmers living solely off of the land and free from finance capitalism, may well have had an admirable legacy which reached back to the very origin of the republic, but it was outmoded even at the moment of their re-imagining of it. However, one cannot deny the metaphorical influence such a conception has maintained over the Southern imagination.

A moment the Agrarians truly dreaded opens *Child of God*, where their ideal is dispossessed by the machinations of aggressive

---

[3] Ransom, "Reconstructed but Unregenerate," 1.
[4] Lytle, "The Hand Tit," 205.

finance capitalism manifested in this instance by a real estate auction. Of course, we must always remember not to become pastorally deluded when reading McCarthy, as there is ample evidence to suggest that the Ballards were awful farmers and Lester, their sole and pitiful progeny, would maintain the disastrous family tradition. Still, the auction takes place in the "mute pastoral morning" with a grim reminder of his father's suicide (another failed, absent father) there for all to see in the form of the rope hanging from the barn roof (COG 4). The auctioneer has an almost evangelical aspect about him as he bows, points, and smiles, reminding the crowd that "they is real future in this property [and also a grim past] ... I believe you all know that ever penny I own is in real estate," adding that "there is no sounder investment than property. Land ... A piece of real estate, and particular in this valley, is the soundest investment you can make" (COG 5, 6). The mythic homestead becomes nothing more than an investment here, and it is most definitely now operating within an aggressive cash nexus which ruptures traditional attachments to place as we learn that it is purchased by the outsider Greer from a neighboring county.

Lester attempts to take his stand against this process by threatening to use his rifle (his only constant companion in the novel) against anyone involved. However, he is reminded that the county is taking his land due to his failure to pay taxes, which hints at a tightening of bureaucratic control and regulation across the novels as we know that John Wesley and his mother were able to live in their house in *The Orchard Keeper* as they were exempt from paying taxes. In a highly symbolic moment, Lester is clubbed unconscious with the result that "he never could hold his head right after that" (COG 9), and this reveals how acts of violence are sanctioned by the normative community that instigates, mythologizes, and perhaps even needs a figure such as Lester within their own historical memory. This violent act leaves Lester bleeding from the ears, and it brutally confirms his dispossession, serving as a catalyst for his later acts in which he attempts to replicate the world he has been evicted from.

The objective narrative voice manages to evoke some sympathy for Lester as it shows us how he fails to establish an identity in other mythic forms. Following the scene where he is accused of raping the prostitute, Lester finds himself in town and is beguiled by the rhetoric and anti-authoritarian chic (so he believes) of the criminal world he encounters. In one instance, he appropriates criminal rhetoric to impress a fellow prisoner by stating that "all the trouble I was ever was in … was caused by whisky or women or both. He'd often heard men say as much," whilst he also attempts to act the criminal, briefly pretending to be a rogue lawman; as with most things, Lester fails to convince (COG 53, 149). The enshrined national myth of material self-improvement also seems beyond him, as the boys in the store successfully out-trade him when, displaying a degree of entrepreneurial spirit, he tries to sell the watches of his dead victims. Meanwhile, an incredulous store owner asks him, "in twenty-seven years you've managed to [only] accumulate four dollars and nineteen cents," as Lester struggles to pay his bill (COG 126). In the memorable scene where he is attempting to carry his grotesque cargo of meager possessions and corpses across the river, the narrative voice describes him as a "bedraggled parody of a patriotic poster," and parody seems to be the best hope for Lester in the novel (COG 156). He is a sorry parody of the patriotic image here, and Lester also parodies and critiques other culturally encoded icons and narratives such as the pastoral hero and the Horatio Alger myth throughout the narrative.

As he is not part of the established material world that seemingly commodifies everything in its path, it is somewhat inevitable that

Lester will inhabit (and indeed himself become) representative of the anti-commodity. Trash, rubbish, junk, waste, and detritus play an enormously significant role in *Suttree*, but such abject acts and spaces play an equally significant role here. One of the first images we get of Lester is when he is urinating in the barn prior to the auction, whilst the narrative voice gives us the unadorned naturalistic moment where he "trod a clearing in the clumps of jimson and nightshade and squatted and shat" (COG 13). He associates with the dumpkeeper, a veritable robber baron in the trash collecting world, whilst we often see him wandering amidst the cast-off junk from the acquisitive culture that he plays no part in: "At the far end of the quarry was a rubble tip and Ballard stopped to search the artifacts, tilting old stoves and water heaters, inspecting bicycle parts and corroded buckets. He salvaged a worn kitchen knife with a chewed handle" (COG 39). This forlorn backwoodsman we see sadly walking along busy roads "among the beercans and trash" (COG 96) as drivers speed by is a miscast figure that calls to mind Ned Merrill from Jon Cheever's *The Swimmer*. Ned and Lester are contemporized versions of Rip van Winkle and Daniel Boone respectively, and both find themselves stranded on the roadside, excluded by their culture which compels them to live by myths which are in fact denied by their historical moment and material reality.

Place dominates this novel, and it represents another exploration of the theme of "transcendental homelessness" in McCarthy. Lester is dispossessed of his familial place at the opening of the narrative, and his wanderings throughout the remainder of the text—and his subsequent descent into psychosis—take him to some disquieting psychological, sexual, and metaphysical places indeed. This also presents a challenge for the reader as McCarthy makes it increasingly difficult for us to place Lester in ethical, moral, or philosophical terms. *Child of God* therefore asks profound questions about how we map or navigate ourselves around fictional texts, and its initial placement in a clearly delineated geographical place (Sevierville, East Tennessee) is significant in this respect. Eric Bulson's *Novels, Maps, Modernity: The Spatial Imagination, 1865-2000* looks at how novels use maps and concrete geographic locations to comment on the ideological conditions at the moment of their composition. Bulson's claim that "acts of geographic imagining were, and continue to be, part of a larger process by which people construct social, ethical, political, and cultural boundaries" helps us to see how McCarthy uses Lester's story to critique such ethical, political, and cultural boundaries.[5]

The novel once again exhibits a characteristic McCarthy strategy in that its use of place carefully orients and then disorients the reader. As mentioned, the opening of the novel is very deliberately set in Sevierville, but the novel reverts to wilderness and unmapped settings to parallel Lester's inner turmoil. The return to the settled, stable geographic and civil markers at novel's end (state hospitals, Lyons View mental institution in Knoxville, the university medical examination room in Memphis) suggest that Lester has finally been placed, even if the questions which the narrative consciousness raises deny such easy placement and closure. His wilderness condition is intimated at an early stage in the novel when Lester is traveling amongst "toppled monoliths among the trees and vines like traces of an older race of man" (COG 25), suggesting that Ballard will soon follow a path which challenges the rational mind's ability to map, order, and make sense of space.

---

[5] Bulson, *Novels, Maps, Modernity*, 9.

Elsewhere, he wanders through "old woods and deep. At one time in the world there were woods that no one owned and these were like them," suggesting that Lester seems physically comfortable in settings that are somehow pre-modern and pre-capitalistic (COG 127). There are also several occasions where the narrative consciousness places or attempts to orient Lester using the stars, one of the oldest possible ways to navigate our way through the world. The image of Canis Major is referred to during Lester's triumph at the fair (COG 65), and McCarthy uses such astrological constellations to mark out Lester's "place" during his underground-man stage when he seems to have transgressed all other kinds of ethical, social, and cartographic orders: "In the black smokehole overhead the remote and lidless stars of the Pleiades burn cold and absolute" (COG 133).

Significantly, such ancient cartographic markers prompt Lester into one of his few considered, albeit rather limited, introspective moments, and it is the closest he gets to metaphysical contemplation of what he and the natural world are made of: "When they [bats fleeing from the cave] were gone he watched the hordes of cold stars sprawled across the smokehole and wondered what stuff they were made of, or himself" (COG 141). The reference to the stars as "cold" suggests that Lester's speculation does not result in a moment of Romantic awe or transcendental self-realization. Rather, his increasing existential sense of his own insignificance (and kinship with inanimate matter) is reinforced by these uncaring astrological phenomena that have taken millions of years to form and have looked down upon other Lesters, and will do so again.

The only time that Lester feels he can order the world symbolically comes in a wilderness setting. His historical moment has dispossessed him and left him to his own devices in this landscape where "new paths are needed" for Lester's own sense of self and the world that marginalized him: "Coming up the mountain through the blue winter twilight among great boulders and the ruins of giant trees prone in the forest he wondered at such upheaval. Disorder in the woods, trees down, new paths needed. Given charge Ballard would have made things more orderly in the woods and in men's souls" (COG 136).

As we shall see in the review of the critical responses to *Child of God*, one of the most persuasive critiques of the novel is offered by Gary Ciuba. His critique helps us to resolve the complex question of Lester's place, his disempowerment at the hands of culturally sanctioned violence, and his subsequent ghastly replication of that violence as he creates his own order in his underground world. Ciuba's thesis is indebted to the work of Rene Girard, for whom fiction can reveal "the facts about systematic persecution … that the historical record conceals."[6] We have identified how McCarthy's work repeatedly deals with problems of official history, highlighting how his work gives a voice to those silenced or absented by such records, and *Child of God* is no different in this important respect, especially in the way Lester is systematically (and ritualistically) constructed as this community's nightmare.

In the novel, McCarthy brutally critiques the manner in which normative social or cultural institutions—religion, the law, even the medical profession—shun Lester but ultimately need "his kind" in order to reinforce their sense of moral superiority and self-righteousness. Indeed, the culture within the novel—and perhaps our own—is "a race that gives suck to the maimed and the crazed, that wants their wrong blood in its history and will have it" (COG 156). Remember, Lester is a child of God much like us, so how can we

---

[6] Ciuba, *Desire, Violence and Divinity*, 3.

justify the persecution of such figures? How does McCarthy manage to make us feel sympathetic towards a character as obviously monstrous as Lester? McCarthy's treatment of this theme ensures that the *Child of God* never becomes crassly sensational, as he forces us to interrogate how this process operates within our own culture, our own history.

A central component in the practice of scapegoating is sanctioned rituals in which the community identifies and purifies themselves of their bogeyman, or their surrogate, to borrow Girard's phrase. The real estate auction which opens the novel is one such occasion, as the atmosphere is far from business-like as potential buyers arrive "like a caravan of carnival folk," replete with music and refreshments (COG 3). Elsewhere, in one of the novel's most ironic moments, Lester revels in his success at the shooting gallery at the fair, a moment where his culture rewards him for the very skills it will later punish him for (COG 61-5). Tragically a character of Lester's severely limited cognitive capabilities simply cannot work this paradox out.

He is also systematically identified as a scapegoat by a variety of hegemonic cultural institutions. The sheriff informs Lester that "these people here in town won't put up with your shit" (COG 56), especially as the use of "town" here denotes a settled and stable environment that likes to think it has controlled nature, wilderness, and all the things that Lester Ballard represents. Another bureaucratic representative at the police department reinforces this theme when he tells Lester, "You are either going to have to find some other way to live or some other place in the world to do it in" (COG 123). Location matters not here, but the cultural need for a Lester Ballard most certainly does. On his one attempt to attend church, to become a "regular citizen," he is also completely ignored. Indeed, it is interesting that the most pertinent thing that Lester notices whilst at Sixmile

Church is the amount collected, thereby conflating Christianity with the commodifying processes that have left him without a home (COG 31-2). Denied fair and proper legal protection or the consolation of Christian fellowship, where else is there for Lester to go? His final indignity comes with his placement in a cemetery with others of "his kind," after he has been "flayed, eviscerated, dissected. His head was sawed open and the brains removed. His muscles were stripped from his bones. His heart taken out. His entrails were hauled forth and delineated" in another culturally sanctioned act which rivals anything Lester committed in terms of its gruesomeness (COG 194).

Although he was ultimately captured and the bodies of his victims were recovered (albeit accidentally), Lester manages a small victory in evading his captors, thereby denying the community the spectacle of his public death or execution. Old Man Wade's recounting of the execution of the criminals Tipton and Wynn toward the conclusion of the novel reveals that Lester is only the most recent example of someone with "wrong blood," a character needed by his race "who wants their wrong blood in its history and will have it." Indeed, Wade's tale of the late-Christmas execution once again conflates Christianity with the community's scapegoating impulse, and the celebratory feel expressed here echoes the feeling that attended the auction of Lester's family home at the opening of the novel:

> I remember there was still holly boughs up and christmas candles. Had a big scaffold set up had one door for the both em to drop through. People had started in to town the evenin before. Slept in their wagons, a lot of em. Rolled out blankets on the courthouse lawn. Wherever. You couldn't get a meal in town, folks lined up three deep. Women sellin sandwiches in the street ... Don't ever think hangin is quick and merciful. It ain't. (COG167)

Lester becomes another of those excluded from official historical records and McCarthy, using the more inclusive and flexible form afforded by fiction, gives him an identity and place that had otherwise been denied. Walter Sullivan memorably accused McCarthy of being a writer bereft of community and myth, stating that his work declared war on these "ancient repositories of order and truth."[7] However, the manner in which scapegoating functions in the novel reveals that these "ancient repositories of truth and order" hold within them narratives of violence and exclusion which problematizes Sullivan's humanitarian philosophy.

One of the novel's greatest accomplishments is how McCarthy manages to make readers feel a degree of sympathy for a character as monstrous as Lester. He may well be a child of God like us, but there are numerous occasions throughout the narrative where Lester is described in primordial terms, a "misplaced and loveless simian shape" (COG 20) moving across the landscape. The strongest kinship he feels towards another *living* human is with the idiot child, a "hugeheaded bald and slobbering primate" who tears the legs of the bird Lester gives him as "he wanted it to where it couldn't run off" (COG 77, 79), an act Lester can empathize with as he does exactly the same thing with his succession of corpse-lovers. After hauling his horrific possessions deeper underground Lester places his freezing feet in water, and his crying "echoed from the walls of the grotto like the muttering of a band of sympathetic apes," yet he proves surprisingly agile in his shoeless condition, using "his bare toes [and] gripping the rocks like an ape," suggesting that he is quite a way down on the evolutionary chain (COG 159, 184).

---

[7] W. Sullivan, *A Requiem for the Renascence*, 72.

Lester appears to be a character who, perhaps like Culla Holme, seems condemned to always find "darker provinces of night" (COG 23). Like Culla, he is also hopelessly dysfunctional when he is forced to operate within the world of work and capitalism, as evidenced by his utter bemusement following the blacksmith's detailed demonstration of his traditional craft and in the scene where he is out-traded in the store after attempting to sell the watches of his victims (COG 70-4, 131-2). Following his ritualistic marginalization by the community, Lester—a man of limited analytical or cognitive capability—can only partake in ghastly simulations of the practices that he has been excluded from, such as the following scene where he creates a parody of domestic fulfillment that briefly makes him a little less lonely: "He went outside and looked in through the window at her lying naked before the fire. When he came back in he unbuckled his trousers and stepped out of them and laid next to her. He pulled the blanket over them" (COG 92). We should remember that he fails even in this mock arrangement though, as he over-stokes the fire resulting in the cabin he is temporarily squatting in burning down.

These issues will be more thoroughly dealt with in our overview of the critical responses to the novel, but do such scenes only serve to confirm the character's (and perhaps even the author's) misogyny? What kind of agency do female characters—these "Goddamn frozen bitch[es]" (COG 102)—have in this novel? Is Lester a sexual monster, or can he be read as a critique *of* that very culture's attitude toward women as does he, in his own grotesque way, actually offer a critique of how the feminine is constructed and commodified? Note the scene where Lester "poured into that waxen ear everything he'd ever thought of saying to a woman" (COG 88), but where did Lester come by these romantic offerings exactly? The fact that he carries his rifle everywhere, an obvious phallic symbol, reveals how his culture actually endorses a particular type of violence that has a unique sexual charge to it. Ralph's daughter (not the only female character in the novel to tease, abuse, or embarrass Lester) tells him that "you ain't even a man. You're just a crazy thing," a statement which has a great deal of truth to it, especially when we consider how Lester was made to be "the crazy thing" that he is (COG 117).

We can also identify a recurrence of themes from *Outer Dark* here, especially in terms of the abject. We have noted how Lester is often depicted when undertaking the most basic human functions such as defecating and urinating, and when he descends underground (and further into madness) the image conflates a particular type of Christian imagery with the menstrual motif evidenced in the appearance of the cave walls. This of course parallels the scene at the end of *Outer Dark* where Culla journeyed into the mire that, according to Nell Sullivan, resembled female genitalia, and the menstrual motif used here does perhaps support the charges of misogyny often leveled against McCarthy: "Here the walls with the softlooking convolutions, slavered over as they were with wet and bloodred mud, had an organic look to them, like the innards of some great beast. Here in the bowels of the mountain Ballard turned his light on ledges or pallets of stone where dead people lay like saints" (COG 135). Elsewhere, in a scene where the imagery suggests a type of re-birth for Lester, he is covered in "slick red mud down the front of him" as he enters and re-enters the cave, another manifestation of the abject which makes it difficult to locate a clearly defined sense of self for Lester (COG 107).

Denied a stable feminine or matriarchal presence within his own family (the opening of the novel informs us that Lester's own mother has run off) or within his own culture, it is no wonder Lester had "cause to wish and he did wish for some brute midwife to spald him from his rocky keep" (COG 189). In one of the most profoundly melancholic moments in the novel, Lester dreams of a settled childhood memory (one of the only times we get a glimpse of such a history) as he imagines his father whistling on his way home, although he wakes to discover that it is a stream running to "unknown seas at the center of the earth" (COG 170). This is a memorable scene as it has within it two dominant McCarthy themes: that of the absent father and of a mapping or cartographic impulse that descends into unknown (and perhaps unknowable) wilderness territories, be they physical or metaphysical.

Moreover, Lester manages to evoke some sympathy in the reader due to the fact that he is such a failure at everything he does. He is the dispossessed yeoman farmer who can't farm, the frontiersman or backwoodsman who occasionally manages to shoot some ragged-looking squirrels, the accomplished marksman who succeeds at a fair but not when it comes to avenging his dispossession by shooting Greer, and the serial killer who botches his final double murder, which eventually leads to his capture. Yet even at a late stage in the novel when he seems to be beyond all hope, Lester finds within himself a voice that was "no demon but some old shed self that came yet from time to time in the name of sanity, a hand to gentle him back from the rim of his disastrous wrath" (COG 158). No matter how weak or insubstantial this voice may be, it suggests that Lester possesses a consciousness, a sense of interiority and selfhood that juxtaposes the manner in which his society and culture have falsely constructed a mythic Lester Ballard, and this mythically constructed Lester has no room for introspection.

On his way back to the mental institution, he is entranced by the image of a boy traveling on a bus, and "he was trying to fix in his mind where he'd seen the boy when it came to him that the boy looked like himself. This gave him the fidgets and though he tried to shake the image of the face in the glass it would not go" (COG 191). This moment is infused with a Gothic sensibility as the reflection gives back Lester's doppelganger, a Lester that could have been. For all of his latent self-consciousness, Lester seems to be a character entirely without vanity or a false sense of worth, as evidenced in the scene which echoes the myth of Narcissus where "Ballard leaned his face to the green water and drank and studied his dishing visage in the pool. He halfway put his hand to the water as if he would touch the face that watched there but then he rose and wiped his mouth and went on through the woods" (COG 127). One could even perhaps argue that Lester does indeed develop or mature as the narrative concludes when he returns to the hospital stating the he is "supposed to be here," a moment where he finally recognizes his place (COG 192).

Narrative also plays an important function in humanizing Lester, and the retrospective narratives offered by the anonymous speakers in the first part of the novel do at times show Lester a compassion that was denied him during his life. These narrative sections, which significantly do not make an appearance after the first part of the novel, provide a glimpse at the social and cultural totality underpinning Lester's binary function in the community, his marginalization, and his centrality as the "wrong blood" and surrogate victim this community needs in order to preserve its status and equilibrium. The first of these sections informs us that Lester "never could hold his head right" in any kind of way after his father killed himself, whilst the anonymous teller also reveals that Lester was bleeding from the ears when he was clubbed unconscious after the auction (COG 9). One of these narrators also reveals a degree of sympathy for Lester's plight by drawing attention to the fact that John Greer, the man who purchased Lester's family home, was from "up in Grainger County. Not sayin nothin against him but he was," which betrays perhaps a slight resentment at Greer's outsider status (COG 9).

These narrative vignettes thematically structure the novel, as they are told by a series of anonymous narrators at the opening of the text and by Mr. Wade at the novel's close. Crucially, they also reveal how Lester and others have played the role of community bogeyman, so to speak. The narratives in the first section of the novel also help in disclosing the horrors of Lester's childhood, revealing that his mother ran off and that "they say he never was right after his daddy killed hisself" (COG 21). This represents another absenting of the father figure in McCarthy, and it is a grim tableau that Lester witnessed mutely as a child, revealing that he endured considerable psychic trauma at an early age. Like Culla Holme, Lester is also entirely useless when it comes to operating within the cash nexus, and we learn that he earned the money to buy his rifle by setting fenceposts (which he symbolically sets about removing, in sexual and moral terms, throughout the text) but that he "quit midmorning right in the middle of the field the day he got enough money for it" (COG 57). This particular teller grudgingly admires Lester for his skill with the rifle, saying, "he could by God shoot it," a violent act that receives cultural endorsement here (COG 57).

The final section reveals a characteristically essentialist reading which serves to provide a genealogy of Lester's less than impressive family history and an analysis of the nature of the world that is atavistically evil. Lester's grandfather Leland was suspected of lying about his involvement in the Civil War in order to receive a pension, as he claimed to be in the Union Army. In his shiftlessness and fraudulent war record he calls to mind Kenneth Rattner, and we learn that Leland was hanged in Hattiesburg, Mississippi, perhaps on account of his association with the White Caps. Leland's tale affords the opportunity for some characteristic essentialist philosophizing, as his history "goes to show it ain't just the place. He'd of been hanged no matter where he lived" (COG 81), echoing a pronounced theme in *Outer Dark* that evil is an inescapably endemic fact amongst humans, no matter how much we attempt to deny it. Although this important attempt to frame and better understand Lester comes via narrative, these unidentified tellers depart the novel for more pressing quotidian concerns as one of them has "supper waiting on me at the house" (COG 81), thereby contributing to another form of abandonment experienced by Lester, even when dead.

The mention of the White Caps in this mini-narrative section is also echoed by one of the tales related by Mr. Wade at the novel's conclusion. These tales are significant as another instance where McCarthy deconstructs the conventional Southern mythos, especially in regard to how the Klan—or shadowy groups loosely affiliated with them—supposedly maintained a romanticized myth of extra-legal justice. Contrary to this myth, Old Man Wade reveals that "they was a bunch of lowlife thieves and cowards and murderers" who were "sorry people all the way around" and that they were finally brought to order by Tom Davis, the mythical lawman (COG 165).

The allusions to Whitecapping also reveal how the novel continues McCarthy's dialoguing of myth, history, and fiction, and how Lester's tale is a challenge to conventionalized narratives. He is undoubtedly a perverse extra-legal agency, but his own psychotic appropriation of this traditional feature of his culture's history critiques the role that such myths have played in the South's history. William Joseph Cummings' *Community, Violence and the Nature of Change: Whitecapping in Sevier County Tennessee During the 1890s* reveals that extra-legal violence was actually endorsed by the community, as revealed in the following quote by William Montgomery, editor of the *Sevierville Star*: "There should be some means provided for the legal execution without judge, jury, clergy, or ceremony of all villains who invade the sanctity and destroy the happiness of other people's homes."[8] The sheriff and the auctioneer invade Lester's domestic sanctity and, no matter how tenuous this sanctity may be, it results in Lester taking his revenge in this most grotesque defense of traditional republican and pastoral values.

For all of the novel's taboo-shattering moments and Lester's instances of monstrosity, *Child of God* is surprisingly humorous in places, and this is especially evidenced with McCarthy's treatment of grotesque motifs. After Lester stumbles upon the couple asphyxiated in the car, the radio is still playing and the DJ dedicates the song to "the sick and the shut-in," which applies to the dead couple and Lester in an especially harrowing manner (COG 86). Whilst he struggles to manipulate the dead girl's form, Lester is shocked to discover the "dead man's penis, sheathed in a wet yellow condom, was pointing at him rigidly," although it is not quite enough to prevent him from embarking upon his career as a necrophiliac, becoming "a crazed gymnast laboring over a cold corpse" (COG 88). This "practitioner of ghastliness, a part-time ghoul" ends up grotesquely disfigured in the hospital, with his stub looking like "an enormous bandaged thumb" (COG 174-5). Like Robert McEvoy in *The Gardener's Son*, Lester ends up symbolically castrated here, following his failed attempt to avenge Greer for dispossessing him. The discovery of Lester's remaining victims in the final allegorical section of the novel is a similarly macabre scene, and the bodies here ironically achieve

---

[8] Cummings, "Community, Violence and the Nature of Change," 66.

a type of synthesis or fusion with the natural, inanimate world that Lester was seeking throughout his own life: "The bodies were covered with adipocere, a pale grey cheesy mold common to corpses in damp places, and scallops of light fungus grew along them as they do on logs rotting in the forest" (COG 196).

A large part of the novel's visual power derives from its deployment of cinematic motifs, which hint at the stripped-down eidetic style that is characteristic of much of McCarthy's later work. As noted by many critics, McCarthy makes us see the action in the novel, such as when one of Lester's victims "dropped as if the bones in her body had been liquefied" (COG 151). Many of the horrific images in the novel could have been plucked from a horror movie, such as when we witness him "wearing the underclothes of his female victims but now he took to appearing in their outwear as well. A gothic doll in illfit clothes," whilst Greer discovers that Lester's wig "was fashioned whole from a dried human scalp" (COG 140, 173). In one instance, even the narrative voice portrays Lester as "some slapstick contrivance of the filmcutter's art" (COG 173).

We should also note that the tales offered by (and to) Mr. Wade towards the conclusion of the novel parallel the narrative parts of the first section, and they help us in historicizing Lester; moreover, they also reveal the essentialist philosophy about the nature of our species that is a recurrent theme in McCarthy. In conversation with his deputy Mr. Wade claims that "people are the same from the day God first made one," and the sheriff underpins this belief by stating, in a reading of human nature that pre-empts Sheriff Bell's philosophizing in *No Country for Old Men*, that "some people you cain't do nothin with" (COG 168, 162). In another subtly ironic moment, we discover that thieves have been ransacking homes and stores as Sevierville experiences a flood of biblical proportions, causing one woman to exclaim that she "never knew such a place for meanness" (COG 164). This is another example where the self-righteousness of the community that shunned Lester is punctured, as even in times of trouble the community spirit is manipulated by other children of God. It is a familiar move on McCarthy's part as these essentialist readings and tales of communal woe reveal that another Lester could be lurking within their culture. What we've witnessed here could easily be replicated as the next Lester is sought for and the cycle begins again "as in olden times so now. As in other countries here," as the narrative voice dispassionately (but prophetically) warns us (COG 191).

Child of God is a novel that markedly contrasts in style from the one that preceded it, but it continues McCarthy's deconstruction of some foundational myths of Southern culture, most notably the pastoral. The novel is rescued from crass sensationalism as McCarthy asks us to interrogate how we as a culture construct rules of marginalization and exclusion, and how Lester Ballard's tale therefore allegorically represents an unacknowledged force within our culture, even if we would not like to confront it. The style of the novel is stripped down, yet it is philosophically complex, as the eidetic narrative voice is contrasted with the polyphonic voices from the community who help to frame Lester Ballard in a much broader cultural and historical framework. Lester, this character who has only the most notional "shed self," who above anything else knew "that all things fought" (COG 169), ultimately becomes a parodic figure who develops a grim simulacra of the community and culture he is forcibly excluded from. Despite its economic style, *Child of God* is an undeniably complex text, and we will now turn our attention to see how critics have discussed McCarthy's third novel.

Overview of Critical Responses

One of the most persuasive and theoretically sophisticated critiques of *Child of God* can be found in Gary Ciuba's *Desire, Violence and Divinity in Modern Southern Fiction,* which focuses on the work of Flannery O'Connor, Katherine Anne Porter, and Walker Percy, as well as McCarthy. As mentioned in our textual overview of the novel, Ciuba structures his critique around the work of the French theorist Rene Girard, with particular emphasis on Girard's discussion of violence and the sacred. Ciuba uses Girard to analyze how the novelists under discussion reveal "sites of violence and occlusion," thereby exposing "the exclusions that underwrite culture."[9]

The myth of the benighted or savage South is one that is lodged in the American popular consciousness, thanks in part to fiction and numerous television programs and movies. Ciuba intelligently uses Girard to reverse the stereotype of the South as an aberration, stating that "it might be more accurate to regard the South as a culture of violence because of the violence of culture itself."[10] Cultures sustain their sense of stability (no matter how fragile or illusory this may be, especially in McCarthy) through ritualistic acts of scapegoating and sacrifice, which is how Lester—the child of God—becomes this "paradoxical founding figure" who is both shunned and desperately needed by the very culture that marginalizes him in life but embraces him in death. Lester therefore becomes a powerfully melancholic allegorical figure as his grotesque tale, his wrong blood, is vital in sustaining the culture that turned its back on him. Somewhat ironically, he becomes a founding father, that figure so prominent in

---

[9] Ciuba, *Desire, Violence, and Divinity,* 50, 54.
[10] Ibid., 15.

American and Southern cultural rhetoric, and his fate conforms to this Girardian reading and, as we shall see, to an image of a pastoral/republican hero gone wrong.

With such a theoretical framework in mind, it becomes difficult not to feel sympathy for Ballard, as it is the community that is the villain of the piece here and not Lester. His domestic and family situation also makes readers feel sympathetic towards him. His father is absent from the text as he committed suicide before the narrative commenced, but the rope hanging from the barn roof, which he used to kill himself, is still there at the opening of the novel. As a result, Ciuba notes that "violence is Ballard's true patrimony" in familial, cultural, and mythical terms.[11] His sexual deviancy and necrophilia can also be excused in a similar fashion as in his own deranged manner Lester extends the violence done to women in his own culture. His inanimate, doll-like ideal woman "caricatures the stereotypical image of the Southern woman," which goes some way to countering the charges of misogyny leveled against protagonist and author as it reveals the sophistication of McCarthy's critique.[12]

Ciuba certainly makes a persuasive case here, and he enables us to see how this ostensibly eidetic and stripped-down novel works against—and asks profound questions about—the culture that produced it. We have seen how the worshippers at Sixmile church mechanically ignore Lester, and Ciuba notes that he also "becomes the victim of the violence mediated by law and medicine."[13] Lester, this crude naturalistic figure, assumes an allegorical sophistication as his story asks us to question how our culture produces, needs, and

---

[11] Ibid., 172.
[12] Ibid., 179.
[13] Ibid., 197.

subsequently enshrines such figures within our collective memory and mythos. This is a complex idea and, as a result, it ensures that the novel is a characteristically challenging McCarthy text that transcends the sensational and its Southern gothic setting:

> McCarthy's novel undermines such comfortable closure ... *Child of God* does not rest securely in the decisive expulsion of Lester and the reestablishment of a humane and halcyon order. Rather, it recognizes that the violence embodied in McCarthy's enfant terrible can always erupt in some new Girardian deity run amok. After all, he is a "child of god much like yourself perhaps."[14]

Ciuba's Girardian reading allows us to see how the novel functions on a broad cultural level, but it would be foolish to entirely dismiss its Southernist context, as the narrative derives much of its power from this regional heritage. John Grammer intelligently notes how the novel engages with an aspect of pastoral ideology which is quintessentially American as it "deals with the issue of the pastoral, of the republican or Jeffersonian version of it which has dominated the southern imagination."[15] The subsistent and independent landholding farmer was, for Jefferson, the apotheosis of what the South (and perhaps the nation) could be, an image so evocatively captured in *Notes on the State of Virginia*. The novel gets to the very heart of an epochal moment of crisis in the Southern pastoral dream, and it explores what happens when modernity renders this mythic version obsolete. As Grammer astutely observes, Lester is simply "claiming

---

[14] Ibid., 198-99.
[15] Grammer, "A Thing Against Which," 38.

a role for himself in one of the central dramas in the pastoral republican mythology."¹⁶

One of the grandest ironies in this mythology that likes to propagate an image of man in perfect harmony with nature and each other is that it is predicated on violence. Native Americans were violently dispossessed of their ancestral lands, and the pastoral order itself required the strict management and exploitation of the landscape by African Americans. It reaches its conclusion with the evangelical fervor of property-ownership espoused by the real estate auctioneer at the opening of the novel. Lester absorbs the importance of this myth in his own deranged mental condition (remembering that he could never hold his head right after being clubbed unconscious during the auction) and actualizes it in his own grotesque fashion. Of particular symbolic importance here is his rifle, his only constant companion throughout the novel, and Grammer offers the following observation about the significance of this particular relationship:

> What does the rifle mean to Lester? For one thing it identifies him as an anachronism, left behind by history: a Daniel Boone with only stuffed animals to shoot for … An armed man, prepared to defend the country and his own liberty and property, was for our ancestors the ideal republican citizen, the foundation of stable order.¹⁷

John Cant also offers some insightful readings in terms of the novel's relationship to myth, history, and narrative. For Cant the tragic force of the novel can be attributed to the fact that Lester "is informed by American mythology and values and compelled by his culture

---

¹⁶ Ibid., 39.
¹⁷ Ibid., 39.

to seek a way of life that his American circumstances deny him."[18] Denied his rightfully mythic heritage as modernity destroys the pastoral dream, Lester becomes a "dangerous man" of the text, a mythoclastic inversion. In line with the novel's cinematic techniques, Cant makes the point that "rather than becoming Natty Bumpo, the celibate rifleman hero of the wilderness, he becomes Norman Bates, the cinema's first hero/victim as serial killer in Hitchcock's *Psycho*," an intriguing point which is entirely in keeping with the allusions made with all manner of cultural texts in McCarthy's work.[19] Cant also draws our attention to the fact that there is a possible historical template for Lester in the figure of James Blevins of North Carolina, who was accused of a series of murders in 1964 similar in nature to Ballard's.[20]

Cant reads Lester's sexual couplings as representative of the aridity of the American Wasteland, one of McCarthy's consistent motifs. There are also the usual reminders of "the insignificance of human society in the timescale of the earth," whilst the narrative consciousness displays a characteristic skepticism about the range and limits of "scientific gnosis," as evidenced in the dissection scene at novel's close.[21] Cant also remarks upon the significance of Ballard's name, which echoes the ballad, a musical form (especially its folk version) which is used to commemorate and express collective cultural memory. Ballard is central to the way this community understands itself, as captured in the narrative sections in Part One and Wade's tales at the conclusion, and Cant draws our attention to the function of narrative and storytelling in the novel. These ballad-like tales offered

---

[18] Cant, *Cormac McCarthy and the Myth of American Exceptionalism*, 89.
[19] Ibid., 94-95.
[20] Ibid., 90.
[21] Cant, *Cormac McCarthy and the Myth of American Exceptionalism*, 100, 97.

by the various narrators offer another version of the history of the inarticulate, whilst they also preempt the ideological use of the corrido in *The Crossing*.

For David Holloway, *Child of God* is something of a watershed in the development of McCarthy's aesthetic. Holloway maintains that it "first sets (and problematizes) the existential agenda that he will pursue in *Suttree* and the later western writing," and he argues that we see a "deepening of the Sartrean vision" which, Holloway claims, all of his "mature" works exhibit.[22] Holloway maintains that Lester experiences three regressions—into childhood, then into a state resembling prebirth, and finally into a liberating dissolution of the body in his own death, dissection, and internment—which reflect his desire to "merge with the very soil of the land."[23]

Holloway's analysis is indebted to John-Paul Sartre, especially in how the concept of scarcity represents a foundational principle for Lester's alienation and the catalyst that sends him on his doomed existential quest. Holloway argues that this Sartrean concept allows us to better understand the reasons for Lester's alienation and attraction and association to inanimate matter, which ultimately feeds into his wish to "merge with the very soil of the land":

> Sartre argues that where social relations (capitalism) artificially sustain the experience of scarcity by defining existence as antagonistic competition among human beings for access to scarce things, human life itself is constituted as a "thing" that threatens other human lives … Perceiving every other human existence as a potential

---

[22] Holloway, *The Late Modernism*, 125.
[23] Ibid., 131, 151.

> threat to her own existence, the individual interiorizes the matter that governs her life and becomes a subject who regards both herself and other human beings as objects, as material things to be worked and overcome just as all matter is to be worked and overcome.[24]

Scarcity undermines the notion of community as settled, stabled, and harmonious, because if the material conditions within it are essentially competitive and acquisitive, how could it be otherwise? Lester grasps this contradiction in his own warped manner, which serves as another catalyst for his alienation. The novel opens with an emphasis on this acquisitiveness as Lester is disenfranchised by bourgeois property relations which seek to commodify everything; indeed, Holloway notes that the commodity form naturalizes everything in the text, even the female body. As we have seen, Lester goes on to work out his own deranged replication of the institutions that have dispossessed and shunned him, meaning that, for Holloway, the "occlusion of community by capital" is a pronounced theme in the novel, and the horrific acts which subsequently occur can be attributed to this theme.[25]

Vereen Bell notes how Lester is an archetypal McCarthy character in that he is "uninhibited by even the most basic taboo."[26] Bell also hints at a Girardian reading when he observes that Lester is a "berserk version of fundamental aspects of ourselves" and that the novel is another exploration on the theme of homelessness; indeed, Bell goes so far as to claim that the passion to return home is Lester's

---

[24] Ibid., 130-31.
[25] Ibid., 128.
[26] Bell, *The Achievement of Cormac McCarthy*, 61.

undoing.[27] Whilst his attempt to reestablish his yeoman or pastoral status is doomed to fail, Bell does raise the important point that Lester—obviously unable to care for himself even at the opening of the novel—is abandoned by the civic order that fails to take proper care of him following his eviction.

Bell also locates something of a moral element at play in *Child of God* which was entirely lacking in his nihilistic analysis of *Outer Dark*. Unlike Culla Holme, Bell claims that Lester does retain "the capacity to judge himself," which is notably evident upon his return to the hospital and his "I'm supposed to be here" comment.[28] Bell's critique of the novel preceding *Child of God* was at odds with Edwin Arnold's, but the two critics are in accordance here. Arnold also claims that Lester "arguably faces his guilt with a courage not shown by Culla Holme. He identified himself as Culla never can do," whilst he also claims that the novel is "not about violence, but about companionship."[29] Bell also has some sympathy for Lester, claiming that the underlying fact for all Lester's "mad cruelty is simply the fact of human loneliness," and that tragically "we are most aware of Lester's humaneness at the point at which it is irrevocably extinguished" in the dissection scene, which parallels the opening of the novel in that Lester is the victim of violent acts sanctioned by the community which shuns him.[30]

A significant moment in Bell's analysis of the novel comes with his acknowledgment of the role that storytelling and narrative play. Holloway sees *Child of God* as developing the Sartrean concerns

---

[27] Ibid., 61, 60.
[28] Ibid., 55.
[29] Arnold, "Naming, Knowing and Nothingness," 57, 55.
[30] Bell, *The Achievement of Cormac McCarthy*, 64, 67.

that dominate McCarthy's mature work, but his third novel also has a pronounced emphasis on the act of narrative as a potentially redemptive or corrective act. We have already seen how Cant views the role of narrative as offering something of a counter-hegemonic force, much as the *corrido* does in *The Crossing*, and Bell shares this view. Although he observes that even for McCarthy "an unusual degree of unassimilated raw material impedes—or seems to impede—the central narrative flow," he goes on to claim that the novel is "partly *about* stories and storytelling."[31] This increased focus on the role of narrative, along with the emerging (and highly sophisticated) existential consciousness are perhaps the most important contributions that the novel makes to the development of McCarthy's aesthetic.

Robert Jarrett also maintains that McCarthy's work displays a "highly qualified belief in narrative" and storytelling.[32] Jarrett sees *Child of God* as a version of the modernist underground motif and thinks that Lester has a literary kinship with similar underground protagonists in the work of Fyodor Dostoevsky and Ralph Ellison. In keeping with McCarthy's aesthetic, the work has a hybrid mix of styles, ranging from the crudely naturalistic and cinematic to moments of lyrical perception, all of which are imparted by the narrative consciousness and which Lester is oblivious to. Jarrett is another critic who attempts to frame Lester as a figure deserving our sympathy by claiming that his "unconscious knows what it is that he misses" throughout the narrative, even if he lacks the cognitive abilities to objectively rationalize how he could properly correct this situation.[33]

---

[31] Bell, *The Achievement of Cormac McCarthy*, 53, 55.
[32] Jarrett, *Cormac McCarthy*, 121.
[33] Ibid., 53.

Jarrett also claims that Lester is the first in a triumvirate of characters (the other two are the eponymous protagonist and Gene Harrogate from *Suttree*) who are versions of a single character type. All three are criminals to varying degrees, all live on the margins of society, and all "exist in a state of alienation and anomie."[34] Jarrett's reading is also important in that in anticipates Guillemin's idea of an emerging "wilderness aesthetic" in McCarthy's work, as the setting is a "primal wilderness bereft of human order," in psychological and environmental terms.[35] This also parallels Cant's idea of critics who experience a "pastoral delusion" when reading McCarthy, and Jarrett also warns against attempting to frame Lester as an Adamic figure in line with R. W. B. Lewis's seminal arguments posited in his *American Adam*: "Within its setting of primitive wilderness, *Child of God* reverses Lewis's thesis. Unlike Thoreau at Walden Pond, Ballard's isolation in nature neither regenerates nor restores a lost innocence; it corrupts this contemporary inversion of the American Adam."[36]

Whilst Georg Guillemin isn't convinced by the reading which places Lester as a surrogate or scapegoat for the community—he claims that "the text [does not] allow for a classification of Lester as a scapegoat of the violent collective that first makes him into what he is, then ostracizes him"—he does maintain that the novel can be read in part as a fable on the failed Jeffersonian ideal.[37] Guillemin sees the familiar McCarthy narrative strategy at play whereby the narrator uses a rhetoric that is "too sophisticated to be Lester Ballard's," thereby adding another layer to the complex polyphonic effect at work

---

[34] Ibid., 39.
[35] Ibid., 41.
[36] Ibid.
[37] Guillemin, *The Pastoral Vision*, 42.

here and throughout McCarthy's other work.[38] However, the most pertinent aspect of Guillemin's critique of the novel is his claim that its real achievement is its allegorical development of a "wilderness aesthetic" which forces us to re-examine the way we think about the concept of wilderness, be that in psychological or ecological terms.

In "The Cave of Oblivion: Platonic Mythology in *Child of God*," Dianne Luce reveals how the novel critiques the "grasping and materialistic culture" from which Lester emerges. According to Luce, this culture prevents him from undertaking his own quest for truth, his own search for some kind of organizing principle, which is a foundational principle in Platonic mythology and McCarthy's fiction.[39] The psychic trauma experienced in his childhood gives vitally important clues as to his eventual progress into necrophilia, but Luce outlines that "in accepting the illusion offered by necrophilia, Lester commits himself to progressive blindness, becoming the antithesis of Plato's philosopher-as-seeker."[40] Whilst Lester is unable to fully benefit from the Narcissistic episodes in the novel, primarily as "he cannot perceive a creative order in the world, inferring only the principle that 'all things fought,'" Luce maintains that "the whole novel offers a Narcissistic experience for the reader," another moment when the allegorical subtext of the narrative is revealed.[41]

Jay Ellis provides an insightful reading of the novel structured around his interest in McCarthy's characters' fears about domestic entrapment and the trauma they suffer when attempting to move through American culture, space, and history. Ellis observes that

---

[38] Ibid., 54.
[39] Luce, "The Cave of Oblivion," 171-98.
[40] Ibid., 179.
[41] Ibid., 186.

none of McCarthy's characters have a particularly happy or settled family life and Lester, the "least sane of McCarthy's protagonists, has the least family background" from the outset, placing him beyond the normative ordering institutions of society.[42] Moreover, Lester's experience is archetypal in the McCarthy canon in the respect that his problems "with both houses and graves suggest commingled anxieties about domesticity, entrapment, and death, and thus home and graves are regularly conflated."[43] Perhaps nowhere in McCarthy is this more evident as Lester, in a novel set in the early 1960s, sets about creating his very own perverse underground counter-culture.

Ellis sees Lester's predicament as a recurrent attitude among McCarthy's characters as they, consciously or unconsciously, both "fear and yet desire containment."[44] Lester has an extremely problematic relationship to concepts of domestic stability, and right from the beginning, we as readers are also implicated in his unhousing. Ellis notes that as soon as we meet him, Lester is "marginally housed" in the barn, and even when he spends time with his first corpse as a squatter (not even a legal resident) in Waldrop's cabin, he places the corpse in the attic, which is "within the house, but not in the living space."[45] His subsequent actions, even including his spell in the "womb-grave" as Ellis calls it, are pitiful efforts aimed at replicating a version of domesticity, sexual relationships, and companionship that mirror those practices he sees being carried out in the culture that has rejected him.

---

[42] Ellis, *No Place for Home*, 79.
[43] Ibid., 16.
[44] Ibid., 15.
[45] Ibid., 73, 86.

The critical viewpoints summarized so far are generally sympathetic towards Lester, and they do their best to show us how McCarthy manages to make this ghastly character one worthy of our compassion. Nell Sullivan, however, does not adhere to such readings, and she claims that "the seeds of narrative misogyny lying dormant in *Outer Dark* come to fruition in *Child of God*," arguing that this misogyny is revealed by the fact that the narrative "excludes live women from the text."[46]

Sullivan notes that Lester prefers "inanimate, sleeping women—women whose movements ... he controls."[47] Not only that, but the women who do appear in the novel "suffer almost every indignity a body can. These ladies, like Rinthy, exhibit the grotesque, incontinent bodies often associated with women in Western art and literature." Further, "even years after death, the bodies of his victims exhibit this abject incontinence."[48] For Sullivan, the caves that contain Lester's underground community "represent the generative female body," and she claims that the much-analyzed "I'm supposed to be here" one-line confession from Lester represents the fact that he is supposedly free from the generative female body. We have noted thus far how Lester is different from Culla, mainly due to his ability to judge himself, but Sullivan identifies a similarity between them in that they "both turn away from the feminine bodies that once enticed them ... Lester voluntarily leaves the caves that are at once mother and mausoleum."[49] Ciuba claims that Lester, in his own deranged manner, internalizes the violence done to women in his cul-

---

[46] N. Sullivan, "The Evolution of the Dead Girlfriend Motif," 73, 75.
[47] Ibid., 74.
[48] Ibid., 74, 75.
[49] Ibid., 76.

ture and acts out his own version of it which, in turn, means that his acts actually *critique* that very culture itself, but the representation of female characters is once again a problematic issue here. Conversely, John Lang notes that Lester finally "glimpses enough of his own moral darkness to return to the hospital," but it is unclear "whether the other members of the community divine *their* capacity for evil," thereby adding another layer of complexity to Lester and the cultural forces that produced him.[50]

Whether one views Lester Ballard as an impossibly unsympathetic murdering misogynist, a surrogate victim needed to reinforce fundamental cultural values or an archetypal figure through which a quintessentially American/pastoral drama is played out, what cannot be doubted is the fact that the novel is another remarkable piece of work. For all of its grotesque episodes, *Child of God* can also be read as an exploration into the potential humanistic act of narrative and storytelling itself, and we do see Lester changing and maturing somewhat. He reaches a level of interiorized contemplation that is beyond Culla Holme, and his (and his culture's) attempt to reach an understanding through narrative echoes a theme that is of central importance to McCarthy's work, as Dianne Luce astutely observes: "Myth, parable, philosophy, fiction, it matters not; in the end … the meaning of our lives that can be known and of value to us as we live is the meaning that we put there by exercising our human gift for storytelling."[51] *Child of God* asks us to examine how we construct such knowledge and relate it to the world where we will always talk about Lester Ballards, even when we've supper waiting on us at the house.

---

[50] Lang, "Lester Ballard: McCarthy's Challenge," 94.

[51] Luce, "The Road and the Matrix," 201-02.

CHAPTER 6

Suttree

Although *Suttree* was published in 1979 we know that McCarthy had been working on his fourth novel for a number of years, even while he was working on *The Orchard Keeper*. The most notable contrast with the novels that precede it is that in Cornelius Suttree, the novel's eponymous protagonist, McCarthy provides us with a central narrative consciousness who is fiercely intelligent and haunted by the fear of his own death. The novel takes us from the rural to the urban (without forsaking certain wilderness aspects), and spatial representations are key throughout; indeed, the novel is as jumbled, messy, and anachronistic as the city that inspired it. *Blood Meridian* and the subsequent Border Trilogy brought McCarthy to an entirely new readership and level of academic interest, but *Suttree* is as rich, complex and rewarding as any of the novels set in the geographical territory that Suttree (and McCarthy himself for that matter) lights out for at the novel's close.

We have acknowledged the dangers of making straight biographical readings with McCarthy's work, but we can draw some strong parallels between his own life and the experiences of Suttree. McCarthy was at odds with his family—especially his father—over his chosen career path (one recalls his comment to Richard Woodward that he was not what his family had in mind), and so is Suttree. Over the long course of the novel's composition McCarthy married, became a father himself, and ultimately saw his marriage break up, which contributed to his decision to leave Knoxville and move to El Paso. Suttree also experiences similar dilemmas, as we see him do battle with a largely absent but imposing patriarchal figure, we follow as he suffers the agony of his child dying, and we learn that his own marriage didn't work, all of which suggest that the novel could well offer a commentary on McCarthy's own fears about fatherhood and family, just as *The Road* offers a more hopeful reconsideration of these foundational McCarthy themes. Suttree, like McCarthy, is a University of Tennessee dropout, but not because of any lack of intellectual ability. Suttree is remarkably intelligent, and the lack of access to the interiority of his characters that we have remarked upon in his other novels is more than made up for here; in fact, Suttree is plagued by his hyper-consciousness, especially the crippling fear of his own mortality. McCarthy has remarked upon his problems with alcoholism during this part of his life, and Suttree combats his fear of death in a series of scenes in which he alters his consciousness through a variety of means (most notably alcohol) in an attempt to deny and transcend this knowledge.

Suttree is obviously a central protagonist in the novel but, for the first time in McCarthy, the city itself—especially the destitute riverfront and the sub-region of McAnally Flats with its cast of pariahs—dominates the novel. This is one of the novel's most important themes as McCarthy lovingly evokes the world of Knoxville in the 1950s even while the narrative consciousness and Suttree's metaphysical ruminations remind us again and again of our "transcendental homelessness" in the world. Much of the novel is episodic, fragmentary, and perhaps even picaresque, but a memorable aesthetic unity arises out of this hybridity.

We also cannot ignore the developments in American intellectual life during the period of the novel's composition, which was also a significant period in the evolution of McCarthy's aesthetic. It is no coincidence that McCarthy takes us to the world of Knoxville in the early 1950s as this was a period when McCarthy himself would have been introduced to key texts that were published in America for the first time by writers such as John Paul Sartre and Albert Camus, and Suttree's existential battle to transcend his fear of death in an increasingly absurd and godless world is arguably the novel's key theme. These existentialists heavily influenced the leading figures of the Beat generation such as Allen Ginsberg, William Burroughs, and Jack Kerouac, figures who emerged as voices that challenged the complacency and conformism of post-war American culture, and *Suttree* positively hums with a vibrant anti-hegemonic and oppositional sensibility. Although not driven by any radical political agenda the dispossessed characters in the novel battle against what Brian Jarvis has called the *"embourgeoisement* of large sections of American society [that took place in] the 1950s," and Suttree and his cohorts renounce the culture of business, commerce, regulation, and conditioning represented by the world that Suttree's father inhabits.[1] Carnival motifs and imagery play an important role in celebrating this oppositional sensibility, but one of the more melancholic aspects of the novel is that the *"ruder forms"* referred to in the prologue fall victim to the process of embourgeoisement that Jarvis outlines.

The novel also continues McCarthy's exploration of patriarchal and mythic concerns. Suttree is estranged from his own father, and he renounces his father's world and all that it stands for, but two fig-

---

[1] Jarvis, *Postmodern Cartographies*, 97.

ures in particular (Ab Jones and Gene Harrogate) offer commentaries on the patriarchal theme. Ab is an archetypal McCarthy figure as he provides a link to a historical consciousness that has already vanished, whilst his status as an African American offers a more scathing ideological critique of a form of pariahdom enforced by his culture. On the other hand we have Gene "the city rat Harrogate" and Suttree's compassionate, perhaps even fatherly, acts on behalf of Gene go some way to compensating for his failings as a father to his own son. Gene also reminds us that McCarthy is a fine writer of comedy, and he can be read as a contemporized version of the exaggerated characters created by the Southwestern humorists.

It should come as no surprise that we find other recurring themes in a novel as densely rich as *Suttree*. Wilderness plays a significant role in geographic, psychological, and sexual terms, and Suttree's extended sojourn into the Great Smoky Mountains is one of the most important epiphanic moments in the text. The novel also contains some problematic depictions of female characters, which adhere once again to the aridity of the wasteland motif. For the most part, female characters are portrayed using the most unflattering rhetoric, and those who do feature more prominently (Suttree's mother Grace, Wanda, Mother She, Joyce) only play significant supporting roles in his existential quest to transcend his fear of death.

Death itself is a tangible presence in the book, and it is pronounced from the very opening with the novel's italicized prologue which echoes the prologue to James Agee's *A Death in the Family*. Like the unholy trinity in *Outer Dark*, the knowledge and presence of death opens the novel but stands *outside* of the text proper; although it goes on to haunt Suttree throughout, it is only successfully reconciled with his consciousness at the novel's conclusion as he leaves Knoxville. The actual time of the prologue is fuzzily defined, but it is a remarkable stylistic accomplishment as the narrative consciousness creates for us this shadowed and hidden world as we are taken to the *"dusty clockless hours of the town"* where *"the drunk and the homeless have washed up in the lee of walls in alleys,"* and we get the first instance of a waste-strewn landscape where *"blownout autos sulk on pedestals of cinderblock"* (S 3). We also get a characteristic reminder of the insignificance of human culture when set against geological time as this drama is playing out on *"this once inland sea"* (S 3).

The prologue introduces us to the city of Knoxville itself and the immanent presence of death, both of which could be read as protagonists in their own right. The rhetoric used to depict Knoxville is often dense and antiquated, but it succeeds in capturing the historical materiality of the city in the 1950s, as it was a jumbled, grimy, and anachronistic place. This is a city described as being *"constructed on no known paradigm, a mongrel architecture reading back through the works of man in a brief delineation of the aberrant disordered and mad,"* an *"encampment of the damned"* (S 3-4). One of the most significant metaphors used throughout the novel is that of waste as it parallels Suttree's existential consciousness as well reinforcing the status of the citizens of the city that McCarthy focuses on as discarded from society, an assemblage of human detritus that is viewed as worthless by the normative, regular world. This also contributes to McCarthy's critique of the pastoral, as the river that flows through the city resembles a *"sluggard ooze"* which bears along a *"dread waste"* including *"a wrack of cratewood and condoms and fruitrinds. Old tins and jars and ruined household artefacts that rear from the fecal mire of the flats like landmarks in the trackless vales of dementia praecox"* (S 4).

In Jarvis's discussion of Thomas Pynchon's *Gravity's Rainbow* (a novel with which *Suttree* has a number of thematic similarities), he talks of Pynchon's "poetics of junk amidst the extreme hygiene of America's air-conditioned nightmare," a theme especially pronounced in the conformist 1950s.[2] A key feature of *Suttree's* ideology of spatial representation, of its mapping out of a counter-hegemonic space, is its focus on McAnally Flats and the city's poverty-stricken riverfront which represents a *"world within the world ... that the righteous sees from carriage and car another life dreams. Illshapen or black or deranged, fugitive of all order, strangers in everyland"* (S 4). The righteous could well be those commuters (perhaps even Suttree's father) on their way from their newly created suburbs to the "air-conditioned nightmare" of their version of the American dream that the denizens of McAnally have renounced. This is one of the novel's key themes, as this region that is *"fugitive of all order"* is eventually regulated and cleared at the novel's close to make way for a new federally sanctioned freeway as the process of embourgeoisement becomes complete.

Death itself is imbued with a palpable, tangible presence in the prologue, and it maintains its insidious presence throughout much of the narrative proper. In a memorable phrase the narrator tells us that the city is *"beset by a thing unknown,"* evoking images of 1950s B-movies which tapped into national anxieties about the cold war and the nuclear threat; however, the *"thing unknown"* here is the metaphysical fear of death rather than a metaphorical working out of ideological fears. The presence of death is acknowledged towards the end of the prologue in almost hushed, reverential tones, a mystery that cannot be reconciled or properly accounted for. The greatest

---

[2] Jarvis, *Postmodern Cartographies*, 67.

irony of the passage below is that it warns us not to dwell upon it "*for it is by just suchwise that he's invited in,*" yet it is Suttree's succession of morbid "dwellings" that dominate many of the scenes in which he plays a central part:

> *The night is quiet. Like a camp before battle. The city beset by a thing unknown and will it come from forest or sea? The murengers have walled the pale, the gates are shut, but lo the thing's inside and can you guess his shape? Where he's kept or what's the counter of his face? Is he a weaver, bloody shuttle shot through a timewarp, a carder of souls from the world's nap? Or a hunter with hounds* [as in the novel's conclusion] *or do bone horses draw his deadcart though the streets and does he call his trade to each? Dear friend he is not to be dwelt upon for it is by just suchwise that he's invited in.* (S 4-5)

The prologue concludes with a baroque touch as we see that "*a curtain is rising on the western world,*" and we are invited into the central narrative (S 5). It should perhaps come as no surprise that the novel opens with the recovery of a suicide victim from the "*sluggard ooze*" of the river (one remembers Ownby expressing his disbelief to John Wesley that someone was employed for such a task in *The Orchard Keeper*), and it is significant that Suttree "noticed with a feeling he could not name that the dead man's watch was still running" (S 10). Clocks, watches and reminders of time irrevocably elapsing play an important symbolic role throughout the novel, and the prologue and this opening scene announce the fact that Suttree will forever be up against something that he cannot change or alter.

Although his family's physical presence in the text is somewhat limited, *Suttree* could be read as a family drama, as the tensions and hostilities within his family are responsible for Suttree forsaking the comfortable middle-class life he could have; indeed, his renunciation of his family is itself a form of rebellion. His Uncle John pays him a visit in his houseboat at an early stage in the novel, and their conversation reveals these family tensions, as Suttree ridicules John's acquiescence before the status and ideology that his father's side of the family represents: "You think my father and his kind are a race apart. You can laugh at their pretensions, but you never question their right to the way of life they maintain" (S 19). Their exchange also reveals that his father, in social and economic terms, has married beneath "him," and Suttree maintains that, when this happens, his children are also "beneath" him. John's efforts to make Suttree feel at least some kinship with his estranged family is met with the curt reply of "I'm like me. Don't tell me whom I'm like," which hints at Suttree's fiercely stubborn and independent nature (S 18). Crucially, John, a well-intentioned if somewhat hapless character whose objectives for this visit are undermined by his tipsiness, elicits from Suttree the knowledge not of his brother who is alive but of his stillborn twin (S 17). This is the first instance in the novel where the theme of the double or anti-Suttree is introduced, a phantasmagoric figure modeled on this stillborn sibling who embodies his fear of death.

Very little is said of Suttree's mother in this exchange, and all we learn is that social prejudice plays a part in his family due to the fact that she has "married above her station." It should come as no surprise that his father is the key player here, a figure who casts a large shadow over the novel despite never physically appearing in it. There are two key moments in the early stage of the text that reveal the depths of this familial drama, the first being the exchange with his uncle whilst the second is the letter Suttree receives from his father. The fact that the only contact between the two is a letter is significant as it hints at the estrangement between father and son, whilst the letter itself almost reads as a mandate of rebellion for Suttree, a version of the American dream and conformist culture that the world of McAnally rambunctiously opposes:

> In my father's last letter he said that the world is run by those willing to take the responsibility for the running of it. If it is life that you feel you are missing I can tell you where to find it. In the law courts, in business, in government. There is nothing occurring in the streets. Nothing but a dumbshow composed of the helpless and impotent. (S 13-14)

However, the patriarchal theme is not only expressed through Suttree's renunciation of his family's heritage and social standing. Another crucial if somewhat underdeveloped feature of Suttree's past family life is his relationship with his ex-wife and son, and the death of his child is one of the most sorrowful episodes in a novel not lacking in deeply melancholic moments. Suttree's role as a surrogate father figure to some of the residents of McAnally only partially compensates for his failure to be a genuine father figure for his own son, although his implication in Leonard's ludicrous welfare-cheating scheme is one of the more humorous examples where this theme is explored. Leonard's father inevitably rises to the surface after they attempt to drown him, and Suttree's reply that "fathers will do that" reveals the inescapable fact of patriarchal conflict in McCarthy, and its conciseness echoes Mary Weaver's comment on this very theme in *The Stonemason* (S 417).

All of this patriarchal and familial conflict means that Suttree is what popular parlance would refer to as a tortured soul. McCarthy's fourth novel is significant in that its chief protagonist is at least partly modeled on the Jamesian paradigm which his fiction has thus far eschewed, and we are granted access to Suttree's interiority and death-stalked psychological speculations. This is not to suggest that Suttree is a nihilistic character, and we should remember that, symbolically, he is "a son of Grace" after all, and his tale can partly be read as a spiritual or quasi-religious quest (S 432). Throughout the novel, Suttree undertakes a quest for meaning, altering his consciousness through various methods, in order to uncover some kind of organizing truth, his longing for order made clear in one instance where he muses that "even a false adumbration of the world of the spirit is better than none at all" (S 21).

Although he is a university dropout, claiming that "from all old seamy throats of elders, musty books, I've salvaged not a word," he doesn't convince in his solipsism, and he remains intellectually and philosophically curious and introspective (perhaps overly so) throughout the novel (S 14). We are even afforded a glimpse into the nightmarish visions he summoned as a youth, and it appears that even his childhood innocence was punctured by knowledge of death's grotesque attendants:

> He himself used to wake in terror to find whole congregations of the uninvited attending his bed, protean figures slouched among the room's dark corners in all multiplicity of shapes, gibbons and gargoyles, arachnoids of outrageous size, a batshaped creature hung by some cunning in a high corner from whence clicked and winked like bone chimes its incandescent teeth. (S 148-49)

He is relentlessly harsh when probing the nature of his own selfhood, inquiring if "am I a monster, are there monsters in me?" (S 366) in one instance, whilst we learn that his "subtle obsession with uniqueness troubled all his dreams" (S 113). We shall see that Suttree's maturation and development (and the novel's aesthetic unity) is evidenced by the fact that he relinquishes these dreams to uniqueness at novel's end, and he finally succeeds in recognizing his common humanity, as Douglas Canfield has claimed. Whilst the hedonistic camaraderie afforded by the taverns and pariahs of McAnally does temporarily alleviate his sorrow, melancholy appears to be his one constant companion. Even in the temporary and wholly illusory serenity of domestic and romantic stability he enjoys with Joyce, his true companion is his sorrow, and it stalks him even in this supposedly blissful episode: "She had knelt beside him and nibbled at his ear. Her soft breast against his arm. Why then this loneliness?" (S 408). Suttree suffers through what he sees as his "terrestrial hell" (S 14), a condition which entails the essentialist knowledge of the inescapable fact of human suffering as "there are no absolutes in human misery and things can always get worse" (S 372). Suttree also believes that "the last and the first suffer equally" in what is his own melancholic beatitude (S 414).

The one constant feature of his tortured interior workings is his fear of death, embedded in his consciousness with the knowledge of his stillborn twin and metaphorically represented throughout the novel with the representations of a dread doppelganger or the "anti-Suttree." In the recollection of his visit to the racetrack as a child, we learn that Suttree "had already begun to sicken at the slow seeping of life" (S 136), and in another instance, he slackens his facial features in front of a mirror to see "how he would look in death" (S 295). There are large parts of the narrative where Suttree appears to be all too willing to take up his membership amongst the dead as he feels that "nothingness is not a curse. Far from it" (S 153), although tellingly he never makes the jump that the suicidal victim we see at the novel's opening did, thereby making his tale somewhat existentially heroic. Although he summons enough existential fortitude not to commit suicide as a means of escaping his death-haunted condition, his bout of typhoid fever nearly does the job for him, and in his phantasmagoric fever dreams, we see that death plagues his consciousness even here: "Another door closed, door closed, door closed softly in his skull … While the dead wheeled past in floats of sere and faded flower wreaths with little cards on which the ink of the names had run in the rain" (S 452).

Despite the inescapable morbidity of these examples of Suttree's interiority, there are hints even in his gloomiest psychological workings that he will transcend this fear and liberate himself from it. In a passage recounting a childhood memory (note how once again even childhood memories are death-haunted), Suttree recalls viewing a sickly relative whilst a clock symbolically "hammered like a foundry" on a nearby table. He noted that since the "the dead would take the living with them if they could, I pulled away" (S 13). The young Suttree symbolically pulls away from the dying figure here, and he continues to philosophically and metaphysically pull away from death throughout the remainder of the narrative. Another epiphany occurs following his lengthy wilderness sojourn in the mountains, where Suttree "was seized with a thing he'd never known, a sudden understanding of the mathematical certainty of death," a crucial moment in his transcendence of this crippling knowledge (S 295).

Although *Suttree* is structured around a series of fragmentary episodes as we follow the eponymous hero through his philosophical crisis in varying spatial locations, thematic unity is ultimately achieved. Perhaps surprisingly, the fragmentary structure contains within it a series of passages where Suttree moves towards reconciling his fear of death with his own consciousness and thereby liberating himself from this knowledge that threatens to overwhelm him. In other words, Suttree develops and matures in a relatively conventional novelistic manner, and he successfully emerges from his "chrysalis of doom," which ensures that the novel ends on an upbeat note (S 464).

His wilderness sojourn provides one such example, and another comes when he confesses to his reflected image whilst alone in his riverboat one evening in an ironic treatment of the Roman Catholic sacrament. Suttree acknowledges that he once "spoke with bitterness about my life and I said that I would take my own part against the slander of oblivion and against the monstrous facelessness of it … of that vanity I recant all," which is a key moment in the maturation of his character (S 414). During his fever, he seems to go through a mock trial in another instance of judgment in McCarthy, although this one is somewhat more humorous as he is accused of wasting his time with "derelicts, miscreants, pariahs, poltroons, and other assorted felonious debauchees," to which Suttree memorably replies "I was drunk" (S 457). His comedic response should not cloud the fact that this is another moment where Suttree is moving towards a new liberating knowledge about himself that will enable him to transcend the fears that have plagued him throughout the novel.

There are several key moments towards the conclusion of the text where we can clearly see that Suttree has successfully emerged from the "chrysalis of doom" in which he has been enshrouded for so long, shedding the death visage of the anti-Suttree in the process. One such moment occurs in a concretely mimetic scene when a priest visits him whilst he is recuperating from typhoid fever, and Suttree triumphantly informs him that "there is one Suttree and one Suttree only" (S 461), a reconciliation which is confirmed as he leaves Knoxville and all he takes "for talisman [is] the simple human heart within him. Walking down the little street for the last time he felt everything fall away from him. Until there was nothing left of him to shed" (S 468). This is Suttree's grand moment of triumph and reconciliation where the sure knowledge of his end paradoxically allows him to start anew, to leave Knoxville in what is a liberating act of will and consciousness. Indeed, it appears that he has finally heeded the advice given to him by the sheriff following his son's funeral. This sheriff tells him that "everything's important. A man lives his life, he has to make that important. Whether he's a small town county sheriff or the president" (S 157), and it is clear that we can add university dropout, full-time pariah, and part-time river fisherman to that list.

Whilst the final image of Suttree is that of a character at ease with himself, other protagonists (especially female characters) are not so favorably depicted. Indeed even the cast of pariahs, criminals, and roustabouts who inhabit McAnally receive a more generous treatment than the female characters in the novel. The rhetoric used to describe them is never flattering as women are portrayed as harridans with gnomic appearances, and they are rendered in all kinds of grotesque attitudes. Whilst it is true that hardly anyone in the novel receives a wholly favorable characterization, female grotesqueries tend to be more pronounced than those assigned to male characters, and at times it is hard to see how the mythic reading of such characters overrides charges of misogyny against this aspect of McCarthy's aesthetic.

There are plenty of examples of this throughout the novel, and the feminine presence receives an unflattering treatment in Suttree's unconscious (although this perhaps is no surprise considering the Puritanical repressiveness of his culture) as Suttree lies in a "sexual nightmare" (S 450) whilst suffering from typhoid fever. Following his assault with the floor buffer in one of the novel's barroom brawls, he has the following grim vision: "What waited was not the black of nothing but a foul hag with naked gums smiling and there was no Madonna of desire or mother of eternal attendance" (S 197). The religious connotations to this imagery expose the lie of the Roman Catholic orthodoxy that Suttree had been raised by, and the imagery recurs when Suttree's grieving ex-wife is also described in unflattering religious and mythic rhetoric, a "madonna bereaved, so grief-stunned" (S 150). Her mother (Suttree's ex-mother-in-law) is described as a "demented harridan" (S 151), and Wanda's mother— another grief-stricken female seemingly bereft of any kind of verbal reasoning—is cast as "an image of a baroque pieta ... gibbering and kneeling in the rain clutching at sheared limbs and rags of meat" (S 362). Perhaps even more disturbing is the depiction of the victim of horrific sexual abuse suggesting that women can only appear as howling madonnas or inanimate and inarticulate victims of sexual deviancy and cruelty: "And in the dawn a female simpleton is waking naked from a gang-fuck in the back seat of an abandoned car by the river. She stirs, sweet day has broken. Reeking of stale beer and dried sperm, eyes clogged, used rubbers dangling senselessly from the dashboard knobs" (S 416).

Suttree's female relations also receive very little treatment or serious consideration. His mother pays him a weeping visit whilst Suttree is in the workhouse, and shortly after this visit, Suttree is released, suggesting that his influential family have called in some favors on behalf of their black sheep of a son (S 61-2). The two aunts he visits also seem to have been forsaken by his family, as one resides in contented domestic isolation whilst the other has been placed in the asylum, where only Uncle John visits with the smell of whisky on his breath. Female characters fare little better when portrayed as Suttree's sexual partners, even though Joyce, the hustler who promises not to hustle Suttree, is one of the few women who upon first meeting

Suttree actually expresses a genuine fondness for him (S 386). Their mock-bourgeois courtship soon implodes shortly after Suttree notices the "light tracery of old razor scars on her inner wrists," confirming that this is another damaged female, another problematic and incomplete portrait (S 404).

Mother She, the African American witch who closely parallels a similar character Ownby encountered in *The Orchard Keeper*, is another problematically executed if significant character. Suttree often sees her about the streets "before the world's about. A hookbacked crone going darkly and bent" (S 278), a figure one would expect to find in some antiquated fairytale rather than in a novel set in 1950s America. Whilst temporarily paralyzed after taking one of her potions, Suttree experiences another of his "sexual nightmares" in a disquieting scene that is situated on the border between dream and reality, where he envisions her "shriveled leather teats like empty purses hanging," with the "plaguey mouth upon him," and the air is filled with the "dead reek of aged female flesh, a stale aridity" (S 426-7).

Suttree actually visits her in an attempt to transcend his fear of death and to magic away his seemingly perpetual melancholic sensibility. In some respects, his visit to her displays a willingness to embrace something that has been marginalized by his culture, so it becomes another ideologically defiant gesture. The options available to him in the normative world have been exhausted, so Mother She is a natural step for him on his quest for mythical insight. She says to him that "you can walk ... but you caint see where you goin," and she attempts to "read the weathers in your heart" (S 423, 424). The clock motif is present once again in this scene, and Suttree's consciousness is altered as he is aware of "pieces of a dream unreel[ing] down the back of his brain," a search for some kind of "perfect clarity" that will enable him to be rid of the anti-Suttree, of his fear of death (S 424, 427). This important scene, another of Suttree's epiphanic moments, contains a series of ocular references and revelations, culminating in the prophetic moment where Suttree "knew what would come to be" (S 430), therefore imbuing him with the mystical insight that he has been searching for throughout the novel.

Mother She therefore aids Suttree in his efforts to traverse his interior psychological and sexual wilderness (albeit in something of a racially reductive manner) in order to transcend his fear of death. His extended sojourn into the mountain wilderness provides another instance of Suttree's development, and it is one of the most important epiphanic episodes in the novel. The mountain sojourn is a lengthy scene which combines two of the novel's most important narrative threads, as the fate of Suttree is fused with another example of McCarthy's "wilderness aesthetic" in one of the text's most significant spatial representations. Suttree sets out for the mountains in late October, and he doesn't return to the city until early December. The expedition is akin to a Native American vision quest, and it is another example where Suttree attempts to divest himself of the false illusions of truth and order offered by his culture in an effort to combat the knowledge of his own mortality. In his urban environment, Suttree inhabits the wastes of the cityscape, but when he heads to the mountains, it is significant that he gets as far away as possible from space that is carefully mapped and demarcated, as "first he left the roads, then the trails" into a space where "in an old grandfather time a ballad transpired here, some love gone wrong," a fabled landscape (S 283). It is in this unmarked wild territory that he attempts to map the most unknowable and terrifying realms of his consciousness, of his internalized geography.

In the opening moments of his wilderness excursion, the narrator draws our attention to Suttree's cosmic insignificance as he is situated against the "cold indifferent dark, the blind stars beaded on their tracks and mitered satellites and geared and pinioned planets all reeling through the black of space" (S 284). It is also significant that this important scene includes a series of garish carnivalesque images (significant if we take the carnival to function as a site where things that are otherwise normally repressed are placed on show and are perhaps even celebrated), including a group of "squalid merrymakers," gnomes, a mesosaur, and "a gross and blueblack foetus clopping along in brogues and toga" (S 287-88). Suttree goes further and further into the mountains, which means that he eats less and sleeps only fitfully, all of which results in his becoming more hysterical, allowing the gloomy workings of his subconscious to become increasingly pronounced. Inevitably, he becomes aware that something is stalking him, the nightmarish anti-Suttree, the nemesis he must overcome if he is to ever successfully come out of his "chrysalis of doom": "… In these silent sunless galleries he'd come to feel that another went before him and each glade he entered seemed just quit by a figure who'd been sitting there and risen and gone on. Some doublegoer, some othersuttree eluded him in these woods…" (S 286-87).

The confrontation with this "othersuttree" results in another significant epiphanic moment as Suttree "saw with a madman's clarity the perishability of his flesh" (S 287). Although this is most definitely a wilderness section (there is no gentle contemplation often associated with pastoral imagery here), the excursion does allow Suttree to move towards a more settled sense of self, a more harmonious metaphysical and perhaps even ecological grounding. Of course, he is by no means out of the woods just yet, but he does reach a point where he feels that "everything had fallen from him. He could scarce tell where his being ended or the world began, nor did he care ... He could feel the oilless turning of the earth beneath him" (S 286), and when he returns to society and civilization in Bryson City, North Carolina, his head "was curiously clear" (S 291).

Another ideologically significant spatial representation in the novel is that of the city itself. Downtown Knoxville, its shabby riverfront communities and enclaves such as McAnally Flats are central to the geographic and capitalist spaces that the novel depicts and critiques. Eric Bulson points out that "ways of representing the city are decisively influenced by material conditions, political, historical, and social contexts, and literary traditions" and that "what happens depends a lot on *where* it happens." The cityscapes in *Suttree* enable "the battle against the bourgeoisie" and the conformist "air-conditioned" American nightmare of the 1950s to be carried out and for a counter-hegemonic sensibility to find room to express itself.[3]

We should acknowledge that the city depicted in the novel is not merely the work of McCarthy's artistic imagination. Although some aspects are undoubtedly exaggerated, the "material, political, historical, and social contexts" of Knoxville in the 1950s were very, very grim indeed. Although it irked Knoxvillians for many years after its publication, John Gunther's description of the city in his 1946 volume *Inside U.S.A.* was still applicable in the opening years of the following decade:

> Knoxville is the ugliest city I ever saw in America, with the possible exception of some mill towns in New England. Its main street is called Gay Street; this seemed to

---

[3] Bulson, *Novels, Maps and Modernity*, 11-12.

me to be a misnomer ... it is one of the least orderly cities in the South. Knoxville leads every other town in Tennessee in homicides, automobile thefts, and larceny.[4]

Bruce Wheeler's history of Knoxville includes a chapter on the 1950s that reveals just how out of step the city was, especially when compared to regional and national trends. Wheeler contends that Knoxville in the 1950s was "obviously a city in trouble" due specifically to that fact that it was "designed and developed before the impact of the automobile made itself felt, [meaning that] Knoxville seemed to be a city frozen in time, out of touch with the rapidly changing world," and that even breathing was difficult due to the city's dire pollution problems.[5] The city's industry was not simply stagnating, but it was rendered obsolete by changes which a conservative city leadership were unable to respond to and, as a result, "the percentage of Knoxvillians who were unemployed rose from 5.8 percent in 1951 to a disturbing 9.7 percent in 1958."[6] The city lost a huge percentage of its population in the same period as people out-migrated to the newly emerging suburbs and, beyond even that, to burgeoning Northern industrial centers such as Detroit and Chicago.

It is this grimy, dilapidated, outmoded, and anachronistic city that McCarthy evokes so memorably in *Suttree*. The city itself is yet another example of a mode of life that disappears into history as McCarthy is writing about it and, as Suttree heads out of Knoxville at the novel's close, a new Knoxville is emerging, ready to take its place in the forward-looking, automobile-friendly, and suburban-dwelling

---

[4] John Gunther, quoted in Wheeler, *Knoxville, Tennessee: A Mountain City*, 61-62.

[5] Ibid., 95, 107.

[6] Ibid., 98.

New South. Certain descriptions of the city very much have a cold and inhuman modernist feel to them, resembling something from Dos Passos, such as the following: "The city a collage of grim cubes under a sky the color of wet steel in the winter noon" (S 397).

However, the most striking descriptions of Knoxville are the ones which make it look, sound, and feel like anything but an American metropolis in the early years of the 1950s. Untold cultural discourses and texts—including TV programs, movies, and advertising—would have us believe that the decade was a golden age of security (despite the very real threat of catastrophic nuclear destruction), of material prosperity for all, and that an unshakable optimism in the future of the nation prevailed. We then have McCarthy's Knoxville, elements of which resemble a kind of medieval bazaar, which practices an economic system that is decidedly pre-capitalistic and which includes a cast of urban characters who seem to have been plucked from another age entirely. Although lengthy, it is important to cite the following Market Street scene as it captures the counter-hegemonic and unfashionable vibrancy of a city where an antiquated "country commerce" was practiced and where pariahs, grotesques, and demented preachers populate the sidewalks:

> Market Street on Monday morning, Knoxville Tennessee. In this year nineteen fifty-one. Suttree with his parcel of fish going past the rows of derelict trucks piled with produce and flowers, an atmosphere rank with country commerce, a reek of farmgoods in the air tending off into a light surmise of putrefaction and decay. Pariahs adorned the walk and blind singers and organists and psalmists with mouth harps wandered up and down. Past hardware stores and meatmarkets and little tobacco shops. A strong smell of feed in the hot noon like working

> mash. Mute and roosting pedlars watching from their wagonbeds and flower ladies in their bonnets like cowled gnomes, driftwood hands composed in their apron laps and their underlips swollen with snuff. He went among vendors and beggars and wild street preachers haranguing a lost world with a vigor unknown to the sane. Suttree admired them with their hot eyes and dogeared bibles, God's barkers gone forth into the world like the prophets of old. He'd often stood along the edges of the crowd for some stray scrap of news from beyond the pale. (S 66)

The majority of the characters who inhabit the periphery of the novel provide a gallery of grotesques. In a passage which occurs shortly after the riotous Market Street scene, the narrative consciousness draws our attention to the city residents who represent a "maimed humanity" where "every other face [is] goitered, twisted, tubered with some excrescence" (S 67). Elsewhere, Suttree is confronted by a "mute and shapeless derelict" whose "lower face hung in sagging wattles like a great scrotum" (S 383), whilst he also invokes the vitriol of one of the mad street preacher-prophets who admonishes him when "He knows it's a Sunday for he's drunker than usual" (S 412).

The wasteland motif also plays an important symbolic role in the novel, and it enables McCarthy to develop an oppositional perspective. Suttree, like some of Pynchon's characters in *Gravity's Rainbow*, situates himself amongst "various strata of society's rubbish and its waste [and therefore comes] into contact with the underclass and life in the low-lands of capitalist geographies."[7] Furthermore, we can locate another parallel between McCarthy and Pynchon's work as *Sut-*

---

[7] Jarvis, *Postmodern Cartographies*, 54.

tree also constitutes what the Native American writer William Least Heat-Moon has said of Pynchon's *Vineland* in that both novels resemble a "*Praiyerth*, or 'deep map,' a multilayered cartography which pushes beneath the malls and freeways toward the mythical heart of this locale."⁸ As we shall see, the urban wasteland motif receives a particularly striking treatment with the character of Gene Harrogate, especially his ludicrous scheme to explore the caves underneath the city streets.

At one point, a "frozen pestilential miasma" (S 171) cloaks the town, and the city perpetually seems to be enshrouded by such phenomena, which has repercussions for the physical and spiritual health of its residents. The river which flows through the city and from which Suttree fishes and thereby earns his meager living is not immune from being depicted as waste-strewn and filthy, bearing along all manner of junk which makes it hard to believe that any kind of life could flourish within it. In one memorable example, the "swollen river" bears along "garbage and rafted trash" (which includes a dead sow and a dead baby), and it is also another moment in McCarthy where the human form (in this case Suttree) is placed on the same level with inanimate matter: "Bloated, pulpy rotted eyes in a bulbous skull and little rags of flesh trailing in the water like tissuepaper. Oaring his way through the rain among these curiosa he felt little more than yet another artifact leached out of the earth and washed along" (S 306).

The urban wasteland scenes in the novel led one critic to claim that McCarthy is a veritable "Tolstoy of trash."⁹ The following example occurs when Suttree awakes after another night of wild drunken

---

⁸ Ibid., 75.

⁹ Cawelti, "Cormac McCarthy: Restless Seekers," 310.

ness, and his "swollen eyes" take in a vista which parallels his inner ruin in a scene that is suitably dystopian:

> He lifted his swollen eyes to the desolation in which he knelt, the ironcolored nettles and sedge in the reeking fields like mock weeds made from wire, a raw landscape where half familiar shapes reared from the slagheaps of trash. Where backlots choked with weeds and glass and the old chalky turds of passing dogs tended away toward a dim shore of stonegray shacks and gutted auto hulks ... Tottering to his feet he stood reeling in that apocalyptic waste like some biblical relict in a world no one would have. (S 80-81)

Domestic spaces also conform to the wasteland motif and virtually all such scenes take place in ruined, desolate, poverty-stricken and confining structures. Suttree's riverboat provides the most striking example, and its situation on the river hints at the protagonist's comfort with the idea of fleeing, of being as close to the natural (or at least what remains of it) as possible, much like John Wesley's penchant for sleeping on the porch in *The Orchard Keeper*. Towards the end of the novel, the houseboat is nothing more than a scene "of old memories and new desolations" when a corpse is discovered there, which is mistakenly believed to be Suttree himself (S 413). On one of his many wanderings, Suttree passes through a ruined plantation house, something of an anachronistic structure for the region. Some critics have claimed that this scene adds to the counter-mythic agenda pursued in the novel, given the symbolic importance of the plantation house in Southern culture (S 136).

The most significant domestic scenes concerning Suttree himself occur just prior to and during his relationship with Joyce, suggesting that the mode of life that he has enjoyed for much of the novel will not last for much longer. Prior to their meeting, Suttree rents a room in one of the city's "poorer quarters" (S 379), and his subsequent efforts to maintain a normative domestic and sexual relationship with Joyce is a prelude to his more acute mental, physical, and metaphysical moment of crisis. In short, Suttree seems inhibited and ill at ease with the arrangement, and his gesture to an anonymous neighbor stirs something in him that other situations and settings in the novel have not given rise to: "He could see an old man washing at a sink, pale arms and a small paunch hung in his undershirt. Suttree toasted him a mute toast, a shrug of the glass, a gesture indifferent and almost cynical that as he made it caused him something close to shame" (S 402).

William Prather claimed that we can read *The Orchard Keeper* as elegy and eulogy, and the same reading could also be applied to *Suttree*. One of the central narrative threads in the novel concerns the counter-hegemonic and oppositional exploits of the residents of McAnally and the manner in which they resist the embourgeoisement of American society that was taking place in the 1950s. Of course, one of the most melancholic aspects of the novel (and McCarthy's work as a whole for that matter) is that it becomes increasingly hard to stand outside of robust finance capitalism and mass culture, and even artistic production becomes increasingly absorbed into commodity production. Still, the cast of characters give it their best shot and even Suttree becomes embroiled in some outlandish anti-authoritarian schemes that exhibit a Beatific sensibility.[10]

---

[10] See Tytell's *Naked Angels: The Lives and Literature of the Beat Generation* for an excellent introduction to Beat culture and the intellectual climate of the postwar period and the 1950s.

McCarthy employs a series of carnival motifs which underpin the novel's interest in sites of resistance and oppositional cultures. One of the workhouse scenes follows the inmates (themselves officially sanctioned as dangerous outsiders) when they clean a deserted fairground (S 50), and elsewhere Suttree has a series of wild carnival imaginings during his mountain pilgrimage (S 283-91), whilst even the nightclub J-Bone and Suttree attend after Suttree's inheritance windfall is called the Carnival Club (S 302). The oppositional stance of the novel is further underlined as much of the action takes place in the dark netherworld of the Puritan dream, played out amidst "all this detritus slid down from the city on the hill" (S 411).

For Suttree, McAnally Flats, with its "complement of pariahs and endless poverty" (S 296), provides a community of kindred souls, a place he calls home for the majority of the novel and where the generosity, warmth, and drunkenness offers a stark contrast to the sobriety and conformity of his father's world. There is a camaraderie in these ruined environs which, for a time at least, delays or offsets his acute metaphysical crisis, and this "fellowship of the doomed" (S 23) offers a community of genuine hospitality which is directly opposed to the spread of suburbia beyond the world of McAnally. In their succession of drunken shenanigans and violent encounters with residents from other enclaves of the city, the counter-hegemonic culture embodied in this "other" world is very much outside of that represented by the coldly detached "men bound for work in the city looking out with no expression at all" (S 45).

The attitude to work amongst the inhabitants of McAnally characterizes the oppositional nature of this culture. The conversation Suttree has with buddy Joe, the opening exchange in the novel, underscores this theme as Joe informs him that the department store Miller's "needed somebody in men's shoes," to which Suttree replies,

"I guess I'll just stick to the river for a while yet" (S 10). Suttree's career as a fisherman has a number of biblical connotations, but it also offers little hope for serious professional advancement or material gain; indeed, the fish that Suttree catches enable him to take part in the town's "country commerce" in which barter and exchange stands in for a tightly regulated cash nexus. Suttree also has a memorably ironic conversation with Ulysses about J-Bone's absences from their riotous gatherings, absences due to the fact that he is "another victim fallen to employment." Suttree expresses sadness at "all these good men" who have been "lost" to employment, rhetoric usually reserved for war heroes as opposed to pariahs forced to join the normative working world (S 170). Suttree also backs up his ideological commitment of opting out with two acts of anti-authoritarian civil disobedience, such as when he assists Leonard in his outlandish welfare scam and when he sinks the police car in the river following the brutal police beating Ab Jones receives (S 243, 442).

Ab Jones is worthy of further consideration as one of the most significant characters within this counter-hegemonic culture. As an African American, he has been disenfranchised from the world that Suttree has had the privilege to renounce, but he nevertheless displays a genuine fondness for Suttree throughout, calling him "Youngblood" and assuring him that he has a "good heart" (S 203). Ab is also another of those archetypal surrogate father figures who embodies the ethos of the community whilst also acting as a link to a mythic past that now exists in narrative and storytelling only. Ab tells Suttree that "I got no use for man [who will] piss backwards on his friends" (S 203), a loyal sentiment that Suttree shares, whilst Ab's recollections about Irish Long's generosity reveals the hypocrisy of the bourgeois world beyond McAnally: "He give away everything he owned. He'd of been rich if he wanted … They is people livin in this town today in big houses that would have starved plumb to death cept for him but they aint big enough to own it" (S 25). One of his anecdotes also reveals the injustices he has suffered at the hands of the police (Ab will ultimately be killed following a heavy-handed beating at the hands of the police), and the nature of the murder described in this anecdote (where the perpetrator was carrying around the head of his victim in a shoebox) evokes a flavor of Knoxville's past as a frontier outpost (S 203).

Gene Harrogate is another memorable character, a figure that evokes a great deal of sympathy from the reader due to his tragic nature and his uncanny ability to become embroiled in a series of ridiculous scams and situations that always end in disaster. Like Suttree, Gene can also be read as a contemporized version of one of the characters we may have found in the writing of one of the Southwestern humorists, especially George Washington Harris. Gene also adds another dimension to the patriarchal theme in the novel as Suttree acts (or at least attempts to act) as a surrogate father figure for Gene, always ready to offer advice which, more often than not, Gene ignores as he presses ahead with his ludicrous money-making schemes. Gene can be read as a critique of the Horatio Alger myth of self-improvement, and his experiences offer a slapstick version of the entrepreneurial spirit so cherished in American culture.

Whereas Suttree is fondly referred to as "Youngblood," Harrogate is bequeathed the title "city rat," confirming that he is more rodent-like than human, a figure who is happy to dwell amongst waste and all manner of discarded artifacts (including feces). He has a sexual predilection for having intercourse with watermelons, a perverse nighttime excursion for which he is captured and placed in the workhouse. It is in the workhouse that he meets Suttree, and the narrator's description of Gene reveals his grotesque status, this figure who "was not lovable," who looked like "a dressed chicken, his skin puckered," and who doesn't even know to tie his own shoe laces (S 54, 37). According to Suttree, Gene is a character that looks wrong "and will always look wrong" (S 60), a viewpoint seemingly shared by the narrator as he is often associated with waste and discarded images, such as the "vinestrangled trees … gorged with sooty drainage" that he finds himself surrounded by in one instance following his release from the workhouse (S 91).

Much like Reese, another of the novel's deluded if sympathetic fools, Gene never doubts that his schemes will help him fulfill the Horatio Alger myth, imploring Suttree to believe him when he tells him that "this time tomorrow you will be talkin to a wealthy man" (S 211). Gene's episodic adventures punctuate the novel's more melancholic passages, and they remind us that McCarthy is a fine writer of comedy. The "damned ingenious" (S 218) bat-killing operation lands him a dollar and a quarter and a mass-produced institutional lunch which he gobbles down, and the description of him prior to his capture by the "telephone heat" is one of his most memorable appearances in the novel. Indeed, Gene's parody of the criminal look here (although he sincerely believes that he looks the part) echoes the parodies of the ranchers, badmen, and cowboys that McCarthy would go on to create in the Border Trilogy, characters who—like Gene—were tragically unaware of the fact that they were entirely unsuited to the culturally proscribed mythic roles they dreamt of playing:

> And this was Harrogate. Standing in the door of Suttree's shack with a cigar between his teeth. He had painted the black one and it was chalk white and he had grown a wispy mustache. He wore a corduroy hat a helping larger than his headsize and a black gabardine shirt with slacks to match. His shoes were black and sharply pointed, his

> socks were yellow. Suttree in his shorts leaned against the door and studied his visitor with what the city rat took for wordless admiration. (S 418)

However, Gene's most symbolic moment occurs when he goes underground to explore the supposed riches hidden in the caves that lie underneath Knoxville. This is his own mythic quest, his own act of underground disobedience, another of the novel's forays into (quite literally) "the low-lands of capitalist geographies."[11] The fact that he gets covered in sewage, waste and feces is highly significant as it confirms just how utterly worthless he is, and how much of a sewer creature he is in material and social terms: "He was engulfed feet first in a slowly moving wall of sewage, a lava neap of liquid shit and soapcurd and toiletpaper from a breached main" (S 270). The cruel workings of fate in the novel prevent Gene from realizing his clownish dreams of wealth and material betterment, and he meets the fate of so many other McCarthy characters at the novel's close, housed in the penitentiary alongside others of his kind, hapless to the end.

Although imprisoned, Harrogate at least survives, which is more than can be said for some of the more tragic marginal characters. For every humorous scheme Gene becomes embroiled in, there is a moment of gruesome violence to counter it, such as when Suttree is knocked unconscious by a floor buffer in a mass barroom brawl (S 187). Some of McAnally's pariahs survive to live a kind of death-in-life in the world of production and consumerism that they have resisted for so long, whereas others fall prey to the "season of death and epidemic violence" that grips the city as the novel moves toward its conclusion (S 416). We learn of the death of Suttree's good friend

---

[11] Jarvis, *Postmodern Cartographies*, 54.

Hoghead (James Henry), and some of the descriptions of violence have a characteristic cinematic quality to them, such as the death of the legendary Brawler Red Callahan: "The roar of the pistol in his face chopped it off and the size of the silence that followed was enormous. Billy Ray was standing there with a small discolored hole alongside his ruined nose" (S 375). Ab Jones receives one too many horrific beatings at the hands of the police, so he joins Hoghead, Callahan, and others in the dark void that has haunted the novel throughout.

The fate of those who survive the novel lies in becoming members of the regular, normative, and conformist world that they have resisted for so long; indeed, we see that McAnally's "complement of pariahs" ultimately cannot indefinitely resist the embourgeoisement of American culture. The conclusion of the novel hints at the subtext of regional economic displacement and out-migration that was taking place in Appalachia during this period, due to the collapse of traditional industries and manufacturing bases. (In Knoxville itself the city struggled to recover from the collapse of its textile industry, a former economic powerhouse.) Indeed, between "World War II and 1965 the region lost three million people to northern cities."[12] We hear about one-time McAnally residents "gone north to the factories. Old friends dispersed, perhaps none coming back, or few, them changed. Tennessee wetbacks drifting north in bent and smoking autos in search of wages. The rumors sifted down from Detroit, Chicago. Jobs paying two twenty an hour" (S 398). Even Suttree himself almost succumbs to the illusory and hollow seductive powers of material possessions, as he "felt himself being slowly anesthetized" by

---

[12] Branscome, *The Federal Government in Appalachia*, 28.

a new Jaguar that he and Joyce purchase, and he is beguiled as "the silver wire wheels gleamed in the good spring sun" (S 405). Harmless characters who are rendered obsolete by the epochal economic changes also fall victim to the new regulatory order which is emerging, as Daddy Watson is placed in the asylum where he mournfully still keeps time on his ancient railroader's clock in a world that has changed beyond all recognition (S 434).

The dramatic nature of the socioeconomic changes is also inscribed upon the landscape of the city itself. In one of his final wanderings, Suttree, more ghost-like than ever, haunts the "sadder verges of the city" in a scene in which the sense of sorrow and loss is palpable, especially if we compare it to the vibrancy inherent in the earlier Market Street passages. The playful irony of his earlier exchange with Ulysses has vanished entirely as we see that Earl Solomon has been "taken" by a trade, a phrase more suited to describe a tragic death, a feeling made stronger as we see him ruefully consulting the officious trade manual he has recently been given. Indeed, the city is now silent and sorrowful, and it is another instance in McCarthy's work where history has swallowed his characters and his fictional places up, and yet they don't even know it, to borrow Jeffrey's insight from *The Stonemason*:

> Anybody seeing him all that forewinter long going about the sadder verges of the city might have rightly wondered what his trade was, this refugee reprieved from the river and its fishes. Haunting the streets in a castoff peacoat. Among the old men in cubbyhole lunchrooms where life's vagaries were discussed, where things would never be as they had been. In Market Street the flowers were gone and the bells chimed cold and lonely and the old vendors nodded and agreed that joy seemed gone from

> these days, none knew where. In their faces signature of the soul's remoteness. Suttree felt their looming doom, the humming in the wires, no news is good. Old friends in the street that he met, some just from jail, some taken to trades. Earl Solomon studying to be a steamfitter so he said. They look through his books and manuals there in the cold wind and Earl seems uncertain, smiling sadly at it all (S 381).

The conclusion of the novel is somewhat paradoxical as the physical destruction of McAnally is contrasted with Suttree's metaphysical reconstruction and restitution. However, the destruction of this "encampment of the damned" means that it is no longer "fugitive of all order" as "Gnostic workmen" (although as readers we know that any attempts to order or somehow better the world in McCarthy are usually revealed to be sheer folly) conduct scenes of "wholesale razing," where "yellow machines groaned over the landscape" creating "heaps of slag" and "ashy fields" where even "the dead [are] turned out of their graves … until nothing stood save rows of doors, some bearing numbers, all nailed to. Beyond lay fields of rubble" (S 464). Key themes and motifs assault the reader in this passage as McCarthy reveals the level of change taking place, fusing the wasteland motif with a nightmarish vision where man-made machines destroy the earth. Even the dead are removed under the rubric of civic improvement in a passage which echoes the "fragmentation of both physical and mental landscapes" the region experienced, a history of fragmentation McCarthy has recorded from *The Orchard Keeper* through to the conclusion of *Suttree*.[13]

---

[13] McDonald and Muldowny, *TVA and the Dispossessed*, 68.

As Suttree wanders these streets, he sees that "they're tearing everything down" in order for the "new roads being laid over McAnally" (S 463), another reference in McCarthy to a site of conflict where a proudly independent folk or oppositional culture is eradicated when confronted by the machinations of the state or federal government. In this instance, the new roads were part of "a massive interstate highway system that was justified on the basis of national defense" and which received federal support with the passing of the Interstate Highway Act of 1956.[14] Thus even Knoxville and McAnally, the city referred to as being designed on "no known paradigm" at the opening of the novel, becomes part of the monolithic Military Industrial Complex by the time this messy, sprawling novel reaches its very neat (at least in terms of civic improvements) end.

There is something of an irony in the fact that Suttree may well leave Knoxville at the novel's conclusion by one of these new roads, but leave he does, and the world he leaves behind is one that will never quite be the same. *Suttree*, which was for many years McCarthy's last Southern novel until the publication of *The Road*, certainly rivals *Blood Meridian* as his finest achievement. Like his first western novel, *Suttree* remains shockingly violent for some, frustratingly episodic and fragmentary for others, and relentlessly moribund for some readers, but our eponymous hero leaves Knoxville metaphysically and philosophically reconstituted at novel's close. Its exploration of the fragile and tenuous nature of subjectivity, its celebration of an anachronistic city with its counter-hegemonic sensibilities, its treatment of the implications of patriarchy, and its moments of humor, compassion, and generosity ensure that it will remain a provocative and challenging novel for many generations to come.

---

[14] Wheeler, *Knoxville, Tennessee: A Mountain City*, 96.

Overview of Critical Responses

Suttree is, by some distance, the lengthiest of McCarthy's Southern novels, and it is also the most structurally, metaphysically, and ideologically complex. If we look at the shape of McCarthy's career we see that he published the two works generally regarded as his masterpieces—*Suttree* and *Blood Meridian*—sequentially, and *Suttree* has, much like the novel that followed it, received a great deal of critical attention; indeed, *Blood Meridian* dominates the critical responses to McCarthy's Western and Southwestern works, and the same can be said of *Suttree* for the Southern texts. For that reason, we will structure our discussion of the critical responses to the novel thematically in the hope that all of the pertinent critical dialogues will be acknowledged and addressed. The objective is to be as inclusive as possible and to give readers a thorough overview of the fascinating critiques of the novel, discussions which address a vast array of philosophical, ideological, moral, and aesthetic issues.

Many early reviews exhibit a degree of ambivalence toward *Suttree* as critics and reviewers struggled to come to terms with this demanding, sprawling, and at times quite shocking novel. The *Memphis Press-Scimitar* ran an angry review entitled "A Masterpiece of Filth: Portrait of Knoxville Forgets to be Fair," whilst Walter Sullivan, writing in the *Sewanee Review*, found that the novel shocked his aesthetically conservative principles, claiming that *Suttree* is "a limited use of an enormous talent."[15] Some early reviews were, however, particularly insightful, such as Guy Davenport's in the *National Review*. Davenport's review stated that "there is something of a portrait of the artist as a young man about this book," a reading that an-

---

[15] Quoted in Arnold and Luce, "Introduction," 6.

ticipates some of the later scholarly critiques of the novel, especially those that look into McCarthy's use of allegory.[16]

Although coming from differing ideological, aesthetic, and philosophical positions, critical consensus acknowledges the fact that *Suttree* is an undeniably complex text. David Holloway comments about "the sophisticated switching of perspective in the novel from protagonist as narrated object and the protagonist as active participant in the action," a narrative strategy that makes it hard for readers to follow the action or plot (as much as there is one) in any consistently linear pattern.[17] This situation is exacerbated as McCarthy is "obedient to the truth of objects," and one of the hallmarks of his style is the "democratic recentering of all things," where non-human inanimate matter is imbued with as much agency as human consciousness.[18] Narrative and structural complexity has been a hallmark of McCarthy's style from his debut novel, and we can find many examples of what Douglas Canfield has called his famous "slippage from consciousness to consciousness" in *Suttree*, compounded by the fact that "although the narrator of *Suttree* is, of course, not Suttree ... the narrator's and Suttree's consciousness often seem to blend."[19] Even our sense of locating Suttree in a fixed and settled domestic or social setting is destabilized as, like many other McCarthy characters, he exhibits a degree of "spatial ambivalence" and in "wanting freedom of movement, he roams," living as he does "in that most liminal form of housing, a house*boat*."[20]

---

[16] Ibid.

[17] Holloway, *The Late Modernism*, 118.

[18] Bell, *The Achievement of Cormac McCarthy*, 78, 112.

[19] Canfield, "The Dawning of the Age," 668, 686.

[20] Ellis, *No Place for Home*, 113, 148.

Our cursory review thus far reveals the metaphysical and structural complexity of *Suttree*, and the challenges it poses for the reader are considerable. Like McCarthy's other texts, it is structured around the tension between orientation and disorientation, of placing us in a concrete and familiar time and place whilst the novel's metaphysical sensibility seems to undermine our claims to ordering and knowing the world depicted in the narrative. Such a hybrid, polyphonic style clearly echoes the voices of the novelists McCarthy has been heavily influenced by, and John Cant is one of several critics who have commented upon the parallels between *Suttree* and Joyce's *Ulysses*. Cant notes that "both are long works in which 'plot' is secondary to detail, especially quotidian detail. Both are related to myth and seek to create an anti-myth."[21] This fusion of quotidian detail and mythoclasm invites and denies mimetic interpretations, conventional textual mappings that are also undermined by McCarthy's very knowing efforts to disorient his readers by changing his characters' names; for example, J-Bone is James Long, and Suttree himself is known as Bud or Buddy or Sut or Youngblood throughout the novel. Moreover, McCarthy also excels at describing "various states of befoulment," points at which the border between the conscious and subconscious world, the known and the unknown, become very deliberately blurred.[22]

The renowned Faulkner scholar Noel Polk has provided an insightful and lively reading of *Suttree* that echoes the sentiments of many students and readers upon their first encounter with the novel.

---

[21] Cant, *Cormac McCarthy and the Myth of American Exceptionalism*, 104.

[22] Arnold "Naming, Knowing and Nothingness," 45-69. For further evidence of McCarthy's anachronistic technique of narrative mapping which very knowingly conflates historical events into his aesthetic vision see Morgan's "A Season of Death and Epidemic Violence: Knoxville Rogues in *Suttree*" and "Red Callahan in *Suttree*: The Actual and the Fictitious."

We will engage with Polk's reading in more detail when we examine its relation to specific Southernist elements, but Polk is quite right when he comments on McCarthy's flirtations with "traditional ways of producing fictional meaning—through symbol, juxtaposition patterns, language, and metaphor." However, like our eponymous hero's own romances, these flirtations are short-lived as McCarthy "cuts them off at the knees" since he understands that "consistency of point of view is a traditional construct, and he will have none of it."[23] Although Polk is quite right in claiming that the novel could never be read as a singular traditional construct, it does contain elements of allegory, the picaresque, and the epistolary novel, and these stylistic elements warrant further investigation.

Given its episodic structure, the picaresque has always made linear mimetic readings problematic, as it lends itself to seemingly random narrative clusters rather than consistent development and maturation of characters. The picaresque thus allows for a degree of hybridity, as noted by Georg Guillemin, who maintains that "*Suttree* combines a picaresque quest for survival with a modernist quest for truth, a baroque style with existentialist despair," whilst Jay Ellis contends that "the novel hardly has so much of a setting as it does an unsettled constant movement," although as we shall see, this confusion can be alleviated somewhat if we view the city itself as a protagonist and ideological player in the novel.[24]

Suttree also lends itself to various allegorical interpretations, as it can be read as an allegory about Suttree transcending his fear of death, about authoring our existence into the world in an act of conscious will to deny the knowledge of an absurd universe, and as an

---

[23] Polk, "A Faulknerian Looks at *Suttree*," 27, 24-5.

[24] Guillemin, *The Pastoral Vision of Cormac McCarthy*, 140.

allegory about the emergence of Suttree's (and perhaps McCarthy's) artistic consciousness. Thomas Daniel Young contends that if we read *Suttree* with an allegorical framework in mind, we can see that the novel "achieves perfect resolution," whilst Guillemin claims that the "allegorical composition ... gathers the emblems, banter, tall tales, and monotonous syntax into a unified aesthetic."[25] The novel's status as an allegory about an emerging artistic consciousness can be explained if we read *Suttree* as an epistolary novel, "a letter from Cormac McCarthy to his father," as William Prather contends. For Prather, "Dear Friend," the first two words of the novel, "can be read as the beginning of a genuine act of communication, as an address to Mr. Suttree from his son," and the letter-as-novel also documents Suttree's transformation from "artifact into artist," an aspect of the novel's allegorical composition that redeems it from charges of nihilism and inhumanism.[26]

Prather's analysis of the prologue as the opening move in an epistolary novel is a persuasive one, and it draws our attention to the significance of the prologue itself, a familiar feature of McCarthy's aesthetic. The prologue's italics suggest a change in the temporal order, and we seem to go back in time in the prologue before we go forward in the novel itself. For Guillemin, this move by McCarthy suggests that the prologue is "all parable" and that it introduces the "baroque idea that the world represents a stage fronting a higher form of being."[27] For Robert Jarrett, the prologue is significant in stylistic and thematic terms as it "suggests that Suttree's dilemma

---

[25] Young Jr., "The Imprisonment of Sensibility: *Suttree*," 120; Guillemin, *The Pastoral Vision*, 11.
[26] Prather, "The Color of This Life," 50-51.
[27] Guillemin, *The Pastoral Vision*, 11.

is our own: how to live authentically within the absurdist world in which he finds himself," whilst he also notes that the novel actually dispenses with italics after the prologue.[28] Noel Polk expands upon this important point when he discusses what he calls a writer's "visual vocabulary," and he discusses how "much noise quotation marks and even dashes create in a text" and how an author uses them (or in this case doesn't use them) to allow us to differentiate between the narrator and the characters.[29] In a reading that in many respects echoes the "spatial ambivalence" that Ellis identifies as motivating Suttree's roaming, Thomas Young claims that the prologue makes us aware of the "elemental and highly ambiguous activity of human 'settlement' which is essentially the subject of all McCarthy's fiction," and the remainder of the novel documents a version of the "pioneering of America" right through to its "eschatological conclusions."[30]

One of the most significant features of *Suttree's* anachronistic narrative design is of course the consciousness of our central protagonist. One of the greatest ironies of McCarthy's work is that he is an author whose aesthetic places him in a profoundly serious novelistic tradition, yet the characters who inhabit his narratives seem so unbookish and unnovelistic. Suttree is a significant change in this respect, and yet many readers are frustrated by his lack of consistency and linearity of behavior, thought, and action. In keeping with the novel's picaresque elements, Polk claims that Suttree isn't really a consciousness at all, as he is more "like a register than a fully developed narrative consciousness," although Jarrett resolves this apparent contradiction by claiming that "Suttree is an instance

---

[28] Jarrett, *Cormac McCarthy*, 50, 141.
[29] Polk, 19.
[30] Thomas D. Young, "The Imprisonment of Sensibility," 97, 121 n1.

of the divided consciousness of modernity."[31] The complex, perhaps even tragic, irony of Suttree's consciousness is that he knows that his own mind's anthropocentric understanding of the world may not be enough to explain the world or his place in it, which anticipates the advice imparted by the old man in *Blood Meridian*: "a man's at odds to know his mind cause his mind is aught he has to know it with" (BM 19). As a result, Bell is entirely correct when he states that "ontological uncertainty" is a "recurring crisis" for Suttree.[32] Edwin Arnold adds a fascinating rider to this argument by claiming that Suttree is plagued by a hyper-consciousness, that he "is almost *too* aware," which means that he is forever getting closer to the thing he is trying to cast off (namely his fear of death) as everything for Suttree, both human and non-human, is pregnant with signs of its own demise and decay.[33]

Suttree is an intelligent character who, despite turning his back on his family's privileged social standing and his college education, has clearly been heavily influenced by the traditions and cultural institutions he has renounced. This makes him unique among McCarthy characters, and for Ellis, his education allows him to have an "ironic consciousness" about the situations he finds himself in that is denied his peer group who have not benefited from the same privileges as he.[34] For Young, Suttree's ambivalence about his education, embodied in his claim that "from all old seamy throats of elders, musty books, I've salvaged not a word" (S 14) is "clearly self-deluding," and, as we shall see, this does raise some ideological

---

[31] Polk, 14; Jarrett, *Cormac McCarthy*, 57.
[32] Bell, *The Achievement of Cormac McCarthy*, 73, 89.
[33] Arnold, "Naming, Knowing, Nothingness," 58.
[34] Ellis, *No Place for Home*, 266.

problems in the narrative. The ambivalence in regard to his education and previous incarnation as one of "the nice people in town" compounds his feelings of alienation, and Canfield reminds us that "from the beginning of the novel, Suttree is already alienated," noting that he is particularly haunted by figures of a Devouring Mother and an identical twin.[35]

Whilst our knowledge of Suttree's dead twin and his dead son engenders a degree of sympathy for him, his divided consciousness, conflicting patterns of behavior, and doubts over the authenticity of his transcendental search for a simpler way of life force us to entertain one relatively straightforward question: Is Suttree actually that likable? Is his consciousness, split as it is between mimetic and quotidian acts and allegorical and mythical striving, a strength or flaw of the novel? If readers find out they don't much like him, should they level these accusations at Suttree himself or the narrative consciousness that created him? Jarrett notes that following his son's death, one of the most important episodes in the novel, Suttree's response seems "overdetermined, expressive more of his own selfishness and his own dread," as opposed to genuine grief. This viewpoint is echoed by Arnold, who claims that Suttree "seems sorrier for himself at this point than for the lost child," and the same could be said of his response following Wanda's death.[36] Furthermore, for all the novel's gloriously decadent and hedonistic moments, for all the passages which memorably capture Suttree's various states of "befoulment" and the metaphysical anxieties that precede or follow them, "there remains the possibility that for all

---

[35] Canfield, "The Dawning of the Age," 667, 676.

[36] Jarrett, *Cormac McCarthy*, 53; Arnold, "Naming, Knowing, Nothingness," 59.

their complexity, the struggles in Suttree's psyche may have as much to do with the more rudimentary Manichean narcissistic habits of an alcoholic brain, as with loftier quarrels with the universe."[37]

In a fascinating article, Louis Palmer engages with (and eventually refutes) Daniel Traber's contention that Suttree goes to the margins of society only to carry within him the controlling impulse of the dominant culture of which he is a product.[38] For Traber, "blood will tell," Mr. Suttree's line that Cornelius appropriates to refute his father's snobbish worldview, reveals that his search will *never* be truly authentic since the privileged bloodline he derided his father for ironically ensures that Suttree will never truly know the immovable social, fiscal, and racial problems endured by the denizens of McAnally. Palmer notes that Suttree continues to benefit from his upbringing and that throughout the novel he gains "respect from those who have internalized the values of the ruling classes."[39] Karissa McKoy echoes these comments as she notes that Suttree is able to maintain "a critical distance from materiality, a distance not afforded to characters like Harrogate" with the result that, however much he seeks to deny it, Suttree's bloodline *does* tell, which means that for some he is nothing more than a faker.[40]

Although his ideological position as a self-elected outcast may be problematic, one thing that is entirely authentic for Suttree is his fear of death. Critics concur that this fear accounts for the most profound metaphysical speculations in the novel, with Jarrett claiming that Suttree's problems "stem from his fear of

---

[37] Ellis, 134-35.
[38] Palmer, "Encampment of the Damned," 149-170.
[39] Ibid., 160.
[40] McKoy, "Whiteness and the 'Subject' of Waste," 94.

death," whereas Bell argues that the struggle with his fear of death is "antecedent to all other philosophical considerations" and that, when all is said and done, this is a "novel about transcending death, of overcoming morbid realism."[41] Although Bell locates a nihilistic sensibility at play throughout McCarthy's work, he concedes, as do many other critics, that the novel concludes on a hopeful and affirmative note, no matter how tenuous that may be.

However, one critic who doesn't view the narrative as transcending such nihilism is D. S. Butterworth. Butterworth shares Traber's skepticism about the balance and aesthetic coherence of *Suttree*, and in "Pearls as Swine: Recentering the Marginal in Cormac McCarthy's *Suttree*," he contends that physical bodies in the novel operate in a "quasi-nihilistic void" where they are nothing more than a material object, and characters remain nothing more than bits of matter due to what Butterworth sees as McCarthy's "geological view of humankind."[42] Critics such as Bell and Holloway see this "democratic recentering" as an important part of McCarthy's aesthetic whereby Suttree ultimately extricates (or at least reconciles) the knowledge of his own materiality and mortality with hope for a more hopeful future, albeit one that takes him away from McAnally Flats. Although he identifies the strategy, Butterworth does not agree with its execution, and for him, McCarthy's geological view fails to bring humanity or warmth to his characters: "*Suttree*, despite its recentering of the marginal, maintains a dehumanized view of its subject by equating them with physical objects. They are trapped in

---

[41] Jarrett, *Cormac McCarthy*, 56; Bell, *The Achievement of Cormac McCarthy*, 98, 69.

[42] Butterworth, "Pearls as Swine," 100, 95.

time, space, social, and economic circumstances, as living fossils, as empty containers in the surrounding sediment of the world."[43]

William Prather's analysis of the novel, modeled around the philosophies of Albert Camus (especially his theory of the absurd) successfully rebuffs Butterworth's claims. In his excellent essay, "Absurd Reasoning in an Existential World: A Consideration of Cormac McCarthy's *Suttree*," Prather takes the important step of contextualizing the intellectual and philosophical climate of the 1950s and 1960s, the period of the novel's setting and early composition. Prather notes that this was "a period in which the influence of existentialism was cresting," and although Camus's *The Myth of Sisyphus* was initially published in France in 1942, it "was not translated and published in the United States until 1955."[44]

In his seminal essay, Camus argues that "a world that can be explained even with bad reasons is a familiar world," but in a "universe suddenly divested of illusions and lights, man feels an alien, a stranger ... This divorce between man and his life, the actor and his setting, is properly the feeling of absurdity," and "one of the only coherent philosophical positions is thus revolt," a position that Suttree maintains throughout the novel.[45] Other characters opt for physical or metaphysical suicide, but the denizens of McAnally imbue Suttree with a posture of perpetual defiance that enables him to transcend his fear of death. For Prather, there is no doubt that Suttree "has been forced to recognize the existence of the absurd world" and that "clearly, the universe depicted in *Suttree* is existential."[46]

---

[43] Ibid., 100-101.
[44] Prather, "Absurd Reasoning," 113 n1.
[45] Camus, *The Myth of Sisyphus*, 13, 53.
[46] Prather, "Absurd Reasoning," 104.

Nihilism is a recourse one can take in an attempt to deny feelings of absurdity, and this "allurement away from the desert of the absurd" is one championed by the ragpicker.[47] However, despite being initially attracted to the ragpicker's desolate, if laconically articulated, brand of nihilism, Suttree ultimately "unequivocally rejects" it, and his position at the end of the novel embodies his philosophy that "no retreat should be made from life."[48] Suttree's rejection of the ragpicker's nihilism also undermines those critics who accuse McCarthy's fiction of championing a similar position, something countered in a persuasive critique by John Cant. Cant claims that "although McCarthy remains a religious writer in a Godless world," he actually "opposes the annihilating notion of human insignificance, of nihilism, with the assertion of subjective meaning that is motivated by man's inherent vitality," embodied in the end of the novel where Suttree embraces flux and movement and the dread inertia of the anti-Suttree appears to have been banished for good.[49]

Other ways of escaping knowledge of the absurd universe are through a commitment to religion and through embracing the chimera of comfort and stability afforded by material wealth and domesticity. Much like McCarthy, Suttree remains a religious figure (perhaps even a would-be writer) in a Godless world, and although he refutes a "primitive brand of Protestantism" and "orthodox Roman Catholicism," what Prather sees as "the two distinct forms" of conventional religion in the novel, Suttree remains open to spiritual and mystical quests throughout, quests

---

[47] Ibid., 105.
[48] Ibid.
[49] Cant, *Cormac McCarthy and the Myth of American Exceptionalism*, 113.

that often entail altering his normative consciousness.[50] Much to the chagrin of his father, Suttree is completely disinterested in the pursuit of material wealth, and he also rejects the "promise of love and the consolations of domesticity." Prather notes that even in the idyllic passages which describe Suttree and Wanda's relationship death "evinces its power to obtrude, to obliterate, to deny."[51]

For Prather, *Suttree*, if "viewed in the light of the sentiment of absurd reasoning," is resolved, is given aesthetic and thematic coherence. This is a novel "not so much about taking things on as it is about casting them off," and Suttree has therefore grown, changed, and matured over the course of the narrative; he has succeeded in removing or stripping away "various obscuring attitudes."[52] Prather contends that our main protagonist *is* fully humanized at novel's close, and we leave him as he heads out west with an "enhanced state of consciousness" and a "whetted appetite for life," an outlook that "underscores shared human nature, human worth," as Suttree is empowered with "freedom and defiance."[53]

David Holloway structures his critique of the novel around the theories of John-Paul Sartre, another towering figure of existentialist philosophy. Holloway configures "Suttree's point of view as a Sartrean existential gaze," claiming that the "existential fate of the self is to be immersed in a realm where the lines dividing human being from a world of animate and inanimate matter become blurred."[54] The Sartrean reading explains why Suttree is able to arrive at some

---

[50] Prather, "Absurd Reasoning," 105.
[51] Ibid., 108-09.
[52] Ibid., 111.
[53] Ibid., 112-13.
[54] Holloway, *The Late Modernism*, 123, 116-17.

kind of tenuous transcendence, and Holloway notes that "the novel is surely remarkable for the lengths to which McCarthy goes in rescuing his protagonist from the existential inertia in which he seems trapped," a "rescue" confirmed in Suttree's confession to the priest following his bout of typhoid fever that there is "one Suttree and one Suttree only." For Holloway, this is "an existential reaffirmation of the self as a powerful mediating influence within and upon the world of matter."[55]

Several recent critiques of the novel structure their arguments around the theories of Julia Kristeva, especially those put forward in *Powers of Horror: An Essay in Abjection*. Abject spaces and places—corpses, refuse, unstable locations—are to be found throughout *Suttree* and, according to Kristevan thought, the abject can be a site of resistance and defiance. Kristeva contends that from "its place of banishment, the abject does not cease challenging its master" and that "we may call it a border; abjection is above all ambiguity," especially "the corpse seen without God and outside of science, is the utmost abjection."[56] According to Brian Jarvis, Kristeva "proposes that resistance can continue, that the centre is in perpetual danger," and her work reveals that "the geography of identity is consistently defined in relation to the 'not-here,' the 'not-us.'" *Suttree* takes us to these abject spaces and places. McCarthy's work, much like Thomas Pynchon's, Paul Auster's, and Jayne-Ann Phillips's, shows "an explicit concern for [abject] products as spatial allegories of the underclass," and *Suttree* brings "in from the margins those social groups treated as 'trash' by the dominant culture."[57]

---

[55] Ibid., 117, 140.

[56] Kristeva, *Powers of Horror*, 2, 9, 4.

[57] Jarvis, *Postmodern Cartographies*, 192-93.

Karissa McKoy and Douglas Canfield are two critics who skillfully demonstrate how *Suttree* can be illuminated via a Kristevan reading. McKoy draws our attention to the fact that abjection is "the unstable process by which the subject attempts to elaborate herself by expelling socially taboo or transgressive elements," an expulsion that "threatens the American body politic" in another example of the novel's counter-hegemonic sensibility.[58] Canfield highlights how the abject is associated with the "slime of life" and is also related to a deep-seated fear of the maternal which, Canfield maintains, manifests itself in some of Suttree's later hallucinations. Furthermore, the "mirrored double" can be explained in Kristevan terms as representing "the deadly collapse of differentiation," which also parallels Camus and Sartre's theories as all three help us to resolve the dense materiality of the novel, along with Suttree's attempt to transcend this condition.[59] Perhaps the two most striking signifiers of the abject are waste and corpses, and *Suttree* is full of "repeated depictions of refuse that hint at apocalypse." We should remember that on our first glimpse of Suttree, he is amidst the refuse and waste of the city, and the motif is underpinned as he views his murky reflection in the river, a scene which adheres to the Kristevan notion of the abject "as a kind of *narcissistic* crisis."[60]

Although they make no direct reference to Kristeva, Vereen Bell and Noel Polk echo some of her theories in their critiques of the novel, as Bell notes that "death is not tucked away discreetly in hospitals" and other institutionally approved centers, and as a result, it is a "crude, apparent fact that has odor and texture." Despite this

---

[58] McKoy, "Whiteness and the 'Subject' of Waste," 89, 97.

[59] Canfield, "The Dawning of the Age of Aquarius," 665.

[60] Canfield, 671, 678. Another psychoanalytical critique is offered by Robert Jarrett, who uses a Lacanian model to explicate the anti-Suttree motif, 58-59.

apparent awfulness, Bell also acknowledges that it is only by spending time in such an abject social and physical space that allows Suttree to move "off the dead center of his nihilistic immobility" which underpins the regenerative capacity of abject spaces.[61] In a strikingly imaginative piece of linguistic play, Polk reminds us that it is no mistake that the word anal sits in the middle of McAnally and, therefore, "the anal sits at the center of *Suttree*."[62] All of these critiques are persuasive ones, and they underscore the explanatory and oppositional power of Kristeva's theory of abjection which offers the potential for re-birth and re-integration into the world.

Nell Sullivan provides an insightful reading which is indebted to Roland Barthes's theory of the text of *jouissance*, and her analysis helps to counter the reactionary critiques offered by figures such as Walter Sullivan, figures who need "ideologically [and morally] correct novels."[63] Instead, Sullivan maintains that "it is more fruitful to discuss 'textual erotics' than morality in these texts," and Barthes provides this "erotic" model as "the text of *jouissance* transcends the question of morality," and it is "characterized by its unsettling effect, the discomfort it produces."[64] The unsettling effect is attributed to the fact that McCarthy locates his fiction in geographic and cultural "seams" or "sites of textual eroticism ... where civilization is threatened by the destructive violence of barbarians such as Suttree's McAnally Flats cohorts."[65] Barthes's theory of *jouissance*, Kristeva's notion of abjection, and Camus's philosophy

---

[61] Bell, *The Achievement of Cormac McCarthy*, 92, 81.
[62] Polk, "A Faulknerian Looks," 13.
[63] N. Sullivan, "Cormac McCarthy and the Text of *Jouissance*," 122.
[64] Ibid., 115-16.
[65] Ibid., 117. Sullivan also analyzes the conversation Suttree has with the deerhunter following his mountain sojourn as a particularly striking example.

of the absurd all help to account for the fractured and disquieting but also hopeful sense that prevails at the novel's conclusion.

Another "seam" that McCarthy explores in the novel is that between rational intelligence and mystical knowledge as Suttree strives for spiritual insight, and Vereen Bell is entirely correct when he states that "rational intelligence is not the only means of knowing in this text."[66] Despite shunning conventional paths to spiritual insight (one thinks especially of Roman Catholicism here), Suttree's tale can be viewed as a spiritual search, a quest for meaning in a world deserted by God. This quest helps to counter charges of nihilism, and Suttree's successful maturation at the novel's conclusion reveals that he has finally reconciled himself with "the world of the spirit," as Arnold points out below:

> Indeed, it is difficult *not* to follow Suttree's movements as a religious or spiritual quest, even as he tries to deny exactly that aspect of it ... Religion, Faith, God, Death, Grace are constant topics of conversation between Suttree and such figures as the ragpicker, the goatman, Daddy Watson, the street evangelists and numerous strangers he encounters ... By the end he has entered that world of the spirit and has acknowledged its power.[67]

Although Suttree rejects what he sees as the false and chimerical promise of religious consolation offered by the Roman Catholic Church, his renunciation of his childhood faith and his subsequent acts of conscious will—of authoring meaning into existence—assumes allegorical and spiritual import. Farrell O'Gorman has pro-

---

[66] Bell, *The Achievement of Cormac McCarthy*, 72.
[67] Arnold, "Naming, Knowing, and Nothingness," 60.

duced some first-class scholarship that examines the relationship between Southern authors and the Catholic faith, and in "Joyce and Contesting Priesthoods in *Suttree* and *Blood Meridian*," he analyzes McCarthy's two masterpieces alongside Joyce's Dedalus novels, *A Portrait of the Artist as a Young Man* and *Ulysses*. O'Gorman starts his article by admitting his admiration for McCarthy's fiction in that it "continually and brilliantly rearticulates religious questions without giving clear answers to them," noting that deriving religious or spiritual insight from them is a complex task as such themes bristle against McCarthy's "harsh naturalism" that seems to deny them. However, by analyzing McCarthy's "own quasi-Joycean identity as an apparently 'defrocked Catholic' of Irish-American background," O'Gorman convincingly views Suttree as "an aspiring artist, a prodigal son," and he suggests that the novel could be read "as an allegory of writing and authorship."[68]

Suttree's status as a spiritual seeker open to paths beyond those encoded in the Judeo-Christian tradition is especially evident in his mountain sojourn, which Thomas Young regards as an important passage that allows him to grasp "more powerfully than ever his covenant with the world precisely along these lines of mortality and facticity."[69] This episode also constitutes another example of where Suttree searches for what the Native American writer William Least-Heat Moon calls *Praiyerth*, or "deep map," another way of "mapping" his sense of being in the world.

The comparison with Native American culture is a vital one. The most persuasive reading of Suttree's mountain sojourn is offered by William C. Spencer in "The Seventh Direction, or Suttree's Vision

---

[68] O'Gorman, "Joyce and Contesting Priesthoods," 101.

[69] Young, "The Imprisonment of Sensibility," 106.

Quest" in which he reads Suttree's wilderness sojourn as a vital step in his spiritual and metaphysical development, which includes genuinely epiphanic moments. Spencer notes how Suttree experiences a "variety of altered states of consciousness" throughout the novel, that he is an "active spiritual seeker" who has lost his childhood faith but who "remains open to supernatural [and mystical] guidance."[70] Spencer is indebted to Vinson Brown's *Voices of Earth and Sky: Vision Search of the Native Americans,* and he likens Suttree to an American Indian who "seeks insight and spiritual power by going alone and unprotected into the mountains, where he connects with nature and undergoes tests of courage and a mystical rite of passage."[71]

Whilst in the mountains, Suttree successfully achieves a "more primitive, truer connection with nature," and this connection (replete with carnivalesque hallucinations and tests by lightning, which Spencer notes is associated with insight in Native American vision quests) enables him to "become more conscious of his fears and psychological problems and thus constitute[s] an important first step in his spiritual development."[72] In another instance of mapping and cartography in the novel (although this time it is associated with Suttree's internalized spiritual geography), Spencer notes that "Suttree is most interested in traveling the path of the seventh direction, into his 'own center' whereby he touches the divine," and his change is emphasized by two "cathartic events: his own tears and the cleansing rain back in Knoxville at the very end of the chapter."[73] Here, Spencer's "own center" echoes the same con-

---

[70] Spencer, "Seventh Direction," 100, 106.
[71] Ibid., 100.
[72] Ibid., 102, 104.
[73] Ibid., 107, 104.

cept as Heat-Moon's "deep map." Spencer also insightfully analyzes Suttree's second trip into the mountains with Joyce, but this time he doesn't benefit from any mystical insight or connection with nature as he has been temporarily seduced and corrupted by the hollow promise of bourgeois romance and domesticity, and this second trip "underlines how corrupted he is at this stage in the novel."[74]

Much like Ownby in *The Orchard Keeper*, Suttree encounters ideological problems when he comes down from his relative wilderness space to the confines of the city and McAnally Flats. *Suttree* is a novel as much about ideology as it is about spirituality, and McCarthy's depiction of the ideology of the city underlines this, especially the manner in which the residents of McAnally challenge "the ideological power structures of capitalism, patriarchy, and white racial hegemony."[75] The residents of McAnally are "the residue of archaic forces by which the city, and all civilization, originally were generated but which have been used up, rejected, or absorbed in that same process." The fate of those who represent these "archaic forces" adds another layer to the novel's allegorical design as it reveals that it is increasingly difficult to uncover "the counter-hegemonic cartography within texts," especially since the 1950s when "aesthetic production has become integrated into commodity production generally and, as a consequence, has lost its oppositional potential."[76] It is significant that the novel concludes in the middle years of this decade when this process was intensifying, and although it does not record the complete eradication of this counter-hegemonic sensibility, it certainly documents its corrosion, as embodied in the fate of McAnally Flats in the conclusion.

---

[74] Ibid., 106.

[75] Jarvis, *Postmodern Cartographies*, 7.

[76] Young, "The Imprisonment of Sensibility," 98; Jarvis, *Postmodern Cartographies*, 80.

However, this Knoxville neighborhood remains a hotbed of civil disobedience for the majority of the novel, and it warrants further critical analysis from an ideological perspective. Henri Lefebvre's concept of the *mundus* from his seminal study *The Production of Space* can be applied to McAnally Flats, as it reveals it to be a site for opposition and resistance which echoes Kristeva's theory of the abject, of a space that contains the expelled and excluded, the marginal cultures that are needed by the powerful center to define the "not-here" and the "not-us":

> The *mundus*: a sacred or accursed place in the middle of the Italiot township. A pit, originally ... It connected the city ... to the hidden, clandestine, subterranean spaces which were those of fertility and death, of the beginning and the end, of birth and burial ... The pit was also a passageway through which dead souls could return to the bosom of the earth and then re-emerge and be reborn. ... In its ambiguity it encompassed the greatest foulness and the greatest purity, life and death, fertility and destruction, horror, and fascination.[77]

Randall Wilhelm's "'The Wrath of the Path': Spatial Politics and Municipal Powers in *Suttree*" guides us through the "topographical nexus of the novel" which Wilhelm sees as an interplay between "civic-sanctioned urban areas and disenfranchised minority slums," such as the *mundus* of McAnally.[78] Wilhelm skillfully highlights how "the members of the underclass are the 'ruder forms' that the city seeks to control, segregate, and ultimately, annihilate," and that the novel has a continued "emphasis on civic structures that attempt

---

[77] Lefebvre, *The Production of Space*, 242.
[78] Wilhelm, "'The Wrath of the Path,'" 118-136.

to block an individual's path through the municipal landscape."[79] Wilhelm notes how at different stages in the novel, police officers seem to materialize out of civic structures (bridges, buildings, and so on) as if by magic in order to enforce the ideology of the center against those who inhabit the abject, oppositional spaces, such as the residents of McAnally. The "wrath of the path" in the title of Wilhelm's article is a direct quote from Ab Jones, and for Jones and others civil disobedience "in the form of perpetual defiance authors meaning" into an absurd, abject, and ideologically-conditioned world.[80]

The apocalyptic tone one can locate in many of the descriptions of the city is a deliberate strategy on McCarthy's part as it shows how "America's so called technological progress ... leaves destroyed lives in its wake."[81] The destructive impulse associated with technology, culture, and progress receives its most ghastly treatment in *The Road*, of course, but for Canfield, McCarthy's ironic reference to Knoxville as the "city on the hill" in *Suttree* "signals the failure of the great Puritan enterprise to found on this continent a New Jerusalem, the beacon of light that would shine around the world as a sign for all that God has shed his grace on." Canfield goes on to argue that "one of the major reasons for this apocalyptic doom is precisely America's neglect of its underclass."[82] However, Jay Watson counters this apocalyptic reading by making the important suggestion that far from signaling the death of a marginalized or subversive culture, we should instead concentrate on the emergence

---

[79] Ibid., 121, 119.
[80] Ibid., 120.
[81] Canfield, "The Dawning of the Age of Aquarius." 674.
[82] Ibid., 674.

of a new one at novel's end with "vibrant new possibilities for racial interaction, cultural ferment, and regional revitalization."[83]

Louis H. Palmer uses the work of Louis Althusser "to help us read the novel as a social critique focused on ideology rather than merely as an individual quest for meaning or identity."[84] William Prather memorably referred to *Suttree* as a "metaphysical manual" about staying afloat in an absurd universe, and Palmer uses Althusser to show how Suttree extricates himself from the "multiple apparatuses of ideological conditioning," emerging as ideologically retrained and reprogrammed after his spell in McAnally Flats.[85] Palmer uses the Althusserian model of Ideological State Apparatuses (ISAs) which "work ideologically to support the ruling classes in a much more pervasive and subtle way than Repressive State Apparatuses (RSAs) which include the courts, the police, and the military" to show how Suttree successfully completes his period of re-conditioning.[86]

In an important move, Palmer also analyzes how class functions in the novel. Although it may be in a "stark and vulgar Marxist structure," the novel gives us a bourgeoisie (an owning elite), a petit bourgeoisie (those who serve the owners), and a lumpen proletariat (an unemployed underclass)," and this crude structure informs an aspect of the novel's ideological critique.[87] Mr. Suttree's letter tells us a great deal about the patriarchal conflict that drives the novel, but Palmer also notes that the letter "exudes contempt for the have-nots," and he

---

[83] Watson, "Lighting out for the Territory," 81.
[84] Palmer, "'Encampment of the Damned': Ideology and Class in *Suttree*," 157.
[85] Ibid., 158.
[86] Ibid., 157.
[87] Ibid., 155.

suggests that it can be read as the "novel's owning class manifesto."[88] Despite their rambunctious denial of the normative world of work, accumulation, and productivity embodied by the world of Suttree's father, one of the novel's complex ironies is that these "ragtag existential heroes" become involved in a series of ludicrous schemes which mirror and seek to replicate the success of the very world that marginalizes them, which is testament to the pervasive force of the rhetoric of the American dream.[89]

Bell also notes how the "sheer presence, in weight and mass, of the physical world of *Suttree* is in itself a powerful thematic pressure," whilst other critics have noted how trash represents "an organizing trope" in the novel.[90] If we recognize that contemporary society is "structured through the segregation of product from by-product" then the denizens of the McAnally and the riverfront can also be read as such worthless by-products, unable to produce or consume.[91] The river therefore assumes an important metaphorical import as, according to Holloway, it "is a place where the detritus of the commodity form comes alive," and the very fact that it is waste-clogged could be as a direct result of the technological and industrial changes pioneered by Suttree's father.[92] The river becomes another representation of apocalyptic ecological disaster in McCarthy's fiction, another example of the destructive impulses wrought by the self-righteous citizens of the city on a hill.

---

[88] Ibid., 155, 156.
[89] Bell, *The Achievement of Cormac McCarthy*, 81.
[90] Bell, 74; McKoy, "Whiteness and the 'Subject,'" 85.
[91] McKoy, 89.
[92] Holloway, *The Late Modernism*, 115; Ellis, *No Place for Home*, 140.

McCarthy's use of humor and the incorporation of carnivalesque motifs also play an important ideological function. Drawing upon the work of Mikhail Bakhtin, Canfield draws our attention to the fact that *Suttree* "celebrates folk humor" as a strategy of resistance and defiance that embodies the subversive ideology of McAnally Flats.[93] Canfield argues that the humor in the novel is "not nihilistic but celebratory" and that "we descend into the abject only to be regenerated by humor. The art of the novel lightens its darkened heart" to such an extent that even Harrogate's "abject engulfing by the sewage is turned into a carnivalesque joke."[94] Robert Jarrett contends that the repeated use of the carnival image evokes "primal scene[s] of the consciousness," whilst he makes the important point that McCarthy's "fond indulgence of the language of the street" is another aspect of the novel's counter-hegemonic attitude, as the language of the characters is loud and crude and contrasts sharply with the rhetoric used by Mr. Suttree and his ilk.[95]

No summary of the critical discussions about the ideological function of humor in the novel would be complete without a consideration of the role that Gene Harrogate plays. Harrogate is the unmistakably alive and cartoonish version of the anti-Suttree who is "innately oblivious to such immobilizing distractions as ontological uncertainty" and who, perhaps tragically, remains unbelievably optimistic that he will transcend his own materiality "even if his experience of the world dictates otherwise."[96] Thomas Young makes

---

[93] Canfield, "The Dawning of the Age," 666.

[94] Ibid., 667-68, 691. Also see Wade Hall's "The Human Comedy of Cormac McCarthy," for a discussion of McCarthy's use of humor.

[95] Jarrett, *Cormac McCarthy*, 54, 129.

[96] Bell, *The Achievement of Cormac McCarthy*, 84, 89.

the important point that Gene "represents a part of Suttree now buried beneath the irreversible accession of culture and consciousness," and by rescuing him from his disastrous underground venture (which McKoy argues confirms his abject status), Suttree goes some way to making up for abandoning his own son, as Arnold posits.[97] Despite the frequent moments of comic relief Harrogate provides, we should also remember that McCarthy critiques the dominant ideology through him, since "Harrogate longs for the economic privilege that Suttree abjures." This longing ultimately proves elusive and, for all his buffoonery, Harrogate experiences a kind of "psychic death" whilst en route to the penitentiary, made all the more tragic as this "knowledge of himself comes too late for redemption."[98]

Gene's fate reminds us that even though the novel celebrates subversive folk humor and documents a counter-hegemonic sensibility, the world of McAnally is brought into line at the conclusion of *Suttree*. It is impossible to underestimate the impact the TVA had on these civic remodeling projects, and the organization's influence caused a great deal of trouble for all kinds of social and cultural groups, including McCarthy's own family. Jay Ellis reminds us that "the TVA was a project that absolutely required the vision and planning of an American government at its height of centralized power" and that it required staggering "abilities of communication and management" that rival any of the federally sponsored programs that appear in the subtexts of the Border Trilogy.[99]

---

[97] Young, "The Imprisonment of Sensibility," 113; Arnold, "Naming, Knowing, and Nothingness," 60.

[98] McKoy, "Whiteness and the 'Subject,'" 92; Jarrett, *Cormac McCarthy*, 44.

[99] Ellis, *No Place for Home*, 325 n18.

In an impressively researched article, William Prather reminds us of the role that Cormac McCarthy's father played in the displacement of thousands of families and the breaking up of traditional communities. Charles McCarthy served as a "top official of TVA during its transformation from agency of 'social experiment' to that of power and weapons production," and, in a pamphlet he was commissioned to write, he theorized about the "abstracted farmer" the agency would be dispossessing. Prather notes that in all cases of condemnation and purchase of land under eminent domain, "the apparatus was devised to deny landowners a trial by jury to determine a just price for their land" and that by 1946 "the year both Cormac McCarthy and TVA celebrated their thirteenth birthdays, TVA had already dispossessed 72,000 people, one-third of them landowners and two-thirds of them tenant farmers."[100] The displaced families swept into Knoxville and then onto the industrial centers of the North as the ideology of what Prather terms "maximum exploitation" increased its stranglehold and initiated a process of irreversible socioeconomic change for traditional Appalachian communities.

In a charmingly insightful article entitled "*Suttree* as Window into Cormac McCarthy's Soul," Richard Marius (whose own collection of novels set in a fictional East Tennessee community are impressive indeed) states that the city of his and McCarthy's childhood was a place where "you learned early to live with contradiction and paradox."[101] However, by the end of the novel it seems as if those abject or paradoxical places, these cultural or cartographic "seams," are becoming increasingly scarce, a fact confirmed by Marius when he states that if Suttree were to hike into the Smokies today, "he could not find

---

[100] Prather, "The Color of This Life," 33-37.
[101] Marius, "Suttree as Window," 2.

that solitude" he is searching for as the mountain wilderness spaces have been carefully marked-out and managed.[102] The triumph of a tightly controlled regulatory order is confirmed by Wilhelm, who states that submission is "unavoidable in the face of overwhelming legally sanctioned municipal power," and it is significant that when Suttree hitches a ride out of Knoxville at the novel's close, the narrator describes him as looking like someone just out of the army or jail, confirming that he has adopted the look of the respectable world he has shunned for so long.[103] Furthermore, although Suttree heads out into the mythic space of the West on the new blacktop, we should remember that this is a "new civic-sanctioned expressway" and that, to borrow from Ellis's reading of McCarthy, both *Suttree* and *Blood Meridian* end with the laying out of cultural artifacts (expressways and fence posts) which give the illusion of making flight possible but which in reality actually constrain his characters' attempts to do so.[104]

A number of critics devote themselves to discussions of the novel's relationship to Southernist questions. Of particular interest is *Suttree's* relationship to Faulkner and the imaginative malaise that plagues Southern critical discourse that goes by the name of the Quentin problem, derived from the character of the same name who commits suicide in Faulkner's *The Sound and the Fury*. Jay Watson claims that the Quentin problem can be boiled down to "the necessity of elite white southerners to come to grips with modernity in all its economic, racial, and sexual fluidity," and, as Georg Guillemin outlines, a comparison between Faulkner's Quentin Compson and McCarthy's Suttree seems to be full of promise as

---

[102] Ibid., 13.
[103] Wilhelm, "The Wrath of the Path," 131, 133.
[104] Ibid., 134.

"both characters have an academic background; both are haunted by their families' past" and "suicidal neuroses articulate themselves in obsessions with time and the chiaroscuro of light."[105]

In his article, Watson also alludes to Michael Kreyling's groundbreaking study *After Southern Modernism* in which Kreyling bemoans the phenomena of the Quentin problem and "the conceptual stranglehold ... the Quentin thesis [has had] on southern literary studies."[106] The complex (and perhaps even overdetermined) question of McCarthy's relationship to Faulkner is dealt with superbly by Noel Polk, who suggests that Faulkner offers "not limitation at all, but possibility," and that we perhaps limit our enjoyment of Southern literature if we reduce it to a crude this is like or not-like Faulkner paradigm.[107] Instead of offering a claustrophobic comparative analysis, Polk skillfully guides us through the differences between the two writers, and he allows us to see how a background in Faulkner may enable us to see what is missing and what doesn't quite work in McCarthy. Polk argues that Faulkner prefers to evoke the physical world rather than exhaustively describe it, as he lets "his reader's minds provide the detail," whereas for all of the virtuoso linguistic range Polk feels that "the closer McCarthy brings us to [the physical world], the less knowable" it is.[108]

Polk, like many readers of McCarthy, feels frustrated by the lack of ordering principles in *Suttree*, the lack of pathologies and histories and backgrounds of what Eudora Welty called the "middle distance

---

[105] Watson, "Lighting Out," 80 & Guillemin, *The Pastoral Vision*, 7.
[106] Watson, "Lighting Out," 73.
[107] Polk, "A Faulknerian Looks," 8.
[108] Ibid., 23, 24.

of history" which provides explanatory order in a text.[109] In short, Polk articulates a frustration felt by many readers of *Suttree* in that they feel somewhat cheated and shortchanged by McCarthy in terms of clarity of ending and resolution, especially when compared to Faulkner's masterful aesthetic, as Polk memorably addresses below:

> For all their modernity they provide a classical moment of revelation, clarification, and insight: a payoff, a climax, an emotional release, for all the work we've done. Nothing in *Suttree* provides this drive; everything in fact frustrates it, resists whatever would provide some sort of resolution for the various tensions that the novel presides over.[110]

Matthew Guinn goes one step further by identifying McCarthy as a mythoclastic writer and Suttree as a character who relinquishes the Southern "compulsion to order experience through the metanarrative of myth," a fact confirmed by the novel's "iconoclastic treatment of history" that is at "odds with southern literary tradition."[111] As we have illustrated throughout, the Appalachian tradition has always been at odds with the imaginative practices of the rest of the South, so this helps to explain McCarthy's iconoclastic treatment. Guinn's analysis of McCarthy's use of myth is also somewhat problematic as, although he certainly critiques cultural myths that are chimerical and destructive, he does not, as John Cant has so intelligently argued, entirely dispense with myths as narrative structures that provide explanatory power, and perhaps

---

[109] Ibid., 15.
[110] Ibid., 20.
[111] Guinn, *After Southern Modernism*, 103, 107.

even mystical insight. Douglas Canfield suggests that McCarthy incorporates the myth of the dawning of the Age of Aquarius to underpin Suttree's transformation, as the waterbearer would seem to be Aquarius who is "anciently associated with Ganymede, cupbearer to the Gods." This reference parallels New Age philosophy with its emphasis on the acquisition of mystical knowledge and was popular during the period of the novel's composition.[112]

The novel's plantation house scene would seem to support the iconoclastic reading, but there is a temptation to perhaps over-read this aberrant episode. Suttree wanders through the ruined mansion and imagines past feasts and scenes of bounty, and Grammer suggests that these visions "refer to the pastoral dream … of an escape from history" and that it is another example in McCarthy that ridicules the "gnostic fallacy" of such an escape.[113] Of course, a persuasive case can be made that this is much more of a universal theme than a strictly regional one, and examples of where McCarthy punctures other such claims to order and permanence can certainly be found in his works set outside of the South. Perhaps because it refuses to indulge in the delusional aspects of pastoral philosophy, of its futile wish to deny or to stand outside of history, Grammer maintains that *Suttree* is the most optimistic of McCarthy's novels as it recognizes "the solidarity which arises from precariousness" and instead opts to embrace "the flux at the heart of existence."[114]

Inevitably, the novel's relationship to the pastoral is somewhat ambiguous, and we would do well to remind ourselves of Guillemin's claim that McCarthy practices a kind of "nature mysticism" here

---

[112] Canfield, "The Dawning of the Age," 683.
[113] Grammer, "A Thing Against Which," 30-31.
[114] Ibid., 40-41.

which evinces a deeper sense of truth in nature. As with *Child of God,* we would be better served by reading *Suttree* within a wilderness rather than a pastoral aesthetic as not only does it favor "undomesticated nature over agricultural land," but it "equates the external wilderness of nature with the social wilderness of the city and the internal wilderness of the human mind."[115]

Suttree also exhibits a concern with patriarchy and family, two extremely important Southernist themes. As we have seen, the entire novel could be read as a letter from son to father explaining the break from the father's world and the son's attempt to emerge as an artist, a view echoed by Cant, who suggests that the father-son struggle can in part be read as a "metaphor for the contemporary writer's struggle to find his own voice."[116] Jay Ellis's reading of patriarchal conflict in McCarthy is consistently provocative and engaging, and he argues that "by the time we reach *Suttree,* the son's behavior seems related directly to the sins of the father," and he suggests that we could perhaps read the novel as "an apology for, rather than to, the father."[117]

In readings that counter Polk's contention that the novel lacks Welty's "Middle Distance" of history with its family narratives and pathologies, several critics suggest that these themes *are* there, although they struggle for attention in this polyphonic novel; indeed, Arnold suggests that "*Suttree* is a story as much about family as about fishing and drinking and hanging out."[118] Whilst he acknowledges that they are spread out and elliptical, Young identifies four key scenes with members of Suttree's immediate and extended

---

[115] Guillemin, *The Pastoral Vision,* 13.
[116] Cant, *Cormac McCarthy and the Myth of American Execptionalism,* 106.
[117] Ellis, *No Place for Home,* 130, 147.
[118] Arnold, "Introduction," 2-6.

family that structure the narrative, and Palmer notes that Suttree's alienation could be explained by the fact that he is the product of a family composed of two opposing classes (his father's snobbish world and his mother's working-class background). This tension is brought to the fore at a very early stage in the novel by Uncle John who, Palmer claims, has internalized "the elite's attitude toward him and his kind, and so he reproduces his own oppression."[119]

The novel's depiction of female characters is once again problematic, and we are forced to ask a familiar question in regards to this: Does McCarthy's mythical/allegorical portrayal of his female characters get him off the hook? Do those narrative strategies override the suggestions of misogyny? Is he fairer to his male characters than his female ones, whether in a mimetic or mythic context? Robert Jarrett makes the excellent point that although Suttree spends the majority of the novel denying his father's worldview and ideology, his treatment of women mimics the very behavior of the father he has repudiated, and Ellis asks if his avoidance of "the encumbrance of a regular connection to a woman" tell us of a deeper cultural prejudice.[120]

John Cant is one critic who persuasively argues that McCarthy's interest in the "pre-patriarchal epistemology of the Goddess" counters charges of misogyny made against him. For Cant, this pre-patriarchal epistemology provides a regenerative mythic framework which offers the potential to revitalize the barren wasteland of patriarchal culture, thereby providing an ordering impulse to existence, especially in regards to the mystical powers held by Mother She:

---

[119] Palmer, "Encampment of the Damned," 160.
[120] Jarrett, *Cormac McCarthy*, 58; Ellis, *No Place for Home*, 22.

> Mother She ... could be thought to be condemnatory but previous texts, particularly *Outer Dark,* have made us aware of McCarthy's acknowledgment of the pre-patriarchal epistemology of the Goddess. The Great Mother was typically represented in three manifestations, nymph, matron, and crone. Suttree encounters all three; Wanda is the nymph, Joyce the matron, and Mother She the crone. The latter is the Queen of the Underworld; the Goddess presides over both life and death, each passing into the other continuously. It was the loss of this epistemology that brought to man the need for 'resurrection,' the conquest of death.[121]

Yet there are many instances in the novel that undermine such a reading. The rhetoric used by the narrative consciousness during his mother's visit to Suttree in the workhouse is one such example, as the language is "that of sympathy for his mother, but somehow Cornelius turns that against her, [and] makes her into the enemy."[122] The companionship offered by first Wanda and then Joyce never seems to be enough to banish his sense of dread and his immobilizing onto logical and metaphysical anguish. This remains the case even though Wanda may well have "supplanted his gauche carbon," something he has failed to do by himself, and that Joyce is "the only other character in the novel who approaches equal footing with Suttree both intellectually and verbally."[123] His relationship with Wanda ends in tragic circumstances, and he becomes estranged

---

[121] Cant, *Cormac McCarthy and the Myth of American Exceptionalism*, 119.

[122] Polk, "A Faulknerian Looks," 16.

[123] Canfield, "The Dawning of the Age," 681; Young, "The Imprisonment of Sensibility," 118.

from Joyce in what could be read as "an enactment of Oedipal bliss in which Joyce serves as the surrogate mother" after they descend into a hollow simulation of bourgeois existence.[124] Both relationships play an incredibly important, perhaps even epiphanic, role in moving Suttree towards his moment of resolution and transcendence, but what of their voices? What of their experience of events?

Suttree's experiences with Mother She—and it can hardly be called a relationship as his dealings with her are brief, hallucinatory, and entirely free of any kind of sustained mimetic or realistic narrative development—are also problematic. As is the case with Wanda and Joyce, Mother She helps to alleviate his metaphysical suffering, and it is one of the few times in the novel where a "strange peace ensues for him." This encounter provides another example where Suttree acknowledges that "rationality alone is not enough to sustain him," suggesting that it is the hegemonic culture's loss for shunning Mother She and demonizing the access to mystical knowledge she possesses.[125] However, both McKoy and Watson identify an element of "racial panic" at work in his dealings with Mother She (especially during the lengthy, drug-induced phantasmagoric episode) where "blackness appears as a nightmarish threat to the intact white self," and Suttree's body "is polluted figuratively by the "plaguey" black body of Mother She."[126] Watson proposes that this scene "undercuts or qualifies the more egalitarian posture Suttree elsewhere displays towards his black friends" and that not long after his experience with Mother She, he "hops into a car to commence what we might

---

124 Polk, "A Faulknerian Looks," 17.

125 Bell, *The Achievement of Cormac McCarthy*, 96; Cant, *Cormac McCarthy and the Myth of American Exceptionalism*, 119.

126 McKoy, "Whiteness and the 'Subject,'" 96.

now recognize as a version of white flight," which problematizes the optimistic tenor that many critics locate as operating in the novel's conclusion.[127]

Watson's analysis of the racial subtext at play in the novel is an enlightening one, and he notes the irony that in this novel about throwing things off, this hugely significant theme remains suppressed or "undernarrrated."[128] Watson argues that this irony is compounded by the fact that the novel is "set in the half-decade when the Civil Rights Movement was beginning to acquire national visibility," years that witnessed the Brown versus the Board of Education decision in 1954 and the Montgomery bus boycott of 1955. It is therefore puzzling that "*Suttree* fails to mention these historical events, or the larger movement of which they were a part."[129] This is an intriguingly complex question that addresses issues such as the commitment of a novelist to documenting social and political problems. Although the Appalachian South shares a different legacy from the Delta South, it would be folly to claim that it was free of racial tension. As such, does McCarthy's failure to address this problem speak, much like his depiction of his female characters, of a personal or cultural bias? Conversely, should he *have* to address such issues at all? What commitment should his art have to politics?

McKoy also identifies several problems with McCarthy's treatment of race. For McKoy, Jones's death amongst the garbage "highlights the materiality of his body and literalizes that body's status as abject," whereas Harrogate's displeasure of living in close proximity to African Americans is a pathetic episode that confirms that

---

[127] Watson, "Lighting Out," 78.
[128] Ibid., 75.
[129] Ibid., 74.

"he is acutely aware of the racialized structure of Knoxville's urban space."[130] Perhaps more worryingly, McKoy also analyzes the novel's closing scene in terms of its treatment of race, a move that undermines the optimistic readings made by other critics. McKoy suggests that the purity at work in this scene is not transcendental or metaphysical but that it is "racial purity," as "it is important to note that this regenerative image is also one visibly marked by racial whiteness."[131]

The "undernarrated" racial subtext is not the only problem with the novel's conclusion. There is something of an irony in the ending to *Suttree* since, in spite of McCarthy's fabled resistance to provide easy closure, to provide neat and settled endings, he does *exactly* that in a novel that has, for the most past, undermined linearity and has denied easily applicable principles of coherence. Wilhelm notes that Suttree appears somehow to be "magically healed" at the end, whereas Peter Josyph argues that "nothing and no one develops."[132] Despite problems with its execution, and the fact that it appears to be ambiguously qualified, hope does prevail at the conclusion of the novel, and this reader concurs with Arnold's claim that it is "difficult to read the end of *Suttree* as anything but affirming."[133]

Jarrett suggests that Suttree's chief dilemma is transcending his fear of death, and the conclusion does suggest he has been successful as "by confronting death in the form of his own unconscious … Suttree is able to thus affirm and presumably reorient his life," albeit

---

[130] McKoy, "Whiteness and the 'Subject,'" 94, 92.

[131] Ibid., 97.

[132] Wilhelm, "'The Wrath of the Path,'" 132; Josyph, "Suttree and the Brass Ring," 220-235.

[133] Arnold, "Naming, Knowing, and Nothingness," 61.

away from Knoxville.[134] In a characteristically perceptive reading Ellis suggests that the most significant change Suttree makes is that he stops drinking and that, compared to the other novels discussed, "*Suttree* is that rare McCarthy novel, as we read about a character who actually *changes*." Ellis is quite right in pointing out that the ambiguity and complexity of the conclusion is entirely in keeping with the narrative that has preceded it, as McCarthy "avoids epiphanies that are followed by a character changing his behavior too soon. As in real life, McCarthy's characters have transformative experiences that take longer to work a change in actions than we are accustomed to in less complex narratives, such as Hollywood films."[135]

Vereen Bell offers one of the most important critiques of the conclusion by stating that the novel ends with two symbolic acts—the drinking of the water and the fleeing of the hounds of death—which confirm that Suttree's newly realized "consciousness is his transcendence."[136] Suttree ultimately heeds the advice imparted by the sheriff at his son's funeral that you have to make things important, assume self-authorship, and realize that "meaning is an act of creative and imaginative will," even if Suttree's own "individual existentialist epiphany" is tempered with a warning against the "utopian gnosticism" that lies at the heart of Southern and American exceptionalism.[137] Although it is pulled down at the end of *Suttree*, McAnally remains something "that he will carry with him," an internalized geography of opposition and re-

---

[134] Jarrett, *Cormac McCarthy*, 62.

[135] Ellis, *No Place for Home*, 18, 327 n34.

[136] Bell, *The Achievements of Cormac McCarthy*, 112.

[137] Cant, *Cormac McCarthy and the Myth of American Exceptionalism*, 120, 106.

sistance which suggests that, like Suttree, we also "have the possibility of grace, the promise of a genuine, creative life."[138]

Despite its flaws, the conclusion of the novel does resolve the major thematic, metaphysical, and ontological issues raised in the narrative. The child waterbearer who ministers to Suttree at the end performs an act of genuine kindness, and Suttree's doubling in the child's eyes "is no longer a threat"; indeed, this act could be read as a payback of sorts for the compassionate acts Suttree has undertaken throughout the narrative, acts that "seem to have redeemed his soul from its dark night of alienation and abjection."[139] For all of its abject spaces, wilderness places, and barren geographies, Suttree succeeds in "recognizing his common humanity" at the close, which speaks to the "simple human heart" in characters and readers alike.[140]

---

[138] Prather, "Color of this Life," 48, 51.
[139] Canfield, "The Dawning of the Age," 665-666.
[140] Ibid., 682.

CHAPTER 7

The Road

The publication of *The Road* in late 2006 ushered in an exciting period for McCarthy scholarship. This reclusive "writer's writer" who had labored for so long in relative obscurity (certainly in terms of popular recognition) was now headline news. The novel almost universally received glowing reviews, and within a matter of months, it was announced that it had won the Pulitzer Prize. Perhaps more surprisingly, it was chosen by Oprah Winfrey as one of her Book Club selections, something which introduced McCarthy to an entirely new readership; gone were the days of foraging around for copies of his novels, as you could quite easily now pick one up in the supermarket alongside Danielle Steele's latest. Rumors also abounded that he was to make an appearance on the Oprah Winfrey show, his first such appearance, and the Coen brothers announced that they were to make a big-budget adaptation of *No Country for Old Men*.

McCarthy's novels have always reminded us of the majesty of the novelistic form in an age when the genre has been pronounced dead, exhausted, and obsolete; his style and linguistic range have reminded us of the capacity language retains to surprise and excite, and many readers have found that they could not easily shake off a McCarthy novel when they were finished with it. All this was certainly true of *The Road*, but there was something else to it as well. Every now and again, a work of fiction will come along that offers a startling critique of the culture that produced it and, despite its bleak or challenging vision, manages to somehow strike a chord with its readership, and *The Road* is one of those novels.

American writers have historically been charged with picking up the check when the nation finds itself in a crisis, and in these situations, succeeding generations of novelists attempt to get to the very root of the malaise affecting the national consciousness. The challenge can be boiled down to one question: What happens when the "city on a hill" has lost its moral force and luster? With McCarthy's most recent novel, there are plenty of causes to explain this dystopian sensibility, and *The Road* succeeded in tapping into this bleak zeitgeist. The conflicts in Iraq and Afghanistan signaled a grim note in the nation's history, and the zeal of American exceptionalist rhetoric used to justify them had worn extremely thin. There was widespread disillusionment with the Bush administration. There was also an increased awareness that the planet was on the cusp of irreversible ecological disaster, and that damage had been done to the environment that would permanently alter our relationship with landscape and wilderness. This last point is a pronounced theme in American literary culture, and the nation's literature has frequently explored the changing nature of this relationship.

It is clear that *The Road* asks some profound questions about American culture and the relationship between myth, history, and the national consciousness. The novel is quintessentially American in many respects, and it continues McCarthy's mythoclastic program. Perhaps no narrative form is more quintessentially American than the road narrative, but the one offered in the novel problematizes the myths of mobility and prosperity associated with it.

In *Postmodern Cartographies: The Geographical Imagination in Contemporary American Culture*, Brian Jarvis draws our attention to the fact that much American literature, film, and cultural theory (even in the postmodern era) exhibits geocentric themes that have characterized the nation's artistic and intellectual life for so long. Jarvis maintains that space has always been of paramount importance to the American literary imagination, and he argues that American fictions are duty bound to mirror the utopian or dystopian sensibility prevalent at the moment of composition, observing that although "the lenses may have altered considerably ... all subsequent observers have been obliged to observe American landscapes through some kind of ideological eyeglass."[1] Borrowing the famous Dickensian refrain, Jarvis notes that the representation of space in American culture—and the mythical paths, tracks, roads, and blacktops which connect these spaces—have been the best of places or the worst of places and that "always the land itself loomed large in the imagination of America."[2] Developing this theme, Jarvis points out the following:

> What is essential ... is a recognition of the following: the central role that geography plays in the American imagination and the way in which that imagination bifurcates towards utopian and dystopian antipodes. Many of the key words in the discourses of American history and definitions of that nebulous entity referred to as "national identity" are geocentric: the Frontier, the Wilderness, the Garden, the Land of Plenty, the Wild West, the Small Town, the Big City, the Open Road. The geographic monumentality of the New World inspired feelings of wonder and terror.[3]

---

[1] Jarvis, *Postmodern Cartographies*, 2
[2] Ibid., 1.
[3] Ibid., 6.

The Road is part of this cultural narrative, and the novel mirrors the dystopian moment of its composition and publication; this is not to suggest, however, that the novel is without elements of hope though, as we shall see. As with other works by McCarthy, its mythic and allegorical power supersedes reductive attempts to assess the novel purely by means of plot, but we should at least sketch the design of the novel here. An unnamed father and son travel through a barren apocalyptic wasteland following a catastrophe of almost unimaginable proportions, and the action takes us to the aftermath of the event, although the narrative consciousness never fully discloses what actually occurred. In fact, details about the event are as spare as the prose style, but we do know that at the epicenter of the event the clocks stopped at 1:17, and this was followed by "a long shear of light and then a series of low concussions" (TR 52). The father and son are on the road heading south in search of a better, perhaps even marginally warmer life, and there are enough hints to suggest that they have been on the road for some time. It should be noted that this ashen world is the only one the child has known as he was born after the event itself, and the father's quest is largely motivated by his wish that his son will experience some of the life, culture, and civilization that he has never known.

The novel actually reverses two major themes in McCarthy—his return to his Appalachian routes actually takes him further into the south, as opposed to away from it and into the west, as many of his other novels have done. Astute readers will recognize that the oedipal theme still dominates although it has been reversed in *The Road*, as the father is a fully realized, protective, and nurturing presence for the majority of the narrative, a character who undertakes this sorry pilgrimage with his child's welfare and future in mind. However, the feminine/maternal presence is once again absent.

Parallels with other McCarthy novels can be found throughout as on their road narrative the pair travel through a wasteland that is littered with dead, dying, and at times ossified corpses. Trouble frequently starts when they stop in whatever shelter they can find. Violent "bloodcults" roam the landscape threatening to unleash all manner of unimaginable violence and break every possible taboo. Aside from the usual catalog of grotesque characters and scenes, the narrative consciousness also challenges our ability to make the world familiar or secure as maps, calendars, currency, and alphabets are all obsolete here, therefore destabilizing our claims to order or accurately represent the world. There are some notable stylistic parallels with earlier texts, especially *Child of God*, as both novels are stripped down, lean, eidetic, and cinematically striking in places.

Intertextual parallels do not end there, and it should come as no surprise that the novel contains a series of familiar themes and motifs as it was written by an author operating at the peak of his mature style. There are several references to ruined orchards and rotten, tasteless fruit, which calls to mind the motif used in *The Orchard Keeper*. However, this is not just a fallen world or ruined garden but one that is seemingly beyond repair or replenishment. Indeed, the leveling of animate and inanimate matter, or an ecological consciousness which challenges anthropocentric claims to superiority and order, is a pronounced theme in the novel, and it offers another sophisticated working out of what Georg Guillemin identified as McCarthy's "wilderness aesthetic."

Like *Outer Dark* the novel opens with a dream which plunges the dreamer (the father) from the total dark of his dream-world to the darkness of the waking world, which is described as follows: "Nights dark beyond darkness and the days more gray each one than what had gone before. Like the onset of some cold glaucoma dimming away the world" (TR 3). The reference to glaucoma, of sight being impaired, is of symbolic importance here, as the characters struggle to see (and at times breathe) further than a few feet in front of them throughout the entire novel, and ash and atmospheric detritus are their constant companions. Here, the comparisons between the father figures in the two novels stop, as Culla never gives a second thought to his violation of the incest taboo, which condemns him to a sorry fate in McCarthy's moral universe. The father in *The Road*, however, is constantly agonizing about whether he *could* violate a sacred taboo and commit infanticide by murdering his son if their condition became too perilous. One of their fellow travelers on the road calls to mind such figures in *Outer Dark* in that he looked "like some storybook peddler from an antique time" (TR 174), whereas the boy stumbles upon the following horrific scene which looks like something the evil triune could have carried out: "What the boy had seen was a charred human infant headless and gutted and blackening on the spit" (TR 198).

The child's mother despairs at her husband's plans, and shortly before her suicide, she ridicules him by exclaiming that "we're the walking dead in a horror film" (TR 55). Whilst this quote represents her increasing sense of hopelessness, it also reflects how the novel retains McCarthy's characteristic ability to make us see the action in prose that is naturalistically and cinematically lucid. The cannibalistic "bloodcults" who roam the landscape resort to behavior and patterns of socialization that become increasingly primordial, and the description of them could have been plucked from a horror film: "They came shuffling through the ash casting their hooded heads from side to side. Some of them wearing canister masks. One in a biohazard suit. Stained and filthy" (TR 60). Elsewhere, in a ruined pharmacy, the narrator draws our attention to a "human head beneath a cakebell at the end of the counter. Dessicated," a viscerally striking image (TR 184).

As with other McCarthy works, nothing ever goes smoothly in terms of domestic settings, and in keeping with many American road narratives, the trouble actually starts when the traveling stops. Prior to the birth of their child, but after the disaster, the mother and father share a moment as close to domestic bliss that we could hope to find in the novel, and the meal is shared against the following apocalyptic vista: "They sat at the window and ate in their robes by candlelight a midnight supper and watched distant cities burn" (TR 59). The father and son (lucky throughout, as the father informs the son toward the end of the novel) happen upon a temporary sanctuary, and their dining arrangements evoke a grandeur that is at odds with the elemental survivalist impulse which otherwise dominates the narrative: "They ate slowly out of bone china bowls, sitting at opposite ends of the table with a single candle burning between them" (TR 209).

One of the most powerful intertextual parallels can be drawn between *The Road* and *Suttree*. At one point, these sorry pilgrims who are "each the other's world entire" (TR 6) wander through a "once grand house" that "was tall and stately with white doric columns" (TR 105) but which is now in ruins, an image which calls to mind the plantation house scene from *Suttree*. Their discovery of this historic plantation house is particularly harrowing for the pair, even in the context of the novel, as it appears that this icon of the pastoral order, this grand house once designed as a refuge from history, has become nothing more than a place to cultivate and ready people for death as they find naked people huddled against the wall whilst "on the mattress lay a man with his legs gone to the hip and the stumps of them blackened and burnt. The smell was hideous" (TR 110). Death is most certainly here in this most ghastly one-time Arcadian site which exemplifies McCarthy's mythoclastic vision.

It wouldn't be a McCarthy novel unless the main protagonists chanced upon a marginal prophet-character who espoused some kind of essentialist reading of the world or doom-laden nihilistic philosophy which the lead characters then attempt to defy or unwittingly fulfill. In *The Road* this role is played by a ragged old man, a "starved and threadbare Buddha" who offers the following advice which mocks the gnostic idea of planning for a settled or knowable future: "People were always getting ready for tomorrow. I didnt believe in that. Tomorrow was getting ready for them" (TR 168). He offers the axiomatic nihilistic pronouncement that "there is no God and we are his prophets," rounding it off with the observation that "where men cant live gods fare no better. You'll see" (TR 170-71). Of course, the fate of the child counters this to an extent, as he carries the light and fire of civilization throughout the book and finds sanctuary at novel's end.

As one should expect after a catastrophic event such as this, the novel features a relentlessly bleak deathscape. Jay Ellis has noted how difficult burials always seem to be in McCarthy's work, how that particular rite expresses deep-seated psychological and cultural anxieties within his protagonists, and how the dead—disinterred, unburied, hanging, swinging, and in various grotesque aspects—often rival the living in his fictional spaces. *The Road* is no different in this respect, although the need for ceremonial burials wouldn't perhaps seem quite so important after an event such as this.

Early on in the novel we are shown "a corpse in a doorway dried to leather. Grimacing at the day" (TR 12), and elsewhere the narrative voice draws our attention to "human bodies. Sprawled in every attitude. Dried and shrunken in their rotted clothes" (TR 47). There is the usual cast of disfigured characters, some barely alive, more often than not horribly ragged, such as the man whose eye has been "burnt shut," which is another use of the impaired sight or blindness motif, and those who look like they've just stumbled out of a death-camp (TR 49,117). Blacktops carry huge symbolic and mythic import in American culture, associated with the dream of the open road and promise of mobility and prosperity, but here they are populated with figures who have merged with them, "clutching themselves, mouths howling," caught in this gruesome pose at the moment their lives came to an end (TR 190). Such images are entirely in keeping with the memorable phrase imparted by the narrative voice that this is one long "tableau of the slain" (TR 91).

The father and son travel through Knoxville on their way further south, and the city is described in a manner which evokes the carnivalesque imagery used in the prologue to *Suttree*. The description that follows is once again replete with images of the dead, another "tableau of the slain," and it is another viscerally striking image which strips away any notion of the inherent dignity of the human form: "The long concrete sweeps of the interstate exchanges like the ruins of a vast funhouse against the distant murk ... The mummied dead everywhere. The flesh cloven along the bones, the ligaments dried to tug and taut as wires. Shriveled and drawn like latterday bogfolk" (TR 24).

One of the recurrent themes throughout McCarthy's work is of our impermanence and irrelevance as individuals and as a species. His fiction repeatedly reveals the fragility of our attempts to control or order the world, and it frequently problematizes the supposed progress of our culture. Indeed, much of his work seems curiously at odds with the historical moment of its production, as his novels often *lack* culture, and they often lack a certain level of materiality in terms of technology, appliances, and material goods, of the things that supposedly make our lives easier but which may in fact contribute to the end of things. This is especially the case in *The Road*, and McCarthy's portrayal of the response to the event suggests how close we are as a species to a primordial existence, how fragile our claims to superiority over the world truly are, and it is another none too flattering portrayal of homo sapiens: "Within a year there were fires on the ridges and deranged chanting. The screams of the murdered. By day the dead impaled on spikes along the road" (TR 32-3).

As alluded to earlier, perhaps one of the most remarkable aspects of the novel is the reworking of the oedipal theme. In McCarthy's other works, fathers and sons have tortuous relationships (if they manage to have one at all), and whilst the father doesn't quite make it to see that his quest was fulfilled, his devotion for his son—perhaps one of the last remaining children of god—imbues the narrative with a profound emotional force. The child becomes the "warrant" for the father, a force of light and civilization, and he frames him in rhetoric which is almost theological: "If he is not the word of God God never spoke" (TR 5). Attempting biographical readings with McCarthy can be a tricky thing (as is any singular interpretation of his work), but critics have persuasively claimed that the reversal of this theme could be attributed to the fact that McCarthy himself became a father once again at a late stage in his life.

The father and son share an intense devotional bond, these two who are "each the other's world entire" (TR 6), and the father promises his son that he too would want to die if the child were to die: "My job is to take care of you. I was appointed to do that by God. I will kill anyone who touches you. Do you understand?" (TR 77). The father embodies a particular type of stoic heroism that we often find in McCarthy's characters as he continues in his "ardenthearted" quest despite his awareness of the futility of his task: "He knew that he was placing his hopes where he'd no reason to. He hoped it would be brighter where for all he knew the world grew darker daily" (TR 213). The father somehow manages to maintain his faith in their quest despite such thoughts and his burgeoning existential consciousness that is aware of "the crushing black vacuum of the universe" (TR 130). Despite his own doubts, he remains a source of moral fortitude for the boy, willing to wash a dead man's brains out of his hair after one close encounter with a member of the bloodcults, and he assures the child that they would never resort to cannibalism "even if we were starving" (TR 128). His heroism lies in his defiance, in his "ardenthearted" perseverance, as John Cant would put it, embodied in his promise to keep trying and not to give up as evidenced in a line that evokes the rhetoric of a western, in situations where right is clearly delineated from wrong: "this is what the good guys do … they don't give up" (TR 137).

The father assures his son that they will not violate the cannibalism taboo, but he agonizes about whether he could actually kill his son if their situation became too dangerous. It is a typically extreme scenario for McCarthy, but it expresses universal fears about the nature, limits, and duties of parenthood. We are granted marginal access to the father's psychological reasoning as he works through this impossible scenario, promising his son that he will not "send you into the darkness alone" (TR 248). His musings also force him to confront the existence of another potential self within him (yet another variation on the doppelganger motif) that would have to be summoned if he were to be called upon to commit infanticide: "Can you do it? When the time comes there will be no time … What if it doesn't fire? Could you crush that beloved skull with a rock? Is there such a being within you of which you know nothing? Can there be? Hold him in your arms. Just so" (TR 114).

Despite the reversal of the oedipal theme, there are instances in the novel where the familiar tension comes to the surface. Admittedly, such passages are few in number, but there is some ambiguity as to whether they are part of the interiorized thought processes of the father or if they come directly from the narrative consciousness. One such example exemplifies the archetypal oedipal tension that McCarthy explores in all of his work, and such a passage could perhaps be read as confirmation of the fact that McCarthy has succeeded in transcending his literary fathers or forebears: "Do you think that your fathers are watching? That they weigh you in their ledgerbook? Against what? There is no book and your fathers are dead in the ground" (TR 196).

For all the improvement in terms of the father-son relationship, the mother (and the feminine presence for that matter) is once again almost entirely absent from the novel. We learn that the mother killed herself rather than face what she saw as the futile and highly dangerous journey south, accusing the father of actually endangering rather than protecting their child. It adds another layer of complexity to the familial and domestic drama that is played out in the novel as readers are forced to confront the following conundrum: Is the mother's frank assessment of their situation more admirable than the father's attempt to *deny* this reality and undertake the mythic journey which gravely endangers both their lives? Is suicide a morally acceptable option here? Of course, it is precisely by taking a stand "when there is no stand to take" that imbues McCarthy's characters with their mythically heroic qualities:

> I'm speaking the truth. Sooner or later they will catch us and they will kill us. They will rape me. They'll rape him. They are going to rape us and kill us and eat us and you wont face it … You talk about taking a stand but there is

> no stand to take ... As for me my only hope is for eternal
> nothingness and I hope it with all my heart. (TR 56-7)

Narrative and storytelling once again operate as a humanizing, redemptive agency in the novel, one of the last remnants of the culture that is otherwise completely absent from the text. Stories of how things were or will be are all that is left to the child, and he often implores his papa to read him a story (TR 7). The wasteland they journey through still has the capability to surprise and catalyze distant memories within the father, and he is occasionally encouraged to codify the experience in language and memory (no matter how illusory it may be), to "make a list. Recite a litany. Remember" (TR 31). Moments of stability and safety are all too rare for the father and son, but when they do manage to achieve such a moment, stories are told to construct a world of moral order for the boy, and to remind the father that the world was not always so: "they sat warm in their refuge while he told the boy stories. Old stories of courage and justice as he remembered them" (TR 41).

A scene such as this could be plucked from the narrative of a trailblazing western or pioneer movie, and in a way, the two are caught up in an apocalyptically revisionist pioneer adventure. The South becomes the mythically reinscribed frontier, motivated in part by the father's belief that it could fulfill a fundamental human need and be warmer there. It could also be motivated in part by one of the father's sublime childhood memories (one of the few times we get *any* kind of such happy memories from a McCarthy character) of a day spent when he was a youth with his uncle, which quite possibly could have been in the South. The day was the epitome of pastoral bliss, so much so that "this was the perfect day of his childhood. This the day to shape the days upon" (TR 13). It is because of his wish that his own son experience such days that they undertake the journey in the first place, and the child "had his own fantasies. How things would be in the south," a thought which evokes the rhetoric enshrined in American popular consciousness of other pioneers and uprooted travelers who traversed the North American landscape to fulfill such mythic dreams (TR 54).

There are some other moments where the natural world (or what remains of it) is able to inspire wondrous feelings. Such an example occurs when the boy is awestruck upon seeing the waterfall and, shortly after, when they hunt and successfully find mushrooms in the forest, hinting at a tenuous potential for the re-creation of the early republic dream of the subsistence or yeoman ideal (TR 37, 40-1). However, such glimpses of a barely functioning ecosystem (pastoral is too much to ask for) are undermined when the woods in which they find the mushrooms are described as "a rich southern wood that once held may-apple and pipsissewa. Ginseng." These details suggest that it could well have been a forest in which a character like Ownby from *The Orchard Keeper* had hunted for his own ginseng, but the duo's experience in the woods implies that such days are long past, perhaps never to return (TR 39).

Like some of the most accomplished American novels, *The Road* reassesses the nation's relationship to the land, to its geography. The catastrophe that has occurred means depictions of the landscape in the novel amount to a catalog of nightmarish visions, a perpetual wasteland representing an apocalyptic ecological consciousness which is a development of the "wilderness aesthetic" Guillemin identified as emerging in *Child of God*. The landscape throughout has been "burned away," the terrain has been "cauterized," the land is "gullied and eroded and barren," including a "jungle of dead kudzu," which represents the extent of the devastation if this invasive species cannot survive (TR 14, 177). One of the most memorable examples of the extent of the ecological devastation comes when the pair finally reach the coast, and the description of the fish skeletons inhabiting the beach is presented in very precise and exact mathematical language: "At the tide line a woven mat of weeds and the ribs of fishes in their millions stretching along the shore as far as the eye could see like an isocline of death. One vast salt sepulchre. Senseless. Senseless" (TR 222).

Interestingly, fish (particularly trout) play an almost parable-like function on two separate occasions. At one point on their journey, the father discovers a pool where "he'd once watched trout swaying in the current, tracking their perfect shadows on the stones beneath" (TR 30). It is intimated here that, in their unpolluted stream, the trout represented something in the world that has been lost and perhaps will never be found again. At the close of the novel, they are the objects of the fullest expression of the novel's dystopian ecological consciousness, of inanimate phenomena that pre-date man, and upon their bodies one can see "maps of the world and its becoming. Maps and mazes. Of a thing which could not be put back. Not be made right again. In the deep glens where they lived all things were older than man and they hummed of mystery" (TR 287). The reference to maps, of a cartographic order that goes beyond the Enlightenment hubris of maps as cultural artifacts, is a reminder here of what we could perhaps have already lost and of the mystery to the world that perhaps no mind can or ever will comprehend, a mythic knowledge that pre-dates other epistemological constructions of knowing the world.

The references to mapping, to structures and systems which order the world, is of critical importance here as McCarthy once again manages to destabilize his readership, to force us to question the validity and permanence of the systems through which we know the world and our place in it. The narrative consciousness increasingly points towards a kind of deeper mythic mapping that goes beyond the materiality of our culture, and throughout the opening sections of the novel, ordering principles familiar to all of us are obsolete. The father hasn't kept a calendar for years (which also suggests that they have been on the road for some time), and this is underlined as the boy doesn't know about Coca-Cola, a once familiar signifier of globalization. This is a world where "everything [is] uncoupled from its shoring" (TR 11), and the novel reveals the folly of our attempts to order the world as it creates a time for us when "the frailty of everything [is] revealed at last" (TR 28). This is a world where even the power of language to accurately or objectively record things is called into question, as all things are "shorn of [their] referents and so of [their] reality" (TR 89). Coins have no value, states have no authority, and even roadside advertisements imploring travelers to "See Rock City" stand as signifiers deprived of any code of meaning.

The father and son are physically and culturally without a place in what is another remarkable representation of the theme of "transcendental homelessness" in McCarthy's work. This relates to another significant theme, namely McCarthy's focus on the illusory nature of memory, of the inability of cultural artifacts to truly represent the thing they claim to, a situation that can only be remedied by narrative and efforts to tell of things that have been lost. This also provides the father with another existential challenge as at times he finds he is unable to evoke "the richness of a vanished world" (TR 139) for the boy as it slowly fades from his memory, and he experiences a philosophical dilemma faced by other McCarthy characters as he agonizes over how he can possibly "enkindle in the heart of the child what was ashes in his own" (TR 154). This new world frustrates any attempt the father makes to order it and, due to the detritus in the atmosphere, he is even denied the possibility of orienting himself using the stars, a grounding tool that was available to a character as ghastly as Lester Ballard: "He looked at the sky out of old habit but there was nothing to see" (TR 103).

One of the most significant strategies McCarthy employs in making his characters and readers not feel at home in the world is his use of maps. He reveals them to be nothing more than an example of Enlightenment hubris, another of our vain attempts to order and neatly represent the world when there is a violence and volatility to it that we will never be able to chart or control. The tattered oil company roadmap is no longer of any use to them as the landscape it once charted, the landmarks it once pointed out, have either been destroyed or changed forever. The father clings to this routine of grounding himself according to cartography as we know that he had "pored over maps as a child, keeping one finger on the town where he lived. Just as he would look up his family in the phone directory. Themselves among others, everything in its place. Justified in the world" (TR 182).

We have seen that through the parable of the trout McCarthy points us towards a new way of seeing and ordering the world and his critique of cartography and mapping is another way he achieves this. In *The Road*, McCarthy succeeds once again in leveling human and non-human phenomena, animate and inanimate matter, and he provokes us into undertaking a kind of deeper mythic mapping that makes us reconsider our relationship to our ecological environment, which is a quintessentially American theme: "Perhaps in the world's destruction it would be possible at last to see how it was made. Oceans, mountains. The ponderous counterspectacle of things ceasing to be. The sweeping waste, hydroptic and coldly secular. The silence" (TR 274). This striking passage is the novel's secular apocalyptic warning; it implores us to acknowledge that we are already witnessing the "ponderous counterspectacle of things ceasing to be," and McCarthy makes us realize what we stand to lose and perhaps what we've already lost.

We have referred to the novel's apocalyptic mood, but we should clarify what we mean by this before we conclude. Much like the pastoral, ideas and myths of apocalypse are contested, unstable, and paradoxical, especially within popular American culture, where Puritanical ideas of the jeremiad and frequently used political rhetoric invokes fears about the imminent end to the nation's innate moral superiority. McCarthy uses the apocalyptic myth as a medium to critique his cultural moment, especially America's relationship to the land, and he offers the child as a kind of secular prophet or hopeful object for the world. In *Apocalyptic Transformation: Apocalypse and the Postmodern Imagination*, Elizabeth Rosen offers the following definition that is entirely applicable to how McCarthy employs the apocalyptic mythic paradigm: "It is an organizing structure that can create a moral and physical order while also holding out the possibility of social criticism that might lead to a reorientation in the midst of a bewildering historical moment."[4]

Somewhat ironically, the apocalyptic paradigm can be an ordering and organizing principle due to its very disorder, and it can potentially offer new beginnings out of a sense of things ending. Rosen goes on to make the vital distinction between conventional apocalyptic narratives which offer hope of the realization of a New Jerusalem and contemporary neo-apocalyptic narratives (of which *The Road* is one) that incorporate elements of the conventional narrative but secularize it, and this fusion of mythic narratives is a hallmark

---

[4] Rosen, *Apocalyptic Transformation*, xiii.

of McCarthy's fiction. Specifically, the child offers hope of something better to come, of a sense of life continuing and of things being restored *after* the novel has come to a close, and this is the secular hope that lies at the heart of McCarthy's neo-apocalyptic vision. The son is therefore a kind of prophet, a sign that civilization will continue as the light moves with him (TR 277). This may well be the only world he has known, but the surrogate family he finds at the end (perhaps a happy domestic ending) means that his father's quest has been fulfilled and that he was entirely correct when he stated: "Goodness will find the little boy. It always has. It will again" (TR 281).

One of the highest accolades we could bestow upon a writer is that they produce something that makes us see the world differently, that makes us reconsider our relationship to our culture and our environment, and *The Road* certainly does that. McCarthy's most recent novel critiques some of the foundational myths of Southern and American culture; it implores us to reconfigure our ecological consciousness, and it encourages us to consider what kinds of stories about our culture and civilization future generations will be able to tell.

Overview of Critical Responses

At the time of writing, *The Road* has received relatively little critical attention, although that will surely change as McCarthy's stock continues to rise in the academic and popular consciousness. Our overview will focus on the four types of critical attention the novel has received thus far, which includes reviews by respected critics—that were for the most part extremely positive—and significant scholarly discussions of the novel. At the time of writing, only one book-length study devoted to McCarthy criticism (John Cant's) actually deals with *The Road*, whilst Georg Guillemin's insightful critique of McCarthy's oeuvre—although published before *The Road* easily accommodates the most recent novel, especially in his treatment of what he terms McCarthy's "wilderness aesthetic." We will also incorporate significant papers from a conference devoted (for the most part) to McCarthy's recent work, along with the most recent issue of the *Cormac McCarthy Journal*.

As highlighted in the textual overview, one of the paradoxes of post-apocalyptic texts is how a writer manages to establish a sense of goodness, morals, or ethics in a work that reveals the death of everything, the destruction of nature, and the atavistic and taboo-shattering behavior we as a species revert to when the normalizing agencies of society and culture no longer operate. Whilst *The Road* does not offer a fully realized version of a New Jerusalem being established at the novel's conclusion, it does offer a form of secular comfort as the boy carries the fire and offers some hope, no matter how precarious, of a future for civilization. It is therefore significant that a majority of the critical discussions of the novel are fundamentally concerned with how McCarthy establishes an ethical sensibility in such a barren, godless, and cultureless world.

In his review, "The Road to Hell," Alan Warner makes the bold claim that "all the modern novel can do is done here," and he argues for the prophetic qualities of the novel, stating that "it does not add to the cruelty and ugliness of our times; it warns us how much we have to lose."[5] The "cruelty and ugliness" refer to traces of Camusean philosophy Warner sees in the text. He also remarks on the father's stoic heroism in the face of unimaginable horrors, of his refusal to abandon all belief which brings an ethical dimension to a world where all seems lost. Warner also comments on perhaps one of

---

[5] Warner, "The Road to Hell."

the few ironic subtleties in the novel, as this is "truly an American apocalypse" if the can of Coke the son drinks is indeed the last one in the world.[6]

In "Getting to the End," James Wood's view contrasts with that of many other critics in that he doesn't see the novel as an allegory or as "a critique of the way we live now."[7] Although he regards *The Road* as a "magnificent novel" he feels that its magnificence is undermined as McCarthy doesn't quite get the balance right, as what the "novel gains in human interest [is lost by] being personal at the moment it should be theological," and this is a serious weakness for Wood who is not convinced with the boy-as-god-theme: "the idea that the boy might be the last God … is a kind of more philosophical version of *The Terminator*."[8] Many readers have struggled with the daunting complexity and the seemingly ever-present doom-laden rhetoric in McCarthy's work, but Wood suggests that McCarthy gets the balance between minimalist polish and profound philosophical interrogations just right here, as he believes that "the writing tightens up as the novel progresses; it is notable that the theatrical antiquarianism belongs largely to the first fifty pages or so."[9]

The highly accomplished minimalist style that Wood praises does not undermine the novel's broader thematic concerns for Michael Chabon. In "After the Apocalypse," Chabon argues that the novel is an "apocalyptic epic" not due to the *goal* of the characters' journey but due to their passage through hell, meaning that the father "is visited as poignantly and dreadfully as Odysseus or Aeneas by ghosts,

---

[6] Ibid., 2.
[7] Wood, *Getting to the End*.
[8] Ibid., 7, 6.
[9] Ibid., 5.

by the gibbering shades of the former world that populate the gray sunless hell which he and his son are daily obliged to harrow."[10]

Warner detects traces of Camusean philosophy, Wood identifies but isn't impressed by the novel's theodicy, and Chabon frames it within epic terms. In other words, all three critics praise McCarthy's aesthetic accomplishment and—although in different ways—all three allude to the manner in which the novel reveals an ethical sensibility, which is at odds with *The Road's* overtly nihilistic setting. We will now turn to other critiques that specifically attempt to explicate the ethical dilemma played out in the novel, along with those that seek to draw intertextual parallels between *The Road* and McCarthy's other work.

Although published before *The Road* Georg Guillemin's *The Pastoral Vision of Cormac McCarthy* anticipates and accommodates the novel within its overarching thesis. *The Road* exhibits an egalitarian quality in that it pronounces "the ecological equality of all creatures," and it perhaps privileges those that were here before (and will be here after) mankind.[11] Guillemin uses the term "nature mysticism" to describe the sense of a deeper truth in nature which McCarthy's work explores, and the ancient "maps and mazes" encoded in the body of the trout at the end of the novel certainly support this reading. It is another instance where "McCarthy's ecopastoralism betrays more affinity with Native American animism (and European mysticism) than with the ecopastoral regionalism of the American South or West."[12]

---

[10] Chabon, "After the Apocalypse."
[11] Guillemin, *The Pastoral Vision*, 13.
[12] Ibid., 146.

One could certainly argue that the most profound *eco-ethical* contribution that the novel makes is that it encourages us to reconfigure the relationship between land, wilderness and American culture. This has been one of the most fascinating discourses in cultural, political and theological terms in the history of the United States, and Guillemin claims that McCarthy has always encouraged us to undertake a constant reassessment of this relationship, with *The Road* offering perhaps the most startling allegorical and ethical critique within his body of work: "Americans have always sought to define their nationhood via their relationship to the land, no matter whether the country's essence be identified as garden or wilderness … Nature in American pastoralism has come to function as a typological chronotope, an allegory."[13]

At the time of writing, John Cant's *Cormac McCarthy and the Myth of American Exceptionalism* is the only published book-length study devoted to an analysis of McCarthy's work that discusses *The Road*. As Cant's monograph was published shortly after the publication of the novel itself, *The Road* is treated in an appendix briefer than other more developed chapters in Cant's study. This does not undermine Cant's perceptive reading, and for him, the novel once again represents the author's "willingness to address fundamental philosophical questions in a manner generally out of fashion in a culture that has lost faith in the very notion of the grand narrative," with grand narratives representing those larger meta-narratives that have received such skeptical treatment from postmodern theory.[14] As we have seen, one such grand narrative that the novel engages with is American culture's relationship to its ecology and landscape.

---

[13] Ibid., 142.

[14] Cant, *Cormac McCarthy and the Myth of American Exceptionalism*, 266.

In terms of the specific nature of the catastrophe, Cant is doubtful that this is a post-nuclear landscape as, if it were, there would be ubiquitous radiation, and he notes that "none of the characters encountered in the novel have any symptoms of radiation sickness."[15] Cant remarks that the style of the novel is characteristically hybrid in that McCarthy (as reflected in the dream sequence which opens the text) again creates for us a world of "Appalachian allegory," yet the structure and style reflect the nature of the journey where the clipped, eidetic descriptions are "produced by sentences that are rich in nouns but devoid of verbs."[16]

We follow the man and boy on their tortuously slow progress en route to the coast in the novel, but we should not forget that *The Road* represents something of an imaginative homecoming for McCarthy, and it is therefore no surprise that intertextual parallels are plentiful. Like *Outer Dark*, the text opens with a nightmarish vision, and the displaced characters then undertake a perilous road journey. However, Cant maintains that *The Road* differs in one vitally important respect as it completely reverses the oedipal theme, since "the entire journey is motivated by a father's heroic quest for a place in which his young son can survive."[17] The father is another McCarthy character whose "ardenthearted vitality" counters the sense of "man's insignificance in a godless universe," and although he doesn't live to see it, his ardenthearted valor is rewarded at novel's close as a qualified sense of hope prevails; furthermore, Cant notes that even the absent female is restored at the end.[18]

---

[15] Ibid., 269.
[16] Ibid., 267.
[17] Ibid., 271.
[18] Ibid., 270, 279.

Cant also makes the important observation about the function that maps play in the novel. The narrative proclaims that maps are false and obsolete in this world, that they cannot accurately represent what they claim to. What, then, takes their place? *The Road* encourages us to construct a new system of ethical and ecological mapping, a new order of "maps and mazes," a new beginning that, ironically, comes out of a work that proclaims the end of things, a paradox that Cant also addresses: "*The Road* expresses that paradox that lies at the heart of all serious pessimistic literature: its literary passion defies the very emptiness that it proclaims. It declares the inevitability of cultural entropy, but is itself an example of cultural vitality."[19]

The majority of the critical responses discussed here are the result of a conference hosted in April 2007 by the University of Tennessee, Knoxville, entitled "The Road Home: Cormac McCarthy's Imaginative Return to the South."[20] The conference represented the first attempts by readers and scholars—including some of the leading figures in McCarthy scholarship, such as Dianne Luce, Edwin Arnold, Rick Wallach, and Jay Ellis—to discuss *The Road*'s relationship (and *The Sunset Limited,* a play also published in 2006) to McCarthy's body of work.

In "Beyond the Border: Cormac McCarthy in the New Millennium," Dianne Luce's introduction to the conference proceedings, she comments on the increasing McCarthy mania taking hold within academia and beyond. This is quite startling for long-term readers, especially when we recall that his early novels had sold fewer than

---

[19] Ibid., 280.

[20] The full conference proceedings can be viewed by accessing the following link: http://www.newfoundpress.utk.edu/pubs/mccarthy/mccarthy3.html. In conjunction with UT's Newfound Press the papers are available in traditional text format, and the original presentations can also be watched in video format.

2,600 copies.[21] This mania is sure to be added to as movie rights for *The Road* were snapped up in the autumn of 2006 by producers Nick Wechsler and Steve and Paula Mae Schwartz, and the adaptation is to be directed by John Hillcoat; at the time of writing, the movie is slated for a late 2009 release, and it will be interesting to see if it can replicate the phenomenal success of 2007's *No Country for Old Men*.[22] Luce also notes that aside from the Pulitzer Prize, the novel also won the 2007 James Tait Black Memorial Prize for fiction, the most long-standing such award in the United Kingdom and that McCarthy made his television debut on the Oprah Winfrey show in June of 2007.[23]

We have outlined the potential rewards and also the inherent dangers with attempting to read McCarthy's works in strictly biographical terms, as his work demands to be read with aesthetic autonomy. However, we should also remember that *The Road* is dedicated to his son John Francis McCarthy and that the reversal of the oedipal theme could well be a reflection of McCarthy's own reassessment of *his* role as a father at a late stage in his life. Luce offers the following important comments about the "genesis" of the novel:

> *The Road* had its genesis in a very specific moment, when McCarthy had checked into an old hotel in El Paso with his young son, John (probably after their relocation to Santa Fe, perhaps not long after September 11, 2001), and stood looking at the still city at two or three in the morning from the window of their room, hearing the

---

[21] Luce, "Beyond the Border," 2.

[22] Ibid., 6.

[23] Ibid., Winfrey's interview can be viewed in a three-part sequence on YouTube. No official recording or transcript of the interview is currently available; http://www.youtube.com/watch?v=iNuc3sxzlyQ

lonesome sound of trains and imagining what El Paso "might look like in fifty or a hundred years" … The image of a wasted El Paso seems to have been fixed in his memory in conjunction with that of his small boy sleeping in the bed behind him…[24]

In "The Route and Roots of The Road," Wes Morgan exhibits his usual level of meticulous and painstaking research, and his paper allows us to firmly locate the route travelled by the father and son. Although he is unable to ascertain exactly how long the two have been on the road before the novel starts, Morgan claims that we join them on their journey at Middlesboro, Kentucky. According to Morgan, we then follow the pair as they travel through East Tennessee and North Carolina on their way to their coastal goal, which he maintains is somewhere in South Carolina. The dam they stop to see is Norris Dam, and they move on from here through Clinton, on to Knoxville where they cross over the Henley Street Bridge en route to the father's (and McCarthy's) childhood home south of the city. They then continue on this road to the Smoky Mountains—where signs advertising Rock City can be seen on the roadside—on their way to the resort town (Gatlinburg) and Newfound Gap, where they cross into North Carolina. According to Morgan, the waterfall mentioned is probably Dry Falls, located in Cullasja Gorge about 20.5 miles southeast of Franklin on the way to Highlands, North Carolina.[25]

Morgan draws our attention to some "apparently geographically challenged" critics who came up with some curious suggestions as to where the narrative action may take place. Morgan cites Mike Shea in the *Texas Monthly* who claimed they "could be anywhere" but that

---

[24] Luce, *Beyond the Border*, 5.
[25] Morgan, "The Route and Roots of *The Road*," 2-10.

the "'See Rock City' signs suggested Georgia." Jerome Weeks of *The Dallas Morning Star* placed the pair "in a barren Southwest" where "they seem to be headed for the coast of California," whereas William Kennedy in the *New York Times* maintains the pair are heading to the Gulf Coast.[26] According to Morgan, the intertextual parallels, especially the novel's descriptions of significant landmarks, clearly aligns the setting with McCarthy's early Appalachian works, as does the potential reading of the father as a double for McCarthy, as both author and protagonist retrace routes into their childhoods.

We have stressed how allegorical and mythical aspects often override standard mimetic conventions in McCarthy's work, especially in regards to the temporal ordering of his narratives. McCarthy is a writer noted for his use of obscure allusions that indicate the timing of his novels, and Morgan reveals how we can date the action by paying close attention to such allusions. According to Morgan, the earliest the novel could have taken place is in the mid- to late-1970s. He cites textual references to plastics: "the first disposable plastic safety razor, the 'Good News!' razor, was introduced in this country by Gillette in 1976. Similarly, Kendall Motor Oil seems to have introduced the first plastic bottles of motor oil in 1978."[27] Furthermore, Morgan speculates that the latest the novel could take place is the late 1990s as they went over the Newfound Gap and not through the Cumberland Gap Tunnel, which was closed until this point, and a route that went through the tunnel would have made their journey considerably easier.[28] Luce's and Morgan's works therefore helps us to locate the genesis of the novel, and their diligent scholarship allows us to see how we can frame the novel in biographical and cultural terms.

---

[26] Ibid., 2.
[27] Ibid., 13.
[28] Ibid.

In his keynote address to the conference, Jay Ellis provided a characteristically lively, engaging, and persuasive reading of *The Road*. Ellis sees what James Wood was unable (or unwilling) to, in that the man and boy might instead be called "the father" and "the son," and he means this "in both biographical and theological senses."[29] For Ellis, the novel also taps into some universal fears about the perils entailed in parenthood: In what possible situation could you countenance the killing of one's *own* son, an act that "negates the most direct biological imperative to advance one's genetic inheritance into the future."[30] Another fear Ellis sees echoing throughout the novel is that "you will not manage to leave your son enough to get by with," further evidence of the extent to which *The Road* reverses the oedipal drama found elsewhere in McCarthy.[31]

Ellis undertakes the stylistic task of noting that the word "scared" appears seventeen times in the boy's dialogue. This is an important point in establishing how old the child actually is, along with noting what the boy is physically capable of, and this allows Ellis to determine that he is six or seven years old: "An older boy will not so readily admit his fears—even in such a space of horror. A younger one would not express them so accurately in time."[32] Ellis also makes some intelligent observations about the subtle tropes McCarthy employs, noting how there is a crucial distinction between "the fires that ravage the hillside and scorch the road, and *the fire* carried forward by the father and son," whilst he also remarks upon the striking, and highly symbolic, image of the shopping cart they use to transport their sorry cargo. Ellis reminds us that the only people

---

[29] Ellis, "McCarthy's Sense of Ending," 2.
[30] Ibid., 5.
[31] Ibid., 7.
[32] Ibid., 14.

we see perpetually pushing shopping carts on our *own* streets are the homeless, so McCarthy captures another memorable image of our "transcendental homelessness" in poetic and political terms.[33]

Any serious reader of McCarthy criticism will be familiar with the insightful readings Ellis provides of McCarthy's treatment of gender and the domestic, and he doesn't disappoint here. Many readers have cause to ask where exactly the women are in McCarthy's works, and Ellis seems to offer tacit support to the wife's decision to commit suicide as he asks, "Why would even a fictional woman, a character, if we imagine she has the free will to choose, wish to inhabit such books?"[34] The wife's suicide therefore becomes a justifiable act, both morally and aesthetically, if considered from this viewpoint. This absence is of course restored at the novel's close, and Ellis makes the important point that this is new ground for McCarthy as "the ending provides us for the first time in a McCarthy novel with a full family," suggesting that the boy has finally found a "space" where *the fire* can still burn.[35]

Ellis also offers some memorable critiques of how McCarthy depicts once settled and supposedly stable domestic residences in the novel. We have identified how McCarthy draws on a number of texts and genres, including cinematic texts, and Ellis allows us to see how *The Road* can be paralleled with certain horror movies. Ellis contends that in films such as *The Texas Chainsaw Massacre*, "the American domestic is the site *not* of refuge from lawless terror, but the site *of* lawless terror" and this is certainly true in the novel where, in keeping with other American road narratives, the trouble often starts

---

[33] Ibid., 12, 17.
[34] Ibid., 13.
[35] Ibid., 26.

when the traveling stops.³⁶ In a phrase as memorable as the original passage is chilling, Ellis comments on the plantation house death-camp scene by stating that "we are seeing an echo of the holocaust brought down to the quotidian possibilities of Home Depot."³⁷

Yet despite these horrors, Ellis, like other critics, also maintains that the novel concludes on a note of hope, even if McCarthy's sense of God increasingly seems to resemble "a kind of absent parent no longer able, *or willing*, to do anything about the suffering of his characters."³⁸ Nevertheless, McCarthy succeeds in wrenching hope from an "unbelievably hopeless situation," and the novel concludes with the "beginning of a new world," however fragile that may prove to be.³⁹

Before we leave Ellis, it is interesting if we include a critique of the novel included in Ellis's address from Peter Josyph, actor, writer, and critic of McCarthy whose work rivals Ellis's for its lucidity and persuasiveness. The comments in question are from a private correspondence between the two, but Josyph's remarks may well strike a chord with those readers—and they are not few in number—who despair of McCarthy's protagonists' do-and-endure-anything stoicism, of the ability of his characters to exhibit, without any overt sense of irony, boundless reserves of masculine fortitude and self-sufficiency, characteristics that are bedrocks of the very myths that his works set about subverting:

> McCarthy just loves to show cunning in his villains, in his heroes. People always know how to do practically

---

36 Ellis, "McCarthy's Sense of Ending," 17-18.

37 Ibid., 18.

38 Ibid., 22.

39 Ibid., 27.

> everything. I find it stifling: there's never any room for slackers or just plain ordinary mortals in his world. I am exhausted by his endless survivalism ... I feel less and less entertained by a story and more and more dared, taunted, inflicted upon. [It is] like having to listen to Burt Reynolds in *Deliverance* every time I turn the page.[40]

Euan Gallivan and Phillip Snyder are two critics who examine how an ethical sensibility can be validated or asserted in a world which is ashen, lawless, and cultureless. Gallivan and Snyder offer two philosophically and theoretically sophisticated discussions of how we can talk about ethics in the novel through the paradigms offered by the German philosopher Arthur Schopenhauer and the French theorist Jacques Derrida, respectively.

The use of Schopenhauer as an "explicatory system" to analyze McCarthy's work is not without precedent, as Dwight Eddins attempted as much with "Everything a Hunter and Everything Hunted," a study which focused on *Blood Meridian*. In "Compassionate McCarthy? The Road and Schopenhauerian Ethics," Gallivan analyses how Schopenhauer's concept of will—that "blind aimless striving" within all of us—situates the self as "the centre of the phenomenal world, opposed to everything else. From this subject-object distinction arises egoism and consequently violence, as each individual attempts to wrest control from the others."[41] So the ethical dilemma becomes clear; if the environment *demands* that his characters exhibit the survivalist impulse that Josyph bemoaned, how can we speak of hope, charity, generosity, and hospitality in such a world? Who is

---

[40] Quoted in Ellis, "McCarthy's Sense of Ending," 15-16.
[41] Gallivan, "Compassionate McCarthy?," 1, 2.

prepared to adhere to, or who can possibly enforce, these foundations of a cultural order in a world that is so brutally cultureless?

One way in which the man and boy ensure that their ethical code stays intact is by remaining "the good guys" even when their hunger (in physical, metaphysical, or philosophical terms) becomes unbearable. The child makes his father promise him that they will never eat anyone, and the promise never to violate this taboo makes them ethically sound as "the concept of wrong in Schopenhauer's model [is] most completely, peculiarly, and palpably expressed in cannibalism."[42] Somewhat ironically, the father's actions can be termed "fundamentally egoistic" in Schopenhauerian terms as he has to *deny* the will and fundamental needs of others in order to preserve his, and more importantly, his son's will. However, even if "the father fails to see his connectedness to other individuals," he does manage to ensure that his son carries on the fire at novel's close.[43]

Gallivan's Schopenhauerian reading of the novel arrives at the same conclusion as other critiques that employ different philosophical or theoretical paradigms in that he identifies the boy as the ethical center. According to Schopenhauer, it is only "the individual who accepts the moral boundary between right and wrong where no State or other authority guarantees it [who] can truly be identified as *just*," and the god-like child is such a figure, the good character who is induced "not to hinder another's efforts of will as such, but rather to promote them and who [is] therefore consistently helpful, benevolent, friendly and charitable."[44] In a world where no regulatory bodies have any validity, all the boy has to sustain him, to keep

---

[42] Ibid., 5.
[43] Ibid., 11.
[44] Ibid., 9-10.

him on the right path, are the "old stories of courage and justice" his father passes down, and these stories (and the child's compassion and hospitality) are enough to counter the pessimism of Schopenhauer's philosophy.

In "Hospitality in Cormac McCarthy's *The Road*" Phillip Snyder sets out to "deconstruct *The Road* according to Derridian notions of hospitality and by so doing to recover ethics," and he asks whether "hospitality [could] possibly reassert itself as a ground for human identity and relation."[45] According to such Derridian notions, hospitality allows the man and boy to be humane in an inhumane world, it enables them to be just in an unjust world, and it engenders (and refers back to) the culture that has been lost, a culture which the boy has never known. For Snyder, hospitality "supplies the ontological ground on which subjectivity enacts itself … whether or not to be hospitable is an ethical dilemma fundamental to the human condition."[46] After instilling the knowledge of the importance of hospitality to the fire of civilization which the boy carries, it is fitting that the child increasingly has to *remind* his father about their duty to be hospitable as the novel progresses, especially as the father's physical condition weakens.

Snyder identifies nine significant encounters in the novel "that demand hospitality," scenes where the man and boy have to display a fundamental respect for the Other.[47] Interestingly, his focus on hospitality provides something of an ethical justification for the mother's suicide as her (or McCarthy's) decision to absent her from the text may "relieve her husband and especially her son of their

---

[45] Snyder, "Hospitality in Cormac McCarthy's *The Road*," 1.
[46] Ibid., 17.
[47] Ibid., 12.

responsibility toward her."[48] This absence acts as another reminder in McCarthy of the poverty of the world his male characters inhabit when the feminine has been absented, and her absence is subsequently embodied "in a startling simile of poignant and irrevocably lost maternal hospitality; 'By day the banished sun circles the earth like a grieving mother with a lamp.'"[49] The son thus becomes the ethical center, and this simile leaves us with a memorable image of maternal hospitality carrying the light and the fire for the boy, replacing the light that has been blotted out from the earth by the acts of men.

Randall Wilhelm offers a fascinating discussion of McCarthy's use of "visual structures," a strategy which raises a series of moral, ethical, and spiritual issues. In "'Golden Chalice, Good to House a God': Still Life in *The Road*," Wilhelm notes how "rhetorically opulent spaces [in McCarthy's work] often double as characters and reveal crucial thematic and tonal information," a motif that is especially pronounced in a novel that exhibits an "obsession with vision as a means of unveiling."[50] Wilhelm acknowledges that still lifes are often looked down on in the hierarchy of fine art, but McCarthy memorably employs them in the novel in a series of striking visual structures.

One of the earliest examples of the still life motif in the novel comes with their very first meal, which Wilhelm claims could be titled "Still Life with Cornmeal Cakes, Syrup, and Pistol." Not only is this a visually striking image that helps to "unveil" their desperate condition, but for Wilhelm, it also reveals a characteristically atavistic "nod to the generations of humanity who have come before."[51]

---

[48] Ibid., 10.
[49] Ibid., 11.
[50] Wilhelm, "Golden Chalice," 2, 4.
[51] Ibid., 7.

The still life motif is often employed in scenes involving eating, and Wilhelm locates forty significant scenes that involve eating and drinking. This offers a parallel with Snyder's reading of the role of hospitality in the novel as the pair's ethical dilemma is therefore presented in visually striking scenes that "unveil" their predicament, providing another instance in McCarthy where an *internal* dilemma is transposed onto the landscape or a visually striking technique, another gesture by McCarthy to "make us see."

Wilhelm notes that a significant function of this visual trope is that the father "imbues agency" on artifacts. The cart, previously a sign of material abundance, now becomes a "post-apocalyptic roadster," and the billfold—previously a signifier of a "stable" sense of identity and the regulative presence of modernity—now threatens to destroy the post-disaster sense of self. The photograph of his wife is also significant as it is another instance in McCarthy where the supposed objectivity of photographs is not trusted, and the father's decision to discard it confirms that he "will suffer no distractions in his sacred guardianship of the boy."[52]

Aside from helping us to gauge the interior condition and processes of his characters, the still life motif also feeds into the novel's "moral message." For Wilhelm, they ask "us to look closer, to think more deeply, and to consider from an extreme point of view the condition and purpose of humanity as a species."[53] For Wilhelm then, the use of this visual trope eventually leads us to ethics, to the question of whether we can live by an "ethical roadmap" (another cartographic metaphor we find employed to explicate McCarthy's work)

---

[52] Ibid., 6, 11.
[53] Ibid., 8-9.

that the father lays out for his son.[54] Indeed, Wilhelm contends that the novel is McCarthy's most "spiritually-concerned text" and that even the melancholic still-life image which occurs close to the novel's conclusion with the father's death does not undermine the sense of qualified hope that prevails, the beginning that once more seems to come out of the end:

> In the end, the father becomes a still life himself in the literal sense of the French *nature morte*, or dead matter, his body wrapped in a blanket, and laid out in the woods. Although the father's end can be seen as tragic and suffering, an ugliness that seems all too at home in this apocalyptic landscape, it is the father's deeds that remain beautiful, that engender in the reader a sense of moral goodness and trenchant humanity that makes *The Road* McCarthy's most spiritually-concerned text.[55]

In "The End of The Road: Pastoralism and the Post-Apocalyptic Wasteland of Cormac McCarthy's *The Road*," Tim Edwards is also concerned with the text's network of "ocular references." Wilhelm suggested that the power of these striking visual images resembled still lifes, but Edwards parallels *The Road* with Emerson's transcendentalist manifesto *Nature*, especially with how both works present landscape as text and therefore critique the relationship between environment and society in American culture. It is significant, therefore, that one of the first ocular references and moments of unveiling is associated with poor sight or vision: we are told that it is as if "some cold glaucoma [was] dimming away the world" (TR 3).

---

[54] Ibid., 21.
[55] Ibid., 19-20.

For Edwards, the devastation we witness in the novel also challenges what language can do, what it can represent, as McCarthy "simultaneously creates and destroys the world through language."[56] Edwards notes that even the blissful memory from the father's childhood, the "day to shape the days upon," is undercut with gothic imagery, suggesting that the "Edenic past seems to carry in it, somehow, the seeds of its own destruction."[57] In his closing sentence Edwards reaches even further back than the transcendentalists, fusing his reading of American cultural history with the manner in which the novel maps out what we are losing, by suggesting that *The Road* "in the end, is a prophetic hieroglyphic of horror, an American jeremiad more terrifying than even the Puritan imagination could conjure."[58]

Louis Palmer offers a considered reading of the novel which also emphasizes the sense of loss that Edwards identified by comparatively analyzing *The Road* and *The Orchard Keeper*. Palmer reads "both novels as elegies with a focus on loss that occludes other thematic material," arguing that the mournful and elegiac temper is so pronounced since, for an ecopastoralist, what greater loss could there possibly be than a world without nature?[59] For Palmer, *The Road* provides us with "multiple ways of looking at loss," although even a book which gives us plenty of reasons to be mournful also gives the father his son, "a focus that keeps him from falling into the suicidal melancholy that took his wife" and which eventually ends on an affirmative note, suggesting that "humans persevere in their basic ori-

---

[56] Edwards, "The End of the Road," 9.
[57] Ibid., 7.
[58] Ibid., 9.
[59] Palmer, "Full Circle," 1, 4.

entations even in the absence of rational reasons to do so."[60] Palmer is another critic who locates an affirmative note at the novel's close, and *The Road* is the novel that perhaps finally counters John Grammer's claim that "it is hard to imagine McCarthy on some platform in Stockholm, assuring us that man will survive and prevail," an assurance Faulkner offered during his Nobel Prize acceptance speech.[61]

Susan Tyburski offers another intertextual reading, but she opts to analyze the two texts that appeared in 2006, *The Road* and the play (or the novel in dramatic form, as the epigraph informs us) *The Sunset Limited*. In characteristic McCarthy style, Tyburski claims that both works "strip the human condition to its bones," and she argues that both investigate "the viability of faith in the face of an apparently Godless world."[62] Tyburski also points out how both works also explore the question of suicide (we see thematic echoes of *Suttree* here also), and she also delineates how both ask if it is ever ethically or philosophically acceptable to commit suicide. In *The Road*, the boy's "holy breath" contains "a spark of hope for the future of the human race," ensuring that his social, cultural (as much as possible in the novel), and ethical "faith in his connection to other humans grows stronger, even as his journey with the man grows more desperate."[63]

In "Sighting Leviathan: Ritualism, Daemonism, and The Book of Job in McCarthy's Late Work," John Vanderheide offers a fascinating assessment of these texts by employing a variety of explicatory systems. Vanderheide takes us back to the opening image of the iron fence growing through the tree at the start of *The Orchard Keeper*, an

---

[60] Ibid., 6-7.
[61] Grammer, "A Thing Against Which," 30.
[62] Tyburski, "The Lingering Scent of Divinity," 1.
[63] Ibid., 9-10.

image which helps to explain the "philosophical largesse" of his work as it consistently combines realistic yet symbolic modes (as noted by Jarrett) and the mimetic and allegorical (as noted by Cant).[64] Furthermore, Vanderheide reads the spiritual aspect of the book via the daemonic challenges played out in the book of Job.

In his analysis of *The Road*, Vanderheide uses Angus Fletcher's *Allegory*, especially Fletcher's concept of allegory as being either battles or progress, and he claims that *The Sunset Limited* represents an allegorical battle, whereas *The Road* represents an allegory of progress. Furthermore, in Fletcher's rubric, he notes that "allegorical characters are often obsessed with only one idea," something that is certainly true of the father, and that the dream sequence which opens the novel has been "a stock of allegorical narrative since the Middle Ages."[65] The repeated use of "OK" in their dialogue can be explained as the "father['s] ... allegorical impulse toward ritual," and the ultimate justification for the novel as allegorical progress is assured because "the father's daemonic desire overpowers everything that would impede the ritual movement south."[66]

Vanderheide notes that the hope of "absolute transcendence" for these two pilgrims is dim indeed and that the mother's suicide actually embodies a "destructive impulse" that is in its way godlike. Vanderheide makes an insightful parallel between the mother in the novel and the character White from *The Sunset Limited*, pointing out how they share the same imagery, rhetoric, and desire: "McCarthy also puts the same words in their mouths, expressing the same desire ... This hope, moreover, leads both to personify death as a lover. So

---

[64] Vanderheide, "Sighting Leviathan."
[65] Ibid., 3, 7.
[66] Ibid., 8.

along with the figure of White, the figure of the woman likewise constitutes an avatar of Leviathan, a personification of that destructive impulse that is part and particle of God."⁶⁷

Linda Woodson's "*The Road* in Post-Postmodernism" acknowledges the need to place the novel in terms of genre but further argues that, like many other McCarthy texts, it goes beyond such singular readings. Woodson likens the novel to Steinbeck's *The Grapes of Wrath* in that both are examples of journey literature, both are written from an oppositional perspective, and both authors shape their narratives around characters who have been disenfranchised and whose journey critiques versions of the American pastoral.

For Woodson though, the novel's most profound accomplishment is that it makes us re-think our understanding of language. Woodson points out that the boy doesn't know any stories with happy endings, "proof again that the boy lives in a world in which the signs have been changed, and the old signifiers no longer hold meaning," and that Ely's tale does not inspire, that he is not a mystical prophet-character, just one who speaks of grimly holding on and surviving.⁶⁸ Of course, one could argue that the boy's ending is his only, and most important, happy ending, and that whilst the role of the mystical character may well have changed here, Ely's tale of survival is perhaps the best we can ask for.

Woodson's critique is underpinned by the deep skepticism that informs many postmodern (or post-postmodern) inquiries, but even this skepticism is perhaps countered by the qualified sense of optimism that prevails at novel's close. Language still retains the power to evoke, to fire, to affirm, but it is the non-verbal languages in the

---

⁶⁷ Ibid., 18.
⁶⁸ Woodson, "The Road in Post-Postmodernism," 10-11.

text, the "maps and mazes" of inanimate matter, which potentially contain the key to our survival and the ethical genesis of our relationship with the natural world.[69]

It is without doubt that *The Road* will continue to generate many more fascinating critical debates, and I have attempted to provide an overview of the earliest attempts here. However, it is clear that the novel is another major accomplishment for McCarthy, a novel where he returns home but which doesn't deal in nostalgia or sentimentality, a novel which asks us to re-evaluate fundamental ethical, cultural, and geo-political questions about our relationship with animate and inanimate matter alike.

---

[69] Ibid., 13-14.

CHAPTER 8

The Stonemason

Published in 1994, *The Stonemason* is McCarthy's first outing as a playwright. Perhaps due to the fact that he remains on familiar thematic and imaginative ground, *The Stonemason* has a reputation as an unplayable play, a dramatic piece of work which is characteristically profound but which, due to its complex narrative structure, is almost impossible to stage. We are not concerned here with the merits of this five-act play as stageable drama, or with its relation to Southern drama, although these are important questions. Rather, I suggest that we will be best served if we read *The Stonemason* as a commentary on McCarthy's own work and artistry. Indeed, his 2006 play *The Sunset Limited* was subtitled "'a novel in dramatic form," and the same could well be applied to *The Stonemason*.

Set in Louisville, Kentucky, in the 1970s, the play is concerned with the inter-generational hopes, struggles, and losses endured by the Telfairs, an African American family. The play is driven by a divisive patriarchal struggle as Ben, the play's narrator, is lovingly devoted to his grandfather (Papaw), a character more mythic than mimetic. Papaw practices an antiquated version of stonemasonry—*the* only trade there is, according to him—which is being abandoned in favor of more contemporary techniques, most significantly by Papaw's son Big Ben, who owns a failing construction company. The youngest progeny is Soldier, Ben's nephew, another of McCarthy's mythical boy-men whose rebellion, coupled with Ben's withholding knowledge of his existence from his mother Carlotta and the rest of the family following Soldier's decision to run off, ensures that the play ends on a tragic note. Although far from a happy home, there are a number of domestic scenes in which the Telfairs—sometimes in aloof theological rhetoric that makes it hard for readers to empathize with them—play out their destiny against the historical (and contemporary) background of racial subjugation and oppression. If we are to read the play as a commentary on McCarthy's artistry, we cannot overlook how Ben often seems to speak directly for McCarthy (in language that seems more like McCarthy's own narrative consciousness than that of one of his characters, no matter how eloquent Ben is) and that masonry metaphorically represents the ancient craft of narrative and storytelling.

The play opens with a lengthy italicized stage direction which immediately reveals the "unplayability" of the play. We are introduced to Ben Telfair, the central narrator (we cannot overlook the symbolism of the name Telfair, as Ben attempts to fairly tell his family's history), and the stage direction also introduces us to the complex structure: *"It is important to note that the Ben we see onstage during the monologues is a double and to note that this double does not speak, but is only a figure designed to complete the scene"* (TS 5). The difficulties are self-evident here, and although McCarthy often employs a version of the doppelganger to manifest the dilemmas endured by his characters, this is a technique that could be more easily incorporated into a novel or a film than a play.

There is also a *"podium or lectern"* that Ben uses to deliver his monologues, and this is significant as it does often feel as if we are being preached at or lectured to during Ben's monologues as they are delivered in language that is infused with a carefully considered philosophy, perhaps even a theodicy (TS 5). The podium may well be intended to isolate *"that space from the world of the drama on stage,"* but it also isolates Ben and the other characters from the readership or audience (TS 5). Efforts to disorient the reader are a familiar strategy in McCarthy, as are speculations about the illusory and fugitive nature of memory, but they are more successfully accommodated by him in novelistic form. Such techniques do help to ensure that we do not *"defraud the drama of its right autonomy,"* but it also makes it hard for us as readers to feel engaged by these characters following these instructions (TS, 5-6). The themes explored here are characteristically weighty, and they are primarily concerned with Ben's salvation and exoneration, and the readership is explicitly cast here as jurors, a role which is often more subtly demanded of us in McCarthy's other works.

There are also some other gaps and inconsistencies in the play which undermine its unity. For example, the reasons for the estrangement and tension between Big Ben and Ben could have been developed, as could the implications for the family following Ben's refusal to loan his father the money to save his company, and perhaps his home. Likewise, we are left wanting to know more about what's happened during Soldier's absence, and the reasons for his rebellion are never truly developed. We fail to see Carlotta's response to her son's absence, and we also fail to see the true nature of her emotions following her discovery of Ben's decision to withhold knowledge of Soldier's existence from her. Finally, Ben's visit to Mary Weaver, his father's mistress, after his father's death feels too forced, too much like a set piece aimed at resolving unanswered questions about Ben's past, although this does add to the tragic nature of Ben's character.

Masonry, or the *only* trade according to Papaw and Ben, provides an explanatory power for these two members of the Telfair family, "for true masonry is not held together by cement but by gravity. That is to say, by the warp of the world. By the stuff of creation itself" (TS 9-10). His craft is "the oldest there is" and the secrets to it cannot be learned from any book (this is one of the many instances in the play which demonstrate a sensibility that is skeptical about knowledge, especially academically acquired knowledge). They are secure in the ordering principle which masonry provides, as it "was like a power and we knew it would not fail us" (TS 32-33). As we have seen, there are many instances in McCarthy where characters and readers alike do not feel at home in the world, do not know how to ground or orient themselves, but Papaw is blessed in this respect. For him there is only one trade, only one life, and he always wondered what people outside of it do, claiming that "to a man who's never laid a stone there's nothing you can tell him" (TS 66).

Of course there is something of an irony in the fact that this trade, this explanatory meta-narrative, ultimately fails to aid Ben in stopping his father and his nephew from fulfilling their grim fates, and Papaw has little to say to them directly (or via Ben). It continues to provide an ordering moral category though, and for Papaw, masonry is "like the workings of Providence" itself; for Ben, it can potentially restore "*a love and reverence for reality*" [emphasis mine] (TS 37, 90). The use of "reverence" is significant here as the trade assumes a quasi-religious or theological function for Ben, which is especially significant given that he abandoned other ordering principles, such as the pursuit of academic knowledge and, seemingly, the consolation of religion. For Ben salvation lies in masonry, whereas narrative and storytelling seem to inspire similar feelings of reverence and potential for salvation in all of McCarthy's work.

It is the religious or theological aspect that masonry assumes in the play that makes Ben something of an aloof character. It provides a guiding principle for him, but his philosophizing about it distances him from the reader and, if we take Ben as a real, fully formed mimetic character, how many people actually *talk* like him? His rhetoric belongs to McCarthy and the narrative consciousness, and although Ben is undoubtedly articulate, with a cultivated intelligence that has benefited from a brief spell at a graduate school (any kind of formal educational training for a McCarthy character is a rare thing indeed), the *lecturing* Ben rather than the dramatically-conceived Ben dominates the play. It is a familiar McCarthy ploy for the narrative consciousness to provide the inner workings of his characters in a language that is too sophisticated for the characters themselves, but in Ben we have a protagonist through which McCarthy seems to speak directly, such as in the following passage where masonry metaphorically stands in for narrative and where the thematic range is unmistakably McCarthyesque:

> The calculations necessary to the right placement of stone are not performed in the mind but in the blood. Or they are like those vestibular reckonings performed in the inner ear for standing up right. I see him standing there over his plumb bob ... pointing to a blackness unknown and unknowable both in truth and in principle where God and matter are locked in a collaboration that is silent nowhere in the universe and it is this that guides him... (TS 66-67).

Ben's gloomy contemplations about mortality can also closely be aligned to McCarthy's narrative consciousness, such as when he speculates about whether "that namelessness into which we vanish [will] taste of us?" (TS 104). However, McCarthy and Ben are surprisingly minimalist in places, most notably when Ben discovers that

Papaw has died, which is the most emotionally challenging moment for him in the entire play (TS 99-100).

The Stonemason is structured around a divisive inter-generational patriarchal struggle that afflicts the Telfairs. It is left to Mary Weaver, Big Ben's mistress and another of McCarthy's marginal prophet-characters, to offer one of the most insightful commentaries on this theme in the play (and McCarthy's oeuvre) when talking to Ben following his father's death, as she succinctly claims that "you caint get around that daddy" (TS 110). We have four generations in the play that either seek to uphold or betray patriarchal legacies, that conform to or renounce their heritage. Papaw is the mythic archetype, the connection to a lost world; Big Ben is the son who renounces the father's legacy, whilst Ben, his son and Papaw's grandson, fulfills it. Soldier, the youngest Telfair male, has a father who is absent completely in the text, and he goes on to betray every line of his patriarchal heritage. In this respect, the Telfairs' patriarchal crisis represents "the radical disjunction between past and present" that Richard Gray identifies as being characteristic of so much Southern literature.[1]

Papaw is the fabled mythic patriarch who is over one hundred years old, and his knowledge of the ancient trade of masonry marks him out as an archetypal figure. He has a connection to a past and a historical consciousness that no one apart from Ben seems to care for, and he even dies a sort of mythic death that we all dream of—in his sleep, apparently painless and untroubled. He is secure in his calling and his destiny as he was only twelve years old when "I seen the way my path had to go if I was ever to become the type of man I had it in my heart to be ... I never looked back. Never looked back,"

---

[1] Gray, *The Literature of Memory*, 85.

a man for whom masonry and the King James Version of the Bible provide all the ordering principles he needs, which explains his refusal to go against scripture and lay hewn stone (TR 49-50, 63). His code is unshakable, and he maintains a faith in the idea that (despite the destinies being acted out by Big Ben and Soldier) our "accounts" get balanced and that there is a "ledger kept that the pages dont never get old" and that a man stands a more favorable chance of salvation if he has a Puritanical work ethic because "a man that will work they's always hope for him" (TS 29, 27).

Ben is devoted to his grandfather, a mythical figure who ironically revolutionizes Ben's worldview with his essentialist philosophy in which masonry makes sense of all things. In many respects, Ben is a conventionally conceived tragic character who is unable to see his own limitations, despite warnings from his wife and his sister, and who claims that masonry enables him to see everything when in fact it blinds him to the problems in his immediate reality. Like Papaw, he comes to the one true calling of masonry inherited from his mythic patriarch, and he is fiercely devoted to it: "But that the craft of stonemasonry should be allowed to vanish from this world is just not negotiable for me. Somewhere there is someone who wants to know" (TS 91). Like Papaw he possesses an admirable Puritanical work ethic and a stoic "ardenthearted" capacity to endure, a familiar trait in McCarthy's characters, as he doesn't "know any other way to do it," a man who sees "failure on every side and I'm determined not to fail" (TS 41, 119). In sentiments such as this, Ben combines the antiquated faith in *the* trade with the rhetoric of the American dream, but both cultural narratives contribute in their own way to his form of self-blindness.

The relationship between Papaw and Ben dominates the play, and their conversations are particularly important. Some of their exchanges, especially the one concerning the murder of Uncle Selman (which includes Ben's question of "do you think it was easier growing up black back then?") have about them a somewhat heavy-handed instructional and perhaps even didactic feel; this is *the* genuine history, this is *the* knowledge that Ben must wrestle with, they seem to say (TS 46-52). This is a familiar feature of McCarthy's work, especially the late novels, and one thinks of the exchange between the ex-priest and Billy in *The Crossing*, John Grady Cole and Mr. Johnson in *Cities of the Plain*, and even Sheriff Bell in *No Country for Old Men*, who admitted that he always liked to hear the old timers talk.

Despite being Papaw's son, Big Ben seems to have renounced his father's creed in his professional and personal life. In one of his first appearances in the play, McCarthy draws our attention to the expensive and smart clothes he is wearing and that he is sporting *"three of four very expensive rings"* (TS 14). It is significant that he is the only character in the novel who is associated with material possessions and who has a very carefully stylized appearance. This is an obvious difference that drives the tension between father and son, and Big Ben is dismissive of his son's stubbornness as he says that "you caint tell him [Ben] nothing," nor does he try to throughout (TS 69).

The real patriarchal tension is generated from what Big Ben sees as Ben's betrayal of him and the family. Big Ben feels betrayed by Ben and Papaw as they left his construction firm, despite Ben working a regular week for him whilst doing additional masonry work with his grandfather. The betrayal is compounded when Ben refused to lend his father money to save his business, and Big Ben states that "I aint goin to get it. Not even in my own house. Under my own roof. Never could and never will," with "it" here representing financial assistance from his son, familial support, and perhaps even sexual gratification from his wife (TS 77-79). Big Ben ultimately commits suicide following his failure to get the assistance his business requires, and Ben's subsequent contemplation of his father reveals the extent of the patriarchal tragedy, compounded by the fact that Ben is also, in part, afflicted by a form of the self-blindness that he identifies as one of his father's major flaws:

> Because I thought of my father in death more than I ever did in life. And think of him yet. The weight of the dead makes a great burden in this world. And I know all of him that I will ever know. Why could he not see the worth of that which he put aside and the poverty of all he hungered for? Why could he not see that he too was blest? (TS 111)

Soldier can be read as a contemporized mythic figure, the boy-man who makes an appearance in a great deal of McCarthy's work. He possesses something of Ben's stubborn individualism embodied in his approach to selection for the basketball team. Ben (an uncle who also stands in for his absent biological father) tells him that "everybody starts on the B team," to which Soldier replies "that's them, this is me," which suggests that he has an "ardenthearted" drive to fulfill his own unique destiny, albeit a tragic one (TS 22). Soldier ridicules Ben for his belief in his supposed superior insight, a knowledge that encompasses everything, which reinforces the view of Ben as something of a tragic character (TS 116). Soldier resembles Bobby McEvoy in that he is the rebellious son, the dangerous man who haunts the text, existing in a curious limbo away from family, the law, and the state, joining hundreds of other lost and transcendentally (and perhaps even physically) homeless souls: "they put the report in a filing cabinet along with about a thousand others, kids that are missing.

Missing or misplaced or lost or people just couldnt remember where they'd left them or maybe no one even noticed they were gone" (TS 68).

Ben is also heavily implicated in the grim end that Soldier meets, alone in an anonymous motel room following a drug overdose. Ben gives him the money with which he buys the drugs that kill him, but more tellingly, he does not tell Carlotta that Soldier is alive and that he has been in contact with him (and that he has been giving him money to go away again) whilst he has been officially categorized as missing (TS 112). His moral fortitude derived from the practice of masonry fails Ben here, and he actually exacerbates Carlotta's misery following Soldier's death when she discovers that Ben withheld knowledge of his existence from her. Whilst Ben does arrive at some form of self-recognition of his deeds, it is all tragically too late:

> And Maven was right. It's worse than a death. More vengeful than a suicide. His absence is like a pall of guilt and humiliation. People would say He'll come back. Or He'll turn up. Then they stopped saying anything. Then they stopped coming around … His birthday is in two more weeks. He would be sixteen. Will be sixteen? In what tense do you speak of them. You dont speak of them. You are simply enslaved to them. And Carlotta was right. I think I can fix everything. The simplest word of consolation sounds like a lie. (TS 84-5)

Mason Ferguson is Carlotta's partner who marries into this patriarchal tragedy, the father figure who could have saved Soldier but who arrives too late to do so. It is ironic that he is a claims adjuster, and Ben teases him about this in a scene where he assumes the role of the patriarch, gently mocking Mason for his ambiguously abstract role which is at odds with his own work and philosophy, not to mention the fact that McCarthy's work generally makes us reassess *our* claims to knowledge and understanding (TS 86). Papaw ends up dead, Big Ben commits suicide, and Soldier dies from an overdose, whilst Ben ends up with a ghostly visage of Papaw which he knows "would guide me all my days and that he would not fail me, not ever fail me" (TS 133). This doesn't really convince though, and Ben is far from exonerated at the conclusion of the play, as much of a ghost as the visage of Papaw, which he claims will guide him though the remainder of his life.

The Stonemason does include a series of relatively fully-formed female characters, which contrasts with McCarthy's often problematic depiction of female protagonists in other texts. Mama is something of a mythic character in her own right, a repository for wisdom who has her own essentialist understanding of the world. She warns of the folly of attempting to change the natural order of the world, telling Carlotta that "you can make up your own plan if you want to, and you can read it in ruin" (TS 45). Although the play contains a series of domestic scenes, which is unusual for McCarthy, Mama also acknowledges the dangers inherent in imagining that the domestic can shelter you from the world's darkness as when "trouble comes to a house it comes to visit everbody" (TS 71). She also seems to possess something of a mystical foresight or vision not available to other characters, as evidenced by her disturbing dream vision of Soldier's fate (TS 84).

For the most part, she is a caring and sympathetic feminine presence although she claims that her daughter-in-law Maven has "just got a lot of high tone ideas" and that "life'll smack a few of em out of her fore it gets done with her" (TS 44). This is another example of one of the Telfairs being blighted by a degree of tragic self-blindness, as

Maven is more realistic and pragmatic than Ben; indeed, it is Ben's romantic notions that get the family into so much trouble. Maven is always on hand to puncture her husband's romantic notions, revealing that her experience at law school is all automated learning and that only "an older generation ... discussed the philosophy of the law" (TS 38). She also warns Ben against his father taking advantage of him, but most significantly, she punctures his ideas about justice, as he denies his sister the very categories that he so dearly cherishes: "You told me that principles were absolute or they werent principles ... You cant know another person's torment. You of all people. Things come easy to you" (TS 124-25). Ben's sister Carlotta also has the measure of Ben, warning him that "you think you can fix everything [but] you cant," meaning that both she *and* her son Soldier concisely reveal Ben's limitations, but he fails to heed their warnings (TS 60).

Much of *The Stonemason* concerns itself with universal dramas and struggles which transcend any singular readings, but one cannot avoid the references to the history of racial oppression and subjugation experienced by African Americans, not to mention the crippling contemporary socioeconomic problems they also face. The Telfair family narrative is enshrined in the cultural narrative of western movement and mobility, and we learn that "the Telfairs black and white came here from South Carolina in the 1820s," and that Papaw's parents, and two of his siblings, were all slaves (TS 31). Members of the family undertook Herculean tasks of self betterment and improvement, such as Ben's grandmother who taught herself to read after a day of grueling domestic work and who would read until "one or two in the morning and then [got] up again at five-thirty to get breakfast for the family" (TS 93). She would go on to become the first black registered nurse in the state of Indiana.

THE STONEMASON

The Telfairs, like many other McCarthy characters, were dispossessed from the material rewards of this mythic narrative on the grounds of their race, and their experience is representative of hundreds and thousands of other African Americans. The brutality of their experience is fully revealed in the story about the murder of Papaw's Uncle Selman, who was killed "over a dispute that had no sense to it" (TS 50). Uncle Selman's murder reveals the injustices suffered by the Telfairs and hundreds of families like them; the man who killed Selman fled but eventually returned, by which time "it was too late to bring him to justice," as Papaw mournfully tells Ben (TS 52).

Although set in the 1970s, the play in no way suggests that such instances of bigotry and oppression are a thing of the past, and the contemporary forms of prejudice and disempowerment the family confront are perhaps even more insidious. Big Ben has to knowingly underbid on jobs for his construction company, as this is the only way that an African American owned and run company will be awarded them, whereas Mama suggests that Maven will encounter prejudice despite her hard work and impeccable academic credentials: "I heard of negro lawyers and I heard of women lawyers but I sure aint never heard of no negro woman lawyer. Not in Louisville Kentucky I aint" (TS 43). Ben also grasps the irony of their social situation, especially in terms of Soldier's truancy record at his high school, as he remarks that "five years ago they were putting us in jail for sending our kids to school, now they want to jail us for not sending them" (TS 68).

Soldier's fate reveals the most brutal reality experienced by African Americans, especially young black males. His school is "just a drug exchange center" according to Ben, and it is riddled with violent gang conflicts (TS 27, 74). Ben mistakenly believes that Soldier is simply a "troublesome kid," but he comes to discover that "he was involved in things I hardly knew existed. The things I found out I couldnt believe," another example where the knowledge and wisdom that masonry imbues renders him completely unable to deal with the modern world that Soldier finds himself immersed in (TS 108). Indeed it is left to Jeffrey, an acquaintance of Soldier's and another of McCarthy's marginal prophet-characters, to offer an assessment of Ben that is applicable to so many McCarthy protagonists: "History done swallowed you up cept you dont know it" (TS 74). Against this backdrop of racial oppression and emasculation, *The Stonemason* therefore becomes another of his works where history transcends the power and validity of myth to ground oneself in the world, as Ben finds out to his cost.

The play also contains several instances where various characters express deeply skeptical views about what formally acquired (especially academic) knowledge can actually teach you. Carlotta claims that "school isn't the answer to everything," and Ben claims that "most people feel that books are dangerous and they're probably right" (TS 60, 39). Ben eschews graduate school and swaps it for the learning-through-telling-and-doing model embodied in Papaw's work ethic where masonry exists in narrative and memory only as "you couldnt learn it in a book if there were any and there are not. Not one. We were taught. Generation by generation. For ten thousand years." (TS 26).

Papaw, of course, is the repository for this knowledge. Ben's reverence toward him assumes a parable-like quality of what we lose if we turn our back on organically acquired knowledge as opposed to the "debris" that collects in Ben's head in graduate school:

> I knew that when I told him I was studying psychology he had little notion of what that meant ... It was only

> when I came home after my first year of graduate school that I realized my grandfather knew things other people did not and I began to clear my head of some of the debris that had accumulated there and I did not go back to school ... I swore then I'd cleave to that old man like a bride. I swore he'd take nothing to his grave. (TS 11)

The Stonemason is not without some of the gothic touches which characterize so much of McCarthy's Southern work. Soldier's face in death is *"compressed in anger and sorrow,"* as he manages to die in the furious rebellion he experienced whilst alive (TS 121). In Ben's final graveyard vision of Papaw, he sees him in a Sisyphean light, perpetually doomed to carry a great stone, suggesting that even in death he carries out the backbreaking labor that was his lot in life. Moreover, Ben sees him as a "man, naked and alone in the universe," which seems to be McCarthy's view of all his protagonists, dead or alive (TS 131-32).

The play is therefore a characteristically profound work which is structured around a divisive patriarchal conflict. Ben's story is ultimately a tragic one, and the tragedy is compounded by the historical reality of subjugation experienced by African Americans, and of the contemporaneous experience of Soldier. Characters are more mythic than mimetic, and the play could well have the subtitle of McCarthy's 2006 effort *The Sunset Limited*, as both are "novels in dramatic form." *The Stonemason* is elaborately structured, and this unplayable play could best be read as a commentary on McCarthy's aesthetic in which the ancient trade of masonry symbolically and metaphorically represents the equally ancient trade or practice of narrative and storytelling.

Overview of Critical Responses

The consensus that emerges from the scholars of McCarthy's work who have discussed *The Stonemason* can essentially be summed up as follows: McCarthy has joined the long list of accomplished novelists in producing an unplayable play, one that is not really suited to theatrical form. Although the play may well be unplayable, due to its structural, logistical, and even ideological problems, critics do agree that *The Stonemason* provides an invaluable commentary upon McCarthy's work and aesthetic vision.

Edwin Arnold's "Cormac McCarthy's *The Stonemason*: The Unmaking of a Play" is a fascinating and authoritative account of the aborted efforts to produce the play at the Arena Stage in Washington, D.C., in the early 1990s (readers should note that although the play was published in 1994 it had been written some years before). Not for the first time in his distinguished career McCarthy would receive a prestigious prize, as *The Stonemason* won the 1991 American Express/John F. Kennedy Center Fund for American Plays grant. Financially the award was invaluable, and it provided a $50,000 financial package, half of which was paid up front to the theater, with the other half awarded when the actual performance was due to commence; McCarthy received an additional $10,000 award as playwright.[2]

What is so fascinating about Arnold's essay is the access he gets to the major figures involved in the attempts to stage the play, and the interviews he conducts with them provide a detailed chain of events (along with some valuable insights into the foundational elements of McCarthy's work). The central figures involved include Wiley Hausam, who at the time was an agent specializing in dramatic works

---

[2] Arnold, "Cormac McCarthy's *The Stonemason*," 141.

at International Creative Management Inc. in New York; Douglas Wager, Artistic Director of the Arena Stage; and his colleague Larry Maslon. We have remarked that the hybridity of McCarthy's novels is one of the characteristic hallmarks and defining features of his work, but it is *exactly* the hybrid nature of his aesthetic that makes *The Stonemason* an unplayable play. As Arnold duly notes, the interviews he conducted revealed the play to be a "remarkable but problematic work."[3]

Both Hausam and Wager were initially drawn to the hyrbridity of the play, with the latter admiring the fusion of fictional, cinematic, and dramatic techniques, although he also located a significant problem with the length and balance of scenes.[4] Maslon also loved the play, but he expressed a feeling shared by many first-time readers or students of McCarthy as he claimed that it "frightened me in a way. The language was intimidating." Maslon is not alone here, as we shall see that other critics also refer to another of the play's problematic hybrids, namely the fusion of profoundly beautiful prose with sermon-like rhetoric and exact naturalistic exchanges.[5] Other stylistic and structural problems soon became apparent as the "two Ben" strategy was "contextually dysfunctional" when staged, the actors involved in the workshop felt that there wasn't enough "there" in their characters, and, according to Maslon, the play's "naturalistic-novelistic-cinematic framework" made those involved realize "that, in some ways, this was not a play meant for the professional theater." These problems were compounded by the fact that McCarthy was unable or unwilling to quickly change or revise lines; literary

---

[3] Arnold, "Cormac McCarthy's *The Stonemason*," 142.
[4] Ibid., 144.
[5] Ibid.

perfectionism is suited to the drawn-out process of novelistic construction, but not for theater workshoping where spontaneity and improvisation is often required.[6]

Attempts to stage the play were also beset by problems of an ideological nature. Because the Telfairs were black, the actors in the company "assumed they were dealing with an unproduced young black playwright" and problems began to surface when an African American woman, a member of the theater's staff, walked out of rehearsals.[7] Wager then received two letters in quick succession from African American women who objected to "the racial stereotypes they perceived in the play," finding the language beautiful but lacking authenticity, whilst they also objected to the deaths of Big Ben and Soldier.[8] Quite understandably, Wager and the other key players were unwilling to become embroiled in a potentially ugly ideological stand-off, so these complaints, coupled with the emerging and seemingly intractable staging difficulties, meant that the production was never actually completed.

The management of the Arena Stage actually returned the grant to the Kennedy Center in a gesture that, although not unprecedented, according to Arnold "seemed unusually political."[9] Although a contributory factor to the aborted effort to stage the play, it is perhaps tempting to overstate the ideological problems the theater encountered; indeed, Maslon expressed concerns about the commercial viability of the play, believing its appeal would have been more intellectual than populist. With hindsight, the aesthetic merits override

---

[6] Ibid., 146-48.
[7] Ibid., 144.
[8] Arnold, "Cormac McCarthy's *The Stonemason*," 148-49.
[9] Ibid., 149.

its ideological problems, and Arnold is quite correct when he states that "the accusation of racial insensitivity seems essentially unwarranted" (especially considering the fact that McCarthy lived with an African American family of laborers for several months as part of his research for the play) and that the "Telfairs' race is far less important than their humanity."[10]

Until recently McCarthy has been reticent to grant interviews or to reveal much about his artistic process and philosophy, which makes Arnold's essay invaluable for the revelations about McCarthy that it provides. One of the most revealing anecdotes is provided by Wager, who recounts the train ride he took with McCarthy from Washington to New York as they were traveling to the awards ceremony for the Kennedy Prize. Wager told Arnold that McCarthy was an exemplary conversationalist, and Wager saw "many similarities between the trade of stonemasonry in the play and McCarthy's attitude to his own writing." Indeed, McCarthy's comments about the importance and function of narrative itself as an ordering principle—perhaps even as an empowering and humanizing act—provide us with one of the most important commentaries on his work that has been derived from McCarthy himself:

> We had a three-hour conversation on the way to New York on Hegel and the nature of narrative. It came out of nowhere. He talked about how narrative is basic to all human beings, how even people who are buried alive go over their life stories to stay sane. Verification of one's story to someone else is essential to living, he said; our reality comes out of the narrative we create, not out of

---

[10] Ibid., 153.

> the experiences themselves ... He has this tremendous ability to synthesize across disciplines.[11]

Wager's comments, along with Arnold's insightful analysis of the play, enable us to situate *The Stonemason* within McCarthy's body of work, to see how it speaks and relates to the other texts. For Arnold, the lengthy italicized passage/stage direction which opens the play provides vital structural clues as to how the drama will play out, but it is also another instance of judgment in McCarthy's work as it "causes the *reader*, if not the viewing audience, to question Ben's reasons from the beginning, to act as 'jury' during the play."[12] Arnold also acknowledges the role that patriarchal conflict plays, claiming that "nowhere is this sad conflict and misunderstanding so clearly delineated as in this drama," a conflict enriched with the biblical connotations (especially Papaw's practice to use only unhewn stone) that McCarthy uses throughout.[13]

Arnold sees Ben as something of a tragic character who eventually learns that "righteousness can become self-righteousness and intense vision a form of willful blindness," whilst he also reads McCarthy's discussion of Hegel as illuminating "the seriousness in which he holds his own craftsmanship in writing."[14] Arnold goes on to offer a thematic reading of the play that manages to identify its relationship with other McCarthy works, acknowledging how it can also be read as a metaphorical commentary on his own craft:

> Thematically it addresses the question of moral choice, familial responsibility, dedication to craft, and the work-

---

[11] Ibid., 145.
[12] Ibid., 151.
[13] Ibid., 153.
[14] Ibid., 143, 152.

ings of fate found in most of McCarthy's writings. It is, in fact, tempting to read the play as a gloss on McCarthy as writer. Certainly it is a celebration of art and the artist ... True masonry, and by extension, true art, is holy, ultimately derived from the spiritual.[15]

Arnold concludes by claiming that *The Stonemason* is "McCarthy's most clearly religious work" and that it comes closer to *All the Pretty Horses* and *The Crossing* in philosophical and theological terms than the earlier books. Arnold's essay is an invaluable resource for allowing us to see the structural and ideological problems involved in the aborted attempt to stage the play, and he also offers some insightful commentary about the play and its intertextual relationship to other works by McCarthy. Indeed, Arnold sees a great deal of aesthetic merit in *The Stonemason*, claiming that it "deserves to be read and studied and performed" and that "this play may someday be seen as the moral touchstone of his work."[16]

Peter Josyph's articles on McCarthy are written in a style that is fluent, erudite, engaging, and imbued with a sophisticated sense of irony and good humor; indeed, they are as hybrid in nature as the work of the writer he is critiquing. In "Older Professions: The Fourth Wall of *The Stonemason*," Josyph has produced an essay that can be read as a critique of the play itself, an inquiry into the nature of art and its relationship to reading and criticism and, partly, it also serves as a travelogue of Paris, with Josyph as our flâneur with a fetish for stone and the stonemason's craft. Josyph also manages to humorously puncture McCarthy's aura, and he shares many readers'

---

[15] Ibid., 152.
[16] Ibid., 153.

(and indeed Larry Maslon's fears) about the ponderously pretentious nature of his style.

Josyph starts his essay by briefly sketching the rather less-than-glorious history of novelists attempting to become playwrights. He observes: "That Cormac McCarthy's first published play, *The Stonemason*, is a failure places him even more securely in the tradition of great novelists."[17] Josyph identifies a series of flaws with the text as a piece of dramatic fiction, and chief amongst them is the fact that McCarthy remains a novelist and not a playwright as he fails to let his "players play," as he "persistent[ly] call[s] for novelistic detail," which undermines everything, and as he creates characters whose depth and complexity do not match up with the depth and complexity of the plot and theme; as a result, in "a house full of flammable materials, nothing combusts."[18]

Josyph offers some insightful analysis about the unavoidable logistical and structural problems one would have to overcome in order to make a successful production of the play. Josyph notes that a willing producer would need "more than faith to mount *The Stonemason*. He would need a bloody fortune, the world's widest stage, and a team of weightlifters," whilst he also notes than an author who is renowned for his startling depictions of landscape has opted instead for clutter when he switches genres.[19] The double-Ben strategy also causes a seemingly insurmountable problem if anyone were to attempt to stage the play, as Josyph argues that McCarthy "misses the fundamental fact that in theater, no matter what you do, *every-*

---

[17] Josyph, "Older Professions," 119.
[18] Ibid., 122, 127.
[19] Ibid., 121-22.

thing is happening in the present because the audience is sitting there in front of you."[20]

Josyph talks about how the play wears him down due to its ponderous nature, especially Ben's monologues; indeed, another of the subtle ironies of the play is that Ben repeatedly speaks about the craft of stonemasonry, of how it is a force which holds his world together, yet he is completely blind to the forces tearing his *family* structure apart. Josyph contends that Ben may have been able to fix things if he'd spent a little less time theorizing in his monologues and more time actually talking to those around him. Far from being some kind of essential moral, social, and intellectual glue, the craft of stonemasonry ultimately undermines Ben, and Josyph notes that he "is so sullen, so truculent over *the* trade that no joy of stone is communicated," noting that "Ben's teleology for his profession … is positively medieval" and that although he is not "the first man to make a religion out of his job … he is one of the most obnoxious" to do so.[21] In one of the essay's more irreverent moments, Josyph expresses sympathy for Soldier as he feels that he too would have "been driven to shooting dope" if he had had to listen to Ben.[22]

The biggest problem for Josyph is that Ben is "less a character than a McCarthy sound-off," a major problem considering how much he dominates the text, resulting in the play having about it the "sense of an illustrated lecture."[23] The dramatic impact of the play loses out to Ben's relentless moralizing and sermonizing from (quite literally) his pulpit, as "this sermonizer so monopolizes the stage …

---

[20] Ibid., 122.
[21] Ibid., 126, 124.
[22] Ibid., 128.
[23] Ibid., 128, 123.

he keeps the action off it." For Josyph, Ben represents "McCarthy's prose voice at its most misguided and misplaced," imbuing the play with an instructional rather than a dramatic sensibility.[24] Indeed, Ben's sermonizing dominates the play to such an extent that the patriarchal conflict explored in the play—that foundational McCarthy theme—is nowhere near as powerful as in his other works: "the father-son relationship, even the lack of such a relationship, is sketched too sparsely to mean much at all and there is little to suggest that an improvement in relations might have spared Big Ben his suicide."[25]

Wade Hall also sees McCarthy's use of "the stage as a lecture hall" as one of the play's greatest flaws. Despite its didactic elements, the play has universal appeal for Hall due to McCarthy's skillful depiction of the Telfairs, a family who represents the "archetypal family—indeed the human family—of mixed ambition and achievement. It is also a black family that comes on stage with the added burdens of slavery and discrimination."[26] Ironically, Hall notes how the play also links McCarthy with Henry James, another writer whose talent "does not easily transfer to the stage. *The Stonemason* is nonetheless worth reading as a closet drama for its insights into the mind of its author."[27] Like Arnold, Hall identifies many parallels between the play and *The Crossing,* the second installment of the Border Trilogy which was also published in 1994, especially in terms of their treatment of philosophy and theology. Both works also contain some of the most sophisticated contemplations about the importance of nar-

---

[24] Ibid., 124.
[25] Ibid., 130.
[26] Hall, "The Hero as Philosopher," 189-90.
[27] Ibid., 189.

rative in McCarthy's work, one of the most significant components of his aesthetic.[28]

Although he sees much to admire in the play, John Cant insightfully writes about the burdens that author, characters, and readers encounter upon their dealings with the text. There is the burdensome structure and logistics for potential actors, the burden of patriarchal culture and false mythologies the characters have to deal with, and the burden of Ben's rhetoric that readers have to put up with. Cant adds his voice to those critics who have noted that the play's structure is also problematic, as "the dual structure means the drama cannot come to life" as it "undermines the relationship between characters and audience" and that the involved stage directions "challenge the practical limits of the form."[29] Cant also feels that the ideological aspects of the play can be overstated. Although the Telfairs are black (Cant also remarks upon the significance of their name, Tell-fair), the "play is not about race," as the characters are representative figures, like the mythic archetypes to be found throughout McCarthy's work.[30]

Cant sees the Telfairs as another group of McCarthy characters who are informed and seduced by a mythology that is ultimately destructive. The family especially struggles with the patriarchal theme as each successive generation "rejects the values of the father and reacts against patriarchal power. In each case the result is destructive," especially in McCarthy's configuration of the theme where "maleness

---

[28] Ibid., 194. Also see Jarrett's *Cormac McCarthy*, 143-46, for a brief comparative discussion of *The Stonemason* and *The Crossing*.

[29] Cant, *Cormac McCarthy and the Myth of American Exceptionalism*, 123-24.

[30] Ibid., 125.

is about power" and is, therefore, unavoidably destructive.[31] Ben's status as a conventionally tragic character is confirmed by the fact that he "remains unaware of the role of the old man's apparent perfection has had in the tragedy of all their lives," and his greatest weakness is that he has bought into the "patriarchal myth of the provident father as all knowing and all wise"[32] Families often play a significant part in McCarthy due to their absence, but it is the one-hundred-years-plus *presence* of Papaw that means that every member of the Telfair clan suffers from a kind of blindness, and with this they represent "the archetypal American family [who struggles] under the burden of the deeds and values of its own mythic patriarchs."[33]

Ben's faith in the practice and craft of masonry, the very thing which he claims makes him see, know, and understand things others can't, is ultimately revealed to be another false myth, another problematic system of belief. Ben's and the Telfairs' entire experience has been structured around the choice of whether to adhere to or rebel against this "false [patriarchal] mythology," and it is yet another instance in McCarthy's work where an ordering principle is revealed to be deeply problematic: "The 'happy family' and the loving father-provider are powerful aspects of America's mythology and the representation of both, presented in McCarthy's texts in general, and *The Stonemason* in particular, are essential aspects of his mythoclastic project."[34]

---

[31] Ibid., 126, 128.
[32] Ibid., 131.
[33] Ibid., 130.
[34] Ibid., 126.

The Stonemason is a characteristically complex McCarthy text, but it is one that is also fundamentally flawed, especially when it comes to its viability for dramatic performance. The hybridity that is such a strength in his novels proves to be a fatal weakness here. Some critics, especially Peter Josyph, claim that its status as a play is undermined because McCarthy remains a novelist and doesn't become a playwright—and not only does he remain a novelist, but a sermonizing one at that. But we shouldn't let the structural and stylistic issues cloud the fact that the play remains a powerful piece of work and that it serves a valuable purpose as a commentary on McCarthy's aesthetic, especially as indicated by the incisive commentaries offered by Jeffrey and Mary Weaver. A reading of *The Stonemason* enriches our understanding of the texts which both preceded and followed it, and it is hard to disagree with Edwin Arnold's assertion that the play may well come to be seen as the "moral touchstone" to McCarthy's work.

CHAPTER 9

The Gardener's Son

Despite being a slim volume that represents McCarthy's first venture into the world of screenwriting, *The Gardener's Son* is a characteristically multifaceted and complex work. Although McCarthy switches genres his thematic and stylistic interests remain familiar, as all the classic McCarthy motifs are dealt with: first, he once again refuses to grant his readers access into the interior landscapes of his characters. Then, in Robert McEvoy, we have another of his anguished outsiders; the narrative of the McEvoy and Gregg families allows him to critique the evolving ideologies of American culture, especially those of the New South. As in most of McCarthy's work, death is a palpable, grotesque presence, and the drama hinges on one violent deed. Further, it is a historical drama, but the omniscient authorial voice encourages readers to think about how we *think* about history, who tells it, and how our historical consciousness and sense of the past is shaped. We even have a legal drama in which the voice of the powerless defendant is silenced by a controlling hegemonic power.

We can find numerous parallels to his other works here as well. The action makes sudden jumps forward and backward in time, with little information given to explain such temporal jolts. A succession of marginal characters—at times they are even unnamed and unidentified—impart philosophical insights about the dark, secretive workings of the world which seem at odds with their down-home and folksy personas. The drama is intensely associated to a particular place (in this instance the South Carolina mill town of Graniteville), yet it resonates (thematically and metaphysically) far beyond the familiar as McCarthy explores the relationship between cultural and individual narrative, memory, and storytelling and official and unofficial history. This is perhaps the most important theme explored in *The Gardener's Son,* and McCarthy uses the text to suggest that fiction may well present a more inclusive and comprehensive account than "official" history ever can.

Like many of his characters, McCarthy has often seemed to be something of an outsider in terms of his relationship to contemporary developments in literary and intellectual life. His work seems to have more in common with the complex work of the high modernists than with the ironic, highly self-conscious and self-reflexive offerings of some postmodern authors. However, it is useful at this juncture to turn to Michel Foucault, a figure who has made an immeasurable contribution to contemporary intellectual and philosophical movements that have heavily influenced the way we talk about literature and culture. Foucault stresses that it is vitally important that we analyze:

> the full range of hidden mechanisms through which a society conveys its knowledge and ensures its survival under the mask of knowledge; newspapers, television, technical schools, and the high school … In every society the production of discourse is at once controlled, selected, organized and redistributed according to a certain number of procedures *including rules of exclusion.* [emphasis mine][1]

---

[1] Quoted in Best and Kellner, *Postmodern Theory: Critical Interrogations,* 23.

McCarthy has consistently focused on the exploits of what John Cant calls "ardenthearted" protagonists who work against the prevailing culture and ideology of their time. However, this theme is more pronounced in *The Gardener's Son* because of its status as a historical work. Quite deliberately, McCarthy takes us to the world of Graniteville in the 1870s to show how "the hidden mechanisms" (controlled by the Greggs) produced knowledge and discourse (in this case monuments, artifacts, and official, documented historical records) in order to produce "rules of exclusion" (in effect, the legal brokering which meant that Robert McEvoy could not testify during his trial) to ensure that their good "name" and reputation was not damaged by lurid details of James Greggs's predatory sexual advances seeing the light of day, thereby corrupting a legal process that is far from just and objective.

McCarthy structures the narrative around a murder in the South Carolina mill town of Graniteville in the 1870s. The town owed its existence to the utopian vision of William Gregg, a philanthropic industrialist who ensured that, aside from the mill, he provided adequate housing, schools, and agrarian spaces for his workers. The McEvoys are the other family at the heart of the drama, and their move to the town and subsequent struggle to adapt to their new life is representative of the narratives of displacement experienced by thousands of Appalachian families during this period. William Gregg dies at an early stage of the narrative and is succeeded by his son James Gregg, who replaces his father's benevolence with the aggressive and acquisitive creed that prevailed in the South and the rest of the nation at the time.

The oedipal conflict between fathers and sons drives the narrative. Robert McEvoy is the other son involved here, and he offers a bold contrast to James; Robert is unsettled and alienated, and he is plagued by the same sense of existential homelessness experienced by other McCarthy characters. At the opening of the narrative his leg is amputated and the anger generated by this symbolic castration—authorized and witnessed by Mrs. Gregg and the doctor the Greggs employ—is accentuated as he witnesses his father (Patrick McEvoy) becoming increasingly disempowered. Like Marion Sylder, he spends a brief and unsuccessful period employed by the mill before he leaves Graniteville and heads out on the road. He returns two years later after being summoned by his sister who informs him of his mother's poor health; however, she is dead by the time he returns, and the first people he encounters are two grave diggers preparing a space for his mother's corpse. For much of the text, Robert undertakes a doomed quest to honor his mother's wish that she be buried "back home" on the family farm and not in the company-owned graveyard. Robert seeks out but symbolically never finds his father, although he does find temporary solace in Graniteville's well-hidden drinking establishments prior to his explosive (and fatal) encounter with James Gregg. During their showdown he reveals his anger at everything Gregg represents, especially his lascivious advances to Martha, Robert's sister. The machinations of the legal system and the power wielded by the Greggs mean that he is silenced during the trial, and his execution is inevitable; even a visit made by Martha McEvoy, a shrewd and sympathetic character, to Mrs. Gregg cannot alter things, and their exchange reveals a great deal about the class and cultural biases at play here.

The screenplay closes with a visit paid to Martha (who by this point is in the state insane asylum, another legally sanctioned outsider in McCarthy's work) by William Chaffee, the grandson of the Greggs, who we learn was the unidentified young man with whom the timekeeper converses at the opening of the narrative. It seems that Chaffee has not been satisfied by the "official" history of his family, and he turns to Martha for the voice that has been absented, even if she remains one of the excluded in the state institution, still marked out as something of a danger perhaps to the production of "official" knowledge and discourse.

It should be noted at this point that all references to *The Gardener's Son* will be from the 1996 Ecco Press edition. I was fortunate enough to view the screenplay at a conference hosted by the Cormac McCarthy Society, but a single viewing does not lend itself to sustained analysis. The screenplay also came about at an interesting juncture in McCarthy's career, and it demonstrates how skillfully he manipulates historical narratives into his own aesthetic, something he would do at a later stage—and to much critical acclaim—with *Blood Meridian*. The screenplay was written between 1975-76 whilst he was completing *Suttree*, and it was aired on TV in January 1977. McCarthy was approached by the director Richard Pearce to write the screenplay, and the two spent an intensive period of time researching and visiting Graniteville whilst collaboratively working on the project; indeed, Pearce authored a series of research newsletters during this period that documented the progress of the project.[2]

We also know that McCarthy consulted Broadus Mitchell's biography *William Gregg, Factory Master of the Old South* where McCarthy came across the "official" treatment of the Gregg family and James's murder by Robert McEvoy. Mitchell's tone and approach to his subject is as obsequious as that of the speaker who offers the eulogy at Gregg's funeral in the screenplay, and Mitchell portrays him as "the father of Graniteville" (and, according to Mitchell, the father of Southern cotton manufacturing) who was "capable of sustained

---

[2] Luce, "'They aint the thing,'" 29.

exertion of mind and body without exhaustion."[3] The sycophantic tone continues as Mitchell portrays Gregg in the following angelic light:

> Those who knew him spoke of his double virtue of logic and humor ... Living in a period of extraordinary controversy, sectional self-righteousness and bitterness, in which men were flying off on tangents, he kept his balance. There was a spiritual quality about Gregg, which showed in his face; his love of his fellows put him at peace with himself, and this gave a harmony to all he did.[4]

Although Mitchell offers no in-depth analysis of James Gregg, he does provide an account of his murder and the nature of his relationship with Robert McEvoy. Interestingly, Mitchell spells Robert's last name incorrectly (he spells it McAvoy) in what is an extremely sloppy and dismissive gesture. Perhaps unintentionally, Mitchell succeeds in mythologizing Gregg Senior *and* Robert, casting the latter as the "bad boy" of the village who, even after the amputation, remained "remarkably dexterous. He would go hunting all day through the swamps, and could climb a tree like a cat."[5] Although Mitchell quite literally relegates Robert to the footnotes of his official history, he imbues him with some mythical and other-worldly characteristics that mark him as a very McCarthyesque character. McCarthy therefore rescues this "bad boy" from the footnotes of history and places his narrative on center stage.

The Gardener's Son gives us a history of those subjected to "the rules of exclusion" Foucault identifies, and the chief theme of the

---

[3] Mitchell, *William Gregg*, 6.
[4] Ibid., 7.
[5] Ibid., 328.

screenplay concerns the production of historical knowledge and the relationship between our past and our ability to tell or narrate it. The theme is pronounced from the outset of the screenplay where the mythically named timekeeper informs the young man (who by the end we know to be William Chaffee) that "once you copy something down you dont have it any more ... Times past are fugitive" (TGS 5). Memory, therefore, is as "fugitive" as Robert McEvoy was during his own time, and the screenplay gives him the humanizing agency of narrative that was denied him in his own life.

After this characteristically cryptic opening, we find a lengthy italicized passage in which we can most clearly see McCarthy's authorial presence and textual design. The exchange between the young man and the timekeeper frames the opening of the screenplay, and another framing device is represented with the opening italicized passage as it begins with a *"series of old still shots of the town"* that have *"the look of old sepia photographs ... They comprise an overture to the story to follow"* (TGS 5). Thus it can be seen that the screenplay opens with the most prominent theme, which is the conflict between "official" historical consciousness and individual memory and how any kind of authentic testimony is absent from official documents or mechanized reproductions (such as photographs) of the people involved.

There is also a significant scene involving photographs prior to Robert's execution which contributes to the historical "framing" of Robert as the community's sanctioned outlaw and badman. The photographer gets Robert to pose against a backdrop of Greek columns, which could well present the supposed gnostic or pastorally conceived civic order that the Greggs hoped would prevail in Graniteville; Robert, much like Lester Ballard from *Child of God*, is therefore framed as everything that the community isn't, the officially sanctioned scapegoat. The photographer spuriously claims that the money raised from the photographs may help out his family but the real commercial gain will be his, whilst the image itself acts as another artifact of the official historical discourse produced for the Greggs. As an aside it should be noted that Robert is extremely polite in this scene, whilst the guard who is in attendance calls him Bob, hinting at a degree of affection—and perhaps even sympathy—for Robert's plight (TGS 77-79).

In the concluding scene between Martha and Chafee, the photograph is a source of sorrow rather than consolation for Martha. She tells Chaffee that "a person's memory serves better. Sometimes I can almost talk to him. I caint see him no more. In my mind. I just see this old pitcher" (TGS 93). Martha champions individual memory and narrative over "officially" documented history and mechanized reproductions that are anything but objective portrayals. Her account allows Chaffee to fulfill his own search for a genuine historical narrative whilst it also provokes us into analyzing how we develop historical memory or consciousness.

Robert McEvoy is perhaps the most recognizable McCarthy character in the screenplay, and he shares a number of characteristics with many of McCarthy's other protagonists. He is as stoic and loyal (perhaps misguidedly so) as Marion Sylder and John Wesley Rattner. He is made the scapegoat of the community as is Lester Ballard. Like Suttree, he is plagued by a sense of existential alienation or homelessness in the world. The screenplay is as multifaceted as McCarthy's other works in that it is undoubtedly Robert's narrative, but on a more philosophically profound level it can also be read as McCarthy's attempt to rescue all of the Robert McEvoys who are absented from historical discourses.

In our first encounter with Robert, he displays his defiant and anti-authoritarian attitude, even if such gestures will ultimately prove futile. Mrs. Gregg views his wound and summons Dr. Perceval to amputate his leg despite Robert's fiercely stated preference that he would rather be dead than crippled (TGS 15). Mrs. Gregg's will prevails, and his leg is amputated and, symbolically, so is something of his will, his view of the world. The theme of castration or emasculation plagues the McEvoys from this scene onwards, as his father especially becomes increasingly disempowered as the narrative develops.

It seems that Robert has always been angered by the world of Graniteville, and he is perceptive enough to see how the supposed philanthropy of William Gregg actually traps the workers, including his own family, into a harsh life which has limited room for genuine improvement. As we shall see, although it may seem as if James Gregg has betrayed his father's legacy, he may actually be less of a hypocrite in that he has abandoned any philanthropic pretensions in exchange for profits and commercial advancement, which was, after all, at the heart of his father's enterprise. Thus an element of class antagonism drives Robert's anger, as does the developing oedipal conflict with his father and his attempt to defend his sister's honor; all of these factors make a significant contribution to Robert's motivation for shooting James.

Despite their strained relationship, Robert's father, Patrick, provides a reading of his son that is hard to disagree with. He claims that Robert has "infidel ways" (GS 30), mainly due to his predilection for spending time outside (which should not surprise the serious McCarthy reader, as many of his characters display this penchant to be undomesticated), especially in the caves under Graniteville, and for teasing Maryellen about the cow and the family farm (thereby suggesting that they had another life or history which their current situation obscures). However, his father displays no deep-seated antagonism towards Robert, and he reveals an element of his character that gets to the heart of many of McCarthy's chief protagonists: "He's just got a troubled heart and they dont nobody know why" (TGS 31). Whilst the official historical record most certainly frames him as a villain, McCarthy's narrative portrays him in a much more favorable light, and such a view is confirmed by one of the peripheral African American characters Robert meets whilst searching for his father upon his return to the town. The unnamed character calls after him, "I know your heart is full," thereby confirming Robert's essential "ardenthearted" goodness in a phrase that parallels Ab Jones's declaration of fondness for Suttree (TGS 44).

The advice imparted by the unidentified black is done so after Robert returns to Graniteville after an absence of two years. The authorial voice confirms the length of the absence even if it doesn't tell us exactly where he has been or what he has endured. When pressed on this subject in *an old barn used as a doggery for drinkers and cardplayers*," one of the drinkers labeled First Man asks, "[I] reckon you seen a right smart of the world since you left out of here." Robert replies with an uninformative "some" (TGS 46, 48-9). We do know that he has been summoned back to Graniteville by his sister Martha, who has informed him of their mother's poor health, although his mother has died by the time he gets back. His first act upon his return is to try to honor his mother's wishes that she be buried in her family homestead in Pickens and *not* in the graveyard owned by the mill since "she dont belong to the mill" (TGS 35), as he bluntly informs the gravediggers preparing his mother's grave. (These are the first people he meets upon his return.) A parallel can be made here between the McEvoys and the Bundrens in Faulkner's *As I Lay Dying*, who also attempt to honor their matriarch's dying wish to be buried at home, and grotesque motifs operate in both texts. Burials are never straightforward affairs in McCarthy's work, and Robert's desire to ensure that his mother is returned home is somewhat ironic, given the perpetual state of homelessness that he himself seems blighted by. His own death and burial proves just as problematic, as he is placed in "just a nameless grave somewheres" since his father fears that somebody would want to "take it and study it" (TGS 91).

Robert possesses a natural intelligence that allows him recognize his existential homelessness in the world *and* the failing of the community to speak out and defend him at a moment that could save his life; both factors ultimately combine to ensure that he remains a tragically isolated figure. We see this in one of his final exchanges with Martha where we get a rare glimpse of Bobby's interior processes as he claims that he "could have been somebody" in rhetoric that evokes Marlon Brando's similarly rueful declaration in *On the Waterfront* (TGS 80). He also rails against the community members who failed to come to his defense, claiming that they "knew what he [James Gregg] was … They was not one would stand up and…" (TGS 81). Robert never got to finish this sentence, as the ellipses indicate, and McCarthy's text fills this historical gap. It becomes clear that James Gregg was a sexual predator who, as the text intimates, made countless inappropriate sexual advances to mill employees, including Martha Gregg.

The narratives of the two families from different ends of the social spectrum allow McCarthy to continue his critique of the American historical experience; in this instance, it is the New South emerging during Reconstruction and on the cusp of the Gilded Age. However, he subjects both industrial and agrarian myths to a harsh critique, and *The Gardener's Son* suggests that neither exclusively offered a valid social or cultural model. The McEvoys are inexorably caught up in the enforced pattern of migration from mountain farms to industrial mill towns that characterized this period of Appalachian history, whereas the change in the Greggs' management ethos from a civically minded philanthropic benevolence to an overt and aggressive concern for balance sheets and profits reveals the epochal nature of change that Southern communities such as Graniteville experienced during this period. *The Gardener's Son* can be read as a work that is in keeping with McCarthy's own Appalachian discourse, an imaginative project aimed at giving a voice to those individuals and groups who were absented and silenced by official records; the McEvoys can therefore be viewed as an archetypal family, as their experience is representative of a much broader socioeconomic process. The epochal changes taking place during the time of the screenplay's setting are of great significance, as noted by the Appalachian historian Ronald D. Eller:

> Uprooted from their traditional way of life, some individuals were unable to reestablish permanent community ties, and they became wanderers drifting from mill to mill, from company house to company house, in search of higher pay or better living conditions. Most dreamt initially of returning to the land after a few years of public work, but the rising land values that accompanied industrial development soon pushed land ownership beyond the reach of the average miner or millhand.[6]

William Gregg, the founding father of Graniteville and James's biological father, is portrayed as a figure that puts the wealth of the

---

[6] Eller, *Miners, Millhands and Mountaineers*, xxii.

community if not ahead of, then at least equal to, his own personal financial advancement. William Gregg does not physically inhabit the text for long as he is dying at the opening of the screenplay, and Dr. Perceval confirms this by stating to Mrs. Gregg that "he's beyond my or any man's practice" (TGS 9), but his shadow looms large over the rest of the narrative. The unidentified speaker who eulogizes William Gregg confirms his iconic status in the community, and the speaker portrays him as the embodiment of Puritan values of hardwork and self-discipline: "William Gregg was all his life an example of the virtue of hard work ... By force of his own character, by the habits of energy and industry and perseverance" (TGS 18).

The speaker who offers the eulogy draws our attention to the manner in which Gregg was able to realize his utopian dreams in Graniteville, especially with his success in fusing the agrarian with the industrial. It seems that Gregg Senior was blessed with a vision entirely lacking in the indigenous population and that it was only his drive and tenacious perseverance which rescued those he employed from a squalid, poverty-ridden existence:

> There are many among us today who can remember what life held in the way of promise before this man came among us. Too many of us were raised in hunger and poverty to ever forget. To see what he has wrought, the neat homes, the churches and schools, the gardens and the lovely grounds and last but not least the massive factory structure with its beautiful and perfect machinery, these things seem created almost by magic. (TGS 19)

The official record offered here by the eulogizer would suggest that the workers of Graniteville were immeasurably better off due to his altruistic efforts, even though the experience of the McEvoys and that endured by hundreds of families during this period of tumultuous socioeconomic change stands as a corrective to the given historical narrative. Patrick McEvoy is initially given a role as close to the naturally agrarian as he'll find here, even if it is in the somewhat artificial environment of the greenhouse where he pots his plants and attends to the flowers (TGS 31). His fate—as he moves from the greenhouse to the dehumanizing machine, from cultivator to commodity, and the rotting of the flowers and the subsequent decay of the greenhouse (TGS 39)—is one of the most significant metaphors at play within the text.

We learn something of his history prior to his family's arrival in Graniteville, as they "tried to stay on at home after the war but they wasnt no way. I wanted the children to have somethin. If I could have foresaw my life as it's become. I would rather to of been dead than this" (TGS 67-8). McCarthy successfully reveals how the McEvoys are therefore denied two versions of myths that are deeply embedded in American culture, namely the dream of a simple yet fulfilling agrarian existence and the dream of material wealth that was promised (by flyers distributed by the Greggs no less, although they were not alone in this) with the move from country to town. He and his family are as commodified and used-up as the peaches they once farmed (TGS 89), as McCarthy symbolically reveals how both modes of existence (the agrarian and the industrial) are just as exploitative and that there really is very little use in romanticizing a pastoral life that was anything but idyllic. In a typical McCarthy move, it is left to a peripheral character to reveal the melancholy of the situation, as the Old Man informs Robert: "Not big on gardens here no more. Gardens always the first thing to go" (TGS 41).

One of the main contributory factors to this change in philosophy and the loss of any attempts of beautification, no matter how hollow, is ushered in with the stewardship of James Gregg, the only male heir. Where his father was concerned with philanthropy and benevolent gestures, James is driven by a desire for increased performance and higher profit margins; where his father had a caring, paternalistic attitude towards his employees, James displays class-based snobbishness, cynicism, and overt contempt. This is memorably captured in the scene where the ragged man and his family come to the factory after seeing a handbill that promised them "a sealed house and a garden patch" (TGS 22). James claims that this handbill is four years old, and he reluctantly sends them on to the church with instructions for Mrs. Cornish that "some of God's seed has fallen on barren ground" (TGS 24). This is another indication that charity and compassion are found in the church, not in the company, as perhaps was once the case.

It is with his lecherous and inappropriate advances towards Martha where James Gregg reveals his true character. The screenplay suggests that James was renowned for making such sexual advances, a fact confirmed when Robert is searching for his father, and Pinky informs him that the "only way to get ahead down there is to get your wife knocked up by the boss. Give ye a little leverage" (TGS 48). The community's failure to speak out about such transgressions ultimately plays a big part in condemning Robert, and his knowledge of James Gregg's actions justifies the shooting to an extent. Whilst his confrontation with James is partly a defense of his sister's honor, we should note that Martha displays characteristic shrewdness and an ability to comprehend the situation she is facing in her conversation with James. McCarthy inserts "quickly" to demonstrate how rapidly she responds to his offer of a cigar, and she says that she'll "take one to my daddy if you're passin em out" (TGS 27). He teases her by saying that "I bet you'd be just a handful" (TGS 26), with "handful" suggesting here a certain sexual energy that he would like to manage and "own," as he owns the working and social lives of the employees of Graniteville. The fact that he views Martha's sexuality as another thing to be owned and commodified is revealed when he attempts to entice her with a cigar and money (a $10 coin, a considerable sum for her) before "*the full implication of the money strikes her and she looks at James Gregg with an expression partly of disdain but mostly she is just afraid*" (TGS 28). One can only wonder how many times Gregg has tried this before and how many times he has succeeded; if we recall Pinky's advice to Robert, it would suggest that this ploy has worked on numerous occasions on women less shrewd than Martha.

Thus, prior to his fatal confrontation with Gregg, it is clear that Robert is motivated to confront him about the sexual advances he had made towards his sister and about the emasculation of his father, and his anger and long-held resentment about the hegemonic power which the Greggs possess comes to the fore here. Robert asks about the decay of the garden, to which Gregg answers that "we have stockholders to answer to. We're not in the flower business" (TGS 53), revealing the extent to which he has abandoned his father's vision in favor of profits and satisfying the whims of abstract (and absent) finance capitalists. His contempt is revealed when he informs Robert that "we dont need *your kind* here" (emphasis mine, TGS 54), and it is ironic that, prior to the shooting, James Gregg offers Robert exactly the same kind of financial incentive he offered Martha, although his previous success in buying silence will not work here.

It is interesting to note that by the end of the screenplay Mrs. Gregg's way of thinking is more in line with her son's than her husband's, and whilst she stops short of mocking her husband's utopian vision she claims that "my son was right about *you* people ... He used to make fun of my husband's idealism" (emphasis mine,

TGS 76). Through Mrs. Gregg, McCarthy also subtly critiques the changing economic landscape taking hold of the South, since by the drama's end she states that "the directors will take over the mill now. There are always these strangers waiting for those who cannot set their house in order" (TGS 71). These "strangers" are the faceless agents of a robust, acquisitive, and aggressive finance capitalism who revolutionized the economy of the South and whose role in the region would generate considerable chagrin from a group such as the Nashville Agrarians in the opening decades of the twentieth century. Mrs. Gregg reveals how such a change was inevitable, and her own act of empty defiance comes when she oversees the exhumation of the bodies of the dead members of her family as they are moved to Charleston.

McCarthy's characters always struggle when they are forced to follow regulations and bureaucracy, and this is no different in *The Gardener's Son*. We have noted how significant it is that Robert is denied his own narrative and that it is replaced by the formal and cumbersome nature of legal discourse and language; note how the Prosecuting Attorney's summation of the case, with its extensive use of archaically formal terms such as "aforesaid" (TGS 59-60), could never hope to capture the essence of Robert or the true nature of the case. There is also the somewhat farcical scene following his execution where the pressure to conform to bureaucratic requirements obscures the obvious injustice that has been done here, as the doctor and the sheriff quibble about the best way to complete the death certificate (TGS 85-6).

We have attempted to stress in our discussion of *The Gardener's Son* that it is a characteristically multifaceted McCarthy text and that it manages to be a compelling historical drama whilst it also succeeds in asking profound questions about how we acquire historical knowledge. McCarthy's treatment of the changing nature of race relations in the South contributes to this, and the epochal changes that beset the community in the screenplay hint at the upheaval such Southern communities were facing. In the tumultuous period of Reconstruction, we find that Robert is defended by a black lawyer and judged by a black jury and Whipper, his attorney, muses about the nature of justice to an anguished Patrick McEvoy, reminding him of a level of suffering and exclusion that transcends his own (TGS 67). Whilst Robert undoubtedly suffered unjustly here, McCarthy also reminds us that African Americans have also been subject to exclusion from official historical discourses, and the denial of such knowledge is more widespread than we would perhaps like to acknowledge.

Overview of Critical Responses

Despite being a characteristically complex text which in terms of thematic scope comfortably ranks alongside McCarthy's other work, *The Gardener's Son* has received relatively little critical attention. The consensus that prevails among the critics who have discussed the screenplay acknowledges McCarthy's subtle yet complex way of critiquing foundational cultural myths, his depiction of the emerging capitalist landscape of the New South, his continued use of an oedipal conflict to structure his narratives, and his attempt to encourage his readership to ask profound questions about how individual and cultural historical consciousness is formed and passed on.

Dianne Luce has produced two meticulously researched articles on the screenplay which represent very fine pieces of scholarship. In "Cormac McCarthy's First Screenplay: *The Gardener's Son*," Luce provides an account of the history of the project alongside an insightful analysis of the screenplay itself. She notes how the screenplay, "like all of McCarthy's work[,] ... functions through the interplay of finely realized concrete textures and mythic or literary allusiveness to achieve its thematic richness." Within this interplay of allusiveness and myth, Luce remarks that the title of the screenplay alludes both to Adam's sons and to Hamlet, and McCarthy succeeds in linking "its themes of physical and social corruption, fall from grace, and fratricide" and that "the corruption of the social bond ... results largely from man's inability to accept the imperfection in himself."[7]

A particularly illuminating aspect of Luce's article lies in the primary sources she analyzes. Perhaps the most significant of these primary sources is the series of "research newsletters" that the director Richard Pearce sent to the Alicia Patterson Foundation, an organization that helped to finance the project. In the first of these newsletters, Pearce gets to the very heart of the project—and we can see echoes of Pearce and McCarthy working in close collaboration here—as we learn that he wanted to explore "both sides of Graniteville's industrial revolution ... her public mythology of monuments and ceremonial heroes, and at the same time her private underworld of ghost villains and legendary characters, family histories, and photographs."[8] Robert McEvoy is the most notorious of these "ghost villains," and McCarthy and Pearce set about reclaiming his narrative from official historical records and narratives. Indeed, Luce also cites an interview McCarthy granted to the *Knoxville News Sentinel* where he expressed his admiration for Robert McEvoy in that McEvoy had a "certain nobility" which was especially represented in the stand he made against the hegemony of the Greggs and the economic and social inequities perpetuated by the system they controlled.[9]

---

[7] Luce, "Cormac McCarthy's First Screenplay," 75-78.

[8] Ibid., 74.

[9] Quoted in Luce, "Cormac McCarthy's First Screenplay," 75.

These injustices are exacerbated by the manner in which James Gregg has reneged on his father's philosophy as William Gregg was a man who, according to Luce, acted from "a profound sense of social obligation."[10] James Gregg, however, is a man who has wholeheartedly embraced the New South (and early Gilded Age) doctrine of aggressive, profit-centered industrial development.

Luce briefly considers McCarthy's use of history in the screenplay, and this critique is developed in her second article devoted to a discussion of *The Gardener's Son*. Despite the tragedy and melancholy which dominates a first reading of the screenplay, Luce makes the important point that it actually concludes with the two survivors, William Chaffee and Martha McEvoy, "an advocate of memory" who has rescued her brother Robert from the official histories of the town and given him a narrative that was denied during his life. Furthermore, even Chaffee appears to have succeeded in his quest (another to be found in the screenplay) of finding a more authentic history of his family, or at least an alternative version that he couldn't locate in the artifacts available to him. According to Luce, *The Gardener's Son* "would seem to affirm the value of memory and imagination over documentation as an avenue to reality, truth. It may also reflect the idea that documents are created by the literate and powerful and thus do not speak the whole truth."[11]

Luce's "'They aint the thing': Artifact and Hallucinated Recollection in Cormac McCarthy's Early Frame-Works" comparatively analyzes McCarthy's early short story "Wake for Susan," *The Orchard Keeper*, and *The Gardener's Son*. Luce is specifically interested how in each work McCarthy problematizes the supposed fidelity or

---

[10] Ibid., 80.
[11] Ibid., 89.

accuracy that historical or cultural artifacts have in representing the past. Luce notes how such artifacts, be they gravestones, ruins, or photographs, "both evoke the past and obscure memory, but the search to re-imagine the past is valorized."[12] This search forms a crucial feature of McCarthy's aesthetic in these three works and beyond, and it enables his otherwise tragic characters to "recover the past through the human faculties of memory and imagination."[13]

McCarthy's "ardenthearted" protagonists—or "narrator-heroes" as Luce terms them—often meet sorrowful ends, but their quests enable us to develop a more informed and sophisticated "historical imagination" or consciousness which, according to Luce, is something that McCarthy "aspired to from the beginning of his career." This challenge to our historical consciousness and to our expectations of just how much fictional texts can do characterizes McCarthy's work, as does his use of literary allusions, and Luce suggests that the literary forebear looming large here is Melville, especially his *Billy Budd*. Luce notes how both authors use "narratives that carry more authority than the appended [and therefore official] documents they unmask." Ultimately this ambitious imaginative project allows Martha and McCarthy's readership to affirm the role of "memory over artifact."[14]

Photographs are an example of an artifact which plays an incredibly important and symbolic role in the screenplay. Chaffee's search is a direct challenge to the "provoking silence of historical records," and photographs especially are used in his search as "'framing' devices which structure the narrative," according to

---

[12] Luce, "'They aint the thing,'" 21.
[13] Ibid., 29.
[14] Ibid., 32-35.

Luce.¹⁵ The photographs at the opening of the screenplay exclude rather than objectively include, and the images of Robert taken by the professional photographer prior to his execution create a false myth that McCarthy writes against. Photographs therefore distort historical truth rather than objectively capture it, as Luce explains:

> Along with the screenplay's many images of cemeteries, gravestones, and corpses, photographs take on a special weight in the leitmotif of artifacts ... Like gravestones, photographs can be mementos, but as the old Timekeeper says, 'they aint the thing.' Like the court records and histories, they are—for all their illusion of objectivity—man-made and second-hand representations.¹⁶

McCarthy explores this theme in his Southwestern works, most memorably in *The Crossing*, but perhaps the most significant contribution *The Gardener's Son* makes to McCarthy's oeuvre is the faith it expresses in the importance of narrative. McCarthy and Pearce succeed in capturing the "certain nobility" that McEvoy had, and they "sought it precisely in the artifacts and records that would deny [him] worth." Although such worth was denied him in his own life, his quest—and those of his other narrator-heroes—ensured that characters such as Martha and Chaffee could "circumvent the artifacts and records of the past to transcend obscurity, reject falsehood, and find insight."¹⁷

Douglas Canfield's "Oedipal Complexities in Cormac McCarthy's *The Stonemason* and *The Gardener's Son*" focuses on McCarthy's use

---

15 Ibid.
16 Ibid., 32-3.
17 Ibid., 35-35.

of the oedipal conflict in these two dramatic works. Canfield claims that "both are plays in which sons repeatedly attempt to fill the void left by absent fathers" and that, somewhat ironically perhaps, Robert and James are linked because "each rejects what his father stands for."[18]

Canfield also acknowledges how this singular reading doesn't completely satisfy, revealing once again the complexity of the narrative structure and thematic range which McCarthy employs here. Canfield attributes this to the fact that both texts "ultimately resolve themselves into McCarthy's usual cryptic theodicy," and in this instance, it is ironically "a theodicy that is ultimately escapist, nostalgic for a pre-capitalist patriarchy where workers are not alienated from their labor."[19] The oedipal narrative fuses with a critique of the emerging capitalist system whereby James actively promotes this alienation whilst Robert, partly through his attempt to ensure that his mother is buried at the family plot, seeks to transcend this condition caused by modern industrial relations. This feeling of alienation from labor is a phenomenon felt by other McCarthy characters, most notably Marion Sylder in *The Orchard Keeper* when he engineers his firing from the sawmill and in *Suttree* when the eponymous hero refuses to entertain the prospect of "regular" work early on in the novel.

Canfield observes that McCarthy memorably employs a castration motif as part of his critique of this emerging system. The initial castration carried out by the powerful Greggs upon the powerless, voiceless McEvoys is upon Robert itself, as one suspects (although the timekeeper denies) that the accident that led to the amputation of

---

[18] Canfield, "Oedipal Complexities," 97-121.
[19] Ibid., 16.

Robert's leg was actually caused by James himself. Thus the amputation becomes a symbolic castration, and Patrick McEvoy especially is made impotent by the powerful hegemony which the Greggs, especially James, represent. In the fatal confrontation between James and Robert the former displays all the arrogance and blindness associated with the capitalist ethos as he offers to buy off Robert in exactly the same manner, and offering exactly the same money, as he did with Martha. As a result, "Robert shoots him where poetic justice dictates, in his lubricious abdomen. Robert has castrated his rival, momentarily seizing the phallus from the agent of hegemonic power." Furthermore Robert is castrated in terms of legal discourse, as he is left "impotent in his trial, unable to speak to defend himself."[20]

Canfield insightfully draws our attention to how McCarthy's work can be related to Rene Girard's seminal text *Violence and the Sacred*, something Gary Ciuba does in his analysis of *Child of God*. Girard is interested in how cultures "scapegoat" certain individuals or groups in order to reinforce their sense of superiority; the "center" or authoritative agency (in this case the Greggs) says, in effect, "we represent *this* and are therefore moral, trustworthy or so on," whereas the scapegoat (in this case Robert McEvoy) represents everything that the center isn't. The scapegoats are therefore labeled as a threat, as dangerous outlaws when, in reality, all they may simply do is have the courage and integrity to reveal the hypocrisy of the culture they have been excluded by. The inevitable conclusion is an act of often brutal violence carried out (and fully sanctioned by) the "center" in order to cleanse itself of this dangerous other and to reinforce its sense of superiority. Although two very different characters, Robert

---

[20] Ibid., 19-20.

McEvoy shares the fate of Lester Ballard in this respect, as Canfield illustrates:

> This twinning seems related to the mythic conflict between twins analyzed by René Girard in *Violence and the Sacred*. The violence between twins represents a societal implosion, threatening endless reciprocal violence if it is not halted by the sacrifice of a scapegoat. The violence between the patriarchs—a violence destined by the very nature of the antithesis between management and labor—is displaced onto their sons in the absence of their fathers.[21]

Despite the brutal and unjust fate which awaits Robert, Canfield, like Luce, maintains that some vestige of Robert's spirit survives; however, whereas Luce identified Martha as the defiant survivor, Canfield surprisingly opts for his father Patrick. Canfield claims that "thanks to Robert's surrogate patriarchal actions, his father seems momentarily freed to defy the system itself. He defies the company and Catholic doctrine by cremating Mrs. McEvoy's rotting corpse, a kind of ritual immolation."[22] Martha finds some kind of oppositional identity against the prevailing cultural and social doctrine of her time in narrative, in validating Robert's memory in an authentic tale that was denied him in his own life, and Patrick finds his by defying the dictates of capitalist and church power in a characteristically ardenthearted, if perhaps somewhat futile, action.

Like Luce, Canfield succeeds in revealing the multilayered complexity of *The Gardener's Son*, and he does this by drawing our atten-

---

[21] Ibid., 17.
[22] Ibid., 21.

tion to the overlapping themes of the oedipal conflict between father and son, McCarthy's critique of the aggressive New South capitalist system, and the manner in which the collective, hegemonic authority scapegoats Robert and sanctions his removal. The tragedy here, of course, is that James Gregg has also betrayed his father's legacy, and in "killing" his father's ideology—to borrow a phrase from Canfield—he effectively kills the system that had maintained at least some kind of peaceful equilibrium over Graniteville.

John Cant is another critic who has provided an illuminating analysis of *The Gardener's Son*. Cant claims that whilst "the continuing theme of the rebellious son and his relationship with his father is what first strikes one," a further close analysis "reveals it to be interwoven with a number of other concerns which make it a complex and more satisfying work of considerably more depth than *The Stonemason*."[23] A level of critical consensus can therefore be found, and all three critics agree that the screenplay is a challenging work that warrants close textual and historical analysis.

Cant illustrates how McCarthy critiques "the problem of history" by stressing how narrative and storytelling can represent a corrective to official records. Although by no means alone in making an observation such as this, Cant makes the important point that "history and justice are owned by the powerful and … fiction may be used to subvert this cultural hegemony."[24] The fictional text of *The Gardener's Son* therefore gives Robert the justice that was denied him during his life as the trial

---

[23] Cant, *Cormac McCarthy and the Myth of American Exceptionalism*, 137.
[24] Ibid., 139.

reveals how the administration of "justice" is concerned to protect the interest of the governing class. Robert is prevented from speaking by his own lawyers who are mindful of their need to keep on the right side of the Greggs ... Neither activity, judicial process nor the writing of history, is free of the constraints imposed by the power of those who run society.[25]

Cant also comments on the castration motif that Canfield identified as functioning throughout the text. Cant focuses on how Mrs. Gregg, far from sharing in the benevolence of her husband's enterprise, actually revels in how she "arrogates to herself the power of life and death itself over the mill's employees and their families, and that she does this as a function of power inherent in the class system ... She is ruthless in her self-righteousness as she imposes her will on Robert." Furthermore, Cant notes that she "imposes the relentless medical logic of the situation on Robert just as her husband has imposed economic logic on the town."[26] Cant notes how the Greggs implode and bring about their own demise, as when James takes up his position of power "his egotism is one of the principal factors in provoking his own demise." In a move which parallels Patrick's defiant gesture at the close of the text, Mrs. Gregg, "seemingly so strong and stable[,] descends into her own gothic world of death in life: in a bourgeois parody of the Bundrens' [the grotesque family from William Faulkner's *As I Lay Dying*] epic task she has all her family dead exhumed and removed from Graniteville to her place of origin,

---

[25] Ibid., 145-46.
[26] Ibid., 142-143.

Charleston."[27] Thus the narrative of the two families concludes as separately as they began, with Mrs. Gregg fleeing to her place from this *kind* of people, whilst Patrick McEvoy offers a defiant gesture to the type of people that the Greggs represent.

Cant also offers an intelligent and sympathetic reading of Robert. Like some other notable McCarthy characters Robert displays a natural, if uncultivated, intelligence. His ability to grasp the hopelessness of his family's situation propels him upon his quest as Cant notes: "Robert's isolation is increased by his intelligence. His deeper understanding of the world makes it more difficult for him to communicate with those nearest and dearest to him who do not share his perceptions or values." This uncultivated self-consciousness means that, like many of McCarthy's mythic protagonists, Robert "is a man of death" whose "acquiescence in his own death is an existential choice for one who wishes to escape from an intolerable life … His intelligence, initiative, energy, and 'ardentheartedness' have been frustrated and turned to destructive ends by poverty, impotence, misfortune, and the restrictions imposed upon his class." Cant adds that "unlike Suttree, Robert's fate has been too harsh for him to 'choose life.'"[28] Cant's reading of Robert here, identifying his innate characteristics of intelligence, initiative, and energy, reads like a checklist for the self-improvement and material comfort needed to fulfill the much-trumpeted myth and rhetoric of the American dream. However Robert is another in a long line of McCarthy characters who has been tragically aware of how his share in this mythology has been denied.

---

[27] Ibid., 152.
[28] Ibid., 148-49.

Perhaps the most notable aspect of Cant's reading of the screenplay is his informed analysis of how it reveals the changing socioeconomic and racial landscape of the "New South" in the epochal period of Reconstruction. Cant notes that *The Gardener's Son* subtly contradicts the carpetbagger and scalawag stereotypes, and the prominent role given to blacks—especially during the trial—reflects the radical changes taking place during Reconstruction. This is not to suggest, of course, that McCarthy simplifies the trauma of this period (Whipper's remarks to Patrick about the nature of justice in the world support this), but it is another reflection of the complex social, cultural, and political realities of the period that he documents in the screenplay. We should also note how a series of African American characters that have peripheral roles in the narrative impart, as marginal characters so often do in McCarthy's other work, some of the most cryptic yet profound advice in the screenplay. Cant notes that the physical and historical setting of the action allows "McCarthy to deal with the subject of race in a way that his East Tennessee locations do not" and that the "characterization of blacks in the text is significant in that they are presented as inherently the same as the whites, a radical departure from the mythic depictions of the 1870s."[29]

Cant also offers an informed synopsis of the screenplay which allows us to contextualize its place within McCarthy's body of Southern work and as an historical drama in its own right:

> It deals in a convincing fashion with the profound theme of the nature of history, of historical truth as essentially unknowable and of the relation between power and both

---

[29] Ibid., 153.

> history and justice. It presents narrative fiction as the only means of expressing something that approaches the complexity of actual human lives and historical events. It places the story of the deaths of Robert McEvoy and James Gregg in the context of the historical drama of the "New South" and subtly undermines the South's myth of Reconstruction ... [*The Gardener's Son*] exhibits a complex interweaving of profound themes beneath a seemingly simple and melodramatic surface.[30]

We have therefore seen how McCarthy uses the untold story of Robert McEvoy and the community of Graniteville to reveal the "rules of exclusion" that, as Foucault claims, hegemonic discourses attempt to conceal from us. McCarthy's narrative encourages us to reexamine our own historical consciousness, to analyze the relationship between history and fiction, and to recognize the dangers his characters face when denied the power to tell or narrate their own stories. McCarthy's only published screenplay is a typically multifaceted work which denies a singular reading but which reveals the inescapable complexity and paradoxes of Appalachia's historical narrative, as mythically represented in the narratives of the McEvoys and the Greggs.

---

[30] Ibid., 152-3.

Conclusion

The narrator of Peter Taylor's *In the Tennessee Country* opens the novel by referring to members of his family, who were usually male and of varying ages, who had disappeared. The narrator doesn't express shock but attributes their disappearance to the fact that they "very likely felt the urging of some inner compulsion" for flight, for searching out spaces where they could find the mythic identity that was denied them in their contemporary reality.[1] Taylor generally writes about educated, informed, and middle-class Southerners who inhabit an entirely different social and cultural world to McCarthy's characters, but *In the Tennessee Country* explores the malaise which also afflicts McCarthy's protagonists.

In all of the works discussed in this study, McCarthy has written about "ardenthearted" figures who feel "some inner compulsion" for flight and escape. The profound melancholic force his fiction achieves is derived when this compulsion for flight clashes against the material historical realities of a world that cares little for their mythic aspirations. McCarthy's work is undoubtedly complex, but once readers become attuned to his hybrid style which fuses mimetic, mythical, and allegorical tropes, our work in reading his texts is very much rewarded. Although he dispenses with many familiar conventional techniques and narrative strategies that readers may depend upon for establishing meaning and linearity in fiction, McCarthy, by subverting these patterns, reaffirms the majestic scope

---

[1] Taylor, *In the Tennessee Country*, 3.

of the novelistic form. His manipulation of mythical and allegorical narrative strategies is especially notable in this respect.

His Southern work can be viewed as part of a broader Appalachian discourse which critiques foundational Southern and American myths and cultural narratives. This discourse gives a voice to those individuals and groups who inhabit this "other America" and who have been absented from official historical records and artifacts. The works discussed in this study particularly critique pastoral ideology, and the emergence of McCarthy's "wilderness aesthetic" is perhaps the most notable development across these texts.

The oedipal theme is obviously of central importance to McCarthy's aesthetic, but the ecological consciousness represented by McCarthy's Southern texts may well be their most significant feature. *The Road* offers the most apocalyptic configuration of these themes, but this aspect of McCarthy's style, his perhaps even mystical or spiritual ability, as Edwin Arnold has claimed, which "venerates life in all its forms" has been a part of his aesthetic since the publication of *The Orchard Keeper*.[2] All of his Southern works map out new ecological, physical, and internal ethical and moral geographies that reach beyond conventional means of ordering the world.

McCarthy's work obviously reverberates beyond East Tennessee and Appalachia, but we should not underestimate how much the region has informed McCarthy's artistic development. The humor, tall tales, and oral traditions indigenous to the region are lovingly recreated in McCarthy's Southern texts, and this love for narrative informs his Western and Southwestern works. If McCarthy is a "godless writer in a godless world," his belief in narrative as a humanizing

---

[2] Arnold, "McCarthy and the Sacred," 216.

act ultimately rescues his work from charges of nihilism. James D. Lilley remarks that "for McCarthy, storytelling is the definitive human activity," and for Lilley "McCarthy suggests that our agency, our 'faith in being,' can be idealized only to the extent that we accept the role of storyteller and witness."[3]

This study does not claim to be exhaustive, but it is the author's hope that readers are better equipped to navigate around and through McCarthy's texts. At the time of writing we await to hear when McCarthy's next text will be published (the long-rumored New Orleans novel is still hotly talked about on internet message boards, yet no publication date is confirmed), and we have yet to see if the adaptation of *The Road* can replicate the success of *No Country for Old Men*. Whilst his hybrid and multifaceted style is undoubtedly challenging, these characteristics ensure that McCarthy's work will provide a stimulating experience for many generations to come.

---

[3] Lilley, "There was Map Enough," 2-3.

Bibliography

Primary Works

McCarthy, Cormac. *Blood Meridian, or, The Evening Redness in the West*. London: Picador, 1989. [First edition, Random House, 1985].

———. *The Border Trilogy: Omnibus Edition*. London: Picador, 2002.

———. *Child of God*. New York: Vintage, 1993. [First edition, Random House, 1973].

"A Drowning Incident." 1960. *The Phoenix: 40th Anniversary Edition*. University of Tennessee, Knoxville. March 2000.

———. *The Gardener's Son*. Hopewell, New Jersey: The Ecco Press, 1996.

———. Interview with Oprah Winfrey. Online video clip. YouTube. Accessed on 22 July 2008. <http://www.youtube.com/watch?v=iNuc3sxzlyQ>.

———. *No Country for Old Men*. New York: Knopf, 2005.

———. *The Orchard Keeper*. New York: Vintage, 1993. [First edition, Random House, 1986].

———. *Outer Dark*. New York: Vintage, 1993. [First edition, Random House, 1988].

———. *The Road*. New York: Vintage, 2006.

———. *The Stonemason*. London: Picador, 1994.

———. *The Sunset Limited*. New York: Vintage, 2006.

———. *Suttree*. New York: Vintage, 1992. [First edition, Random House, 1979].

———. "Wake for Susan." *The Phoenix*, University of Tennessee, October 1959.

Secondary Works

Agar, Herbert, and Allen Tate, eds. *Who Owns America? A New Declaration of Independence*. Wilmington, DE: ISI Books, 1999.

Arnold, Edwin T. "Blood and Grace: The Fiction of Cormac McCarthy." *Commonweal* 121 (November 4, 1994): 11-16.

———. "Cormac McCarthy's *The Stonemason*: The Unmaking of a Play." In *Myth, Legend, Dust, Critical Responses to Cormac McCarthy*, edited by Rick Wallach, 141-154. Manchester: University of Manchester Press, 2000.

———. "Introduction." *The Cormac McCarthy Journal Special Issue: Suttree* 5, no. 1 (2005): 2-6.

———. "McCarthy and the Sacred: A Reading of *The Crossing*." In *Cormac McCarthy: New Directions*, edited by James Lilley, 215-38. Albuquerque: University of New Mexico Press, 2002.

———. "The Mosaic of McCarthy's Fiction." In *Sacred Violence*, edited by Wade Hall and Rick Wallach, 17-23. El Paso: Texas Western Press, 1995.

———. "The Mosaic of McCarthy's Fiction, Continued." In Hall and Wallach, 2002, 179-87.

———. "Naming, Knowing and Nothingness: McCarthy's Moral Parables." In *Perspectives on Cormac McCarthy*, edited by Edwin Arnold and Dianne Luce, revised edition, 45-69. Jackson: University Press of Mississippi, 1999.

———, and Dianne C. Luce, eds. "Introduction." In *Perspectives on Cormac McCarthy*, 1-16. Jackson: University Press of Mississippi, 1999.

———. "The World of *The Orchard Keeper*." In Holloway, "Proceedings of the First European Conference on Cormac McCarthy," 1-5.

Ash, Stephen, ed. *Secessionists and Other Scoundrels: Selections from Parson Brownlow's Book*. Baton Rouge: Louisiana State University Press, 1999.

Baldick, Chris. *The Oxford Dictionary of Literary Terms*. Oxford University Press, 2008. *Oxford Reference Online*. Oxford University Press. University of Tennessee. 13 August 2008.

Barthes, Roland. *Image-Music-Text*. Translated by Stephen Heath. New York: Hill and Wang, 1977.

———. *Mythologies*. Translated by Annette Lavers. New York: Hill and Wang, 1972.

Bartlett, Andrew. "From Voyeurism to Archaeology: Cormac McCarthy's *Child of God*." *The Southern Literary Journal* 24, no. 1 (Fall 1991): 3-15.

Bell, Vereen. *The Achievement of Cormac McCarthy*. Baton Rouge: Louisiana State University Press, 1988.

Bercovitch, Sacvan. *The American Jeremiad*. Madison: University of Wisconsin Press, 1978.

Berry, Wendell. *A Continuous Harmony: Essays Cultural and Agricultural*. New York: Harcourt Brace, 1972.

Berry, Wesley K. "The Lay of the Land in Cormac McCarthy's *The Orchard Keeper* and *Child of God*." *The Southern Quarterly* 38, no. 4 (Summer 2000): 61-77.

Best, Steven, and Douglas Kellner, eds. *Postmodern Theory: Critical Interrogations*. London: Macmillan, 1991.

"Bildungsroman." *The Oxford Dictionary of Literary Terms*. Chris Baldick. Oxford University Press, 2008. *Oxford Reference Online*. Oxford University Press. University of Tennessee. 27 August 2008.

Billings, Dwight B., Gurney Norman and Katherine Ledford, eds. *Confronting Appalachian Stereotypes: Back Talk from an American Region*. Lexington: University Press of Kentucky, 1999.

Bilton, Alan. *An Introduction to Contemporary American Fiction.* Edinburgh: Edinburgh University Press, 2002.

Bingham, Emily S., and Thomas A. Underwood. *The Southern Agrarians and the New Deal: Essays after "I'll Take My Stand."* Charlottesville: University Press of Virginia, 2001.

Bone, Martyn. *The Postsouthern Sense of Place in Contemporary American Fiction.* Baton Rouge: Louisiana State University Press, 2005.

Branscome, James. *The Federal Government in Appalachia.* New York: Field Foundation, 1977.

Brickman, Barbara. "Imposition and Resistance in *The Orchard Keeper*." In *Myth, Legend, Dust: Critical Responses to Cormac McCarthy*, edited by Wallach, 55-67.

Buell, Lawrence. "American Pastoral Ideology Reappraised." *American Literary History* 1, no. 1, (Spring 1989): 1-29.

Bulson, Eric. *Novels, Maps, Modernity: The Spatial Imagination, 1865-2000.* New York: Routledge, 2008.

Butterworth, D. S. "Pearls as Swine: Recentering the Marginal in Cormac McCarthy's *Suttree*." In *Sacred Violence Volume I: Cormac McCarthy's Appalachian Works*, edited by Wade Hall and Rick Wallach, 131-8. El Paso: Texas Western Press, 2002.

Camus, Albert. *The Myth of Sisyphus.* Translated by Justin O'Brien. London: Penguin Books, 2000.

Canfield, J. Douglas. "The Dawning of the Age of Aquarius: Abjection, Identity, and the Carnivalesque in Cormac McCarthy's *Suttree*." *Contemporary Literature* 44, no. 4 (Winter 2003): 664-96.

———. "Oedipal Complexities in Cormac McCarthy's *The Stonemason* and *The Gardener's Son*." *Cormac McCarthy Journal* 2 (Spring 2002): 12-22.

Cant, John. *Cormac McCarthy and the Myth of American Exceptionalism.* London: Routledge, 2007.

Carr, Duane. "The Dispossessed White as Naked Ape and Stereo-typed Hillbilly in the Southern Novels of Cormac Mc-Carthy." *Midwest Quarterly* 40, no. 1 (1998): 1-9.

Cawelti, John G. "Cormac McCarthy: Restless Seekers." In *An American Vein: Critical Readings in Appalachian Literature*, edited by Danny Miller, Sharon Hatfield, and Gurney Norman, 306-314. Athens: Ohio University Press, 2005.

Chabon, Michael. "After the Apocalypse." Review of *The Road* by Cormac McCarthy. *The New York Times Review of Books* 54, no. 2 (February 15, 2007).

Chollier, Christine, ed. *Cormac McCarthy: Uncharted Territories/ Territories Inconnus*. Reims, France: University of Reims Press, 2003.

Cimprich, John. "Slavery's End in East Tennessee." In *Appalachians and Race: The Mountain South from Slavery to Segregation*, edited by John Roscoe. Lexington: University Press of Kentucky, 2002, 189-198.

Ciuba, Gary. *Desire, Violence and Divinity in Modern Southern Fiction: Katherine Anne Porter, Flannery O'Connor, Walker Percy and Cormac McCarthy*. Baton Rouge: Louisiana State University Press, 2007.

Conkin, Paul K. *The Southern Agrarians*. Nashville, Tennessee: Vanderbilt University Press, 2001.

Coupe, Laurence. *Myth*. London: Routledge, 1997.

Cummings, William Joseph III. *Community, Violence and the Nature of Change: Whitecapping in Sevier County, Tennessee, During the 1890s*. MA thesis, University of Tennessee, June 1988.

Davenport, Guy. "Silurian Southern." *National Review* 31, no. 11 (March 16, 1979): 368-69.

Deaderick, Lucile, ed. *Heart of the Valley: A History of Knoxville, Tennessee*. Knoxville: East Tennessee Historical Society, 1976.

Ditsky, John. "Further Into Darkness: The Novels of Cormac McCarthy." *Hollins Critic* 18, no. 2 (April 1981): 1-11.

Donoghue, Denis. *The Practice of Reading*. New Haven: Yale University Press, 1998.

Dunn, Durwood. *Cades Cove: The Life and Death of a Southern Appalachian Community, 1818-1937*. Knoxville: University of Tennessee Press, 2007.

Eddins, Dwight. "'Everything a Hunter and Everything Hunted': Schopenhauer and Cormac McCarthy's *Blood Meridian*." *Critique* 45, no. 1 (Fall 2003): 25-33.

Edwards, Tim. "The End of the Road: Pastoralism and the Post-Apocalyptic Waste Land in Cormac McCarthy's *The Road*." In *The Road Home: Cormac McCarthy's Imaginative Return to the South* (conference proceedings, April 25-28 2007), edited by Chris Walsh. Knoxville: University of Tennessee Newfound Press, 2007. http://www.lib.utk.edu/newfoundpress/pubs/mccarthy/timedwardsarticle.pdf

Eller, Ronald D. "Foreword." *Confronting Appalachian Stereotypes: Back Talk from an American Region*, edited by Dwight Billings, Gurney Norman, and Katherine Ledford, ix-xi. Lexington: University Press of Kentucky, 1999.

———. *Miners, Millhands and Mountaineers: Industrialization of the Appalachian South, 1880-1930*. Knoxville: University of Tennessee Press, 1982.

Ellis, Jay. *No Place for Home: Spatial Constraint and Character Flight in the Novels of Cormac McCarthy*. New York: Routledge, 2006.

———. "McCarthy's Sense of Ending." *The Road Home: Cormac McCarthy's Imaginative Return to the South*. In *The Road Home: Cormac McCarthy's Imaginative Return to the South*, edited by Walsh. http://www.lib.utk.edu/newfoundpress/pubs/mccarthy/jayellisarticle.pdf

Emerson, Ralph Waldo. *Essays and Poems by Ralph Waldo Emerson.* New York: Barnes & Noble Classics, 2004.

Evenson, Brian. "McCarthy's Wanderers: Nomadology, Violence, and Open Country." Hall and Wallach, 1995, 41-47.

Fielder, Leslie. *Love and Death in the American Novel.* New York: Criterion Books, 1960.

Fisher-Wirth, Ann. "Abjection and 'the feminine' in *Outer Dark.*" In *Cormac McCarthy: New Directions*, edited by Lilley, 125-140.

Foster, Ruel E, ed. *Appalachian Literature: Critical Essays.* Charleston, WV: MHC Publications, 1976.

Foucault, Michel. *The Archaeology of Knowledge.* Translated by A. M. Sheridan Smith. London: Routledge, 1997.

Frye, Steven. "Fate Without Foreknowledge: Style and Image in the Late Naturalism of Cormac McCarthy." *The Cormac McCathy Journal Special Issue:* Suttree. 5, no. 1 (2005): 184-194.

Gallivan, Euan. "Compassionate McCarthy? *The Road* and Schopenhauerian Ethics." In *The Road Home: Cormac McCarthy's Imaginative Return to the South*, edited by Walsh. http://www.lib.utk.edu/newfoundpress/pubs/mccarthy/euangallivanarticle.pdf

Gay, Peter, ed. *The Freud Reader.* New York: W. W. Norton, 1989.

Gifford, Terry. *Pastoral.* London: Routledge, 1999.

Giles, James R. *Violence in the Contemporary American Novel.* Columbia, SC: University of South Carolina Press, 2000.

Girard, Rene. *Violence and the Sacred.* Translated by Patrick Gregory. London: Continuum, 2005.

Graham, Alison. "The South in Popular Culture." In *A Companion to the Literature and Culture of the American South*, edited by Richard Gray and Owen Robinson. Oxford: Blackwell, 2007, 335-351.

Grammer, John. "A Thing Against Which Time Will Not Prevail: Pastoral and History in Cormac McCarthy's South." In *Perspectives on Cormac McCarthy*, edited by Arnold and Luce, 29-44.

Grant, Natalie "The Landscape of the Soul: Man and the Natural World in *The Orchard Keeper*," Hall and Wallach, 1995, 60-68.

Graves, Robert. *The Greek Myths: Complete Edition*. London: Penguin Books, 1992.

Gray, Richard. *The Literature of Memory: Modern Writers of the American South*. Baltimore: John Hopkins University Press, 1977.

———. *Southern Aberrations: Writers of the American South and the Problem of Regionalism*. Baton Rouge: Louisiana State University Press, 2000.

———, and Owen Robinson, eds. *A Companion to the Literature and Culture of the American South*. Oxford: Blackwell, 2007.

Guillemin, Georg. *The Pastoral Vision of Cormac McCarthy*. College Station: Texas A&M Press, 2004.

———. "'Books Made Out of Books': Some Instances of Intertextuality with Southern Literature in *Outer Dark*." In Holloway, "Proceedings of the First European Conference on Cormac McCarthy," 28-34.

Guinn, Matthew. *After Southern Modernism*. Jackson: University Press of Mississippi, 2000.

Hall, Wade. "The Hero as Philosopher and Survivor: An Afterword on *The Stonemason* and *The Crossing*." In *Sacred Violence: A Reader's Companion to Cormac McCarthy*, edited by Hall and Wallach, 1995, 189-94.

———. "The Human Comedy of Cormac McCarthy." In *Sacred Violence: A Reader's Companion to Cormac McCarthy*, edited by Hall and Wallach, 1995, 49-60.

———, and Rick Wallach, eds. *Sacred Violence: A Reader's Companion to Cormac McCarthy*. El Paso: Texas Western Press, 1995. 2nd ed. titled *Sacred Violence*. 2 Vols, Vol. 1: *Cormac McCarthy's Appalachian Works*. Vol. 2: *Cormac McCarthy's Western Works*. 2002.

Higgs, Robert J., Ambrose N. Manning, and Jim Wayne Miller, eds. *Appalachia Inside Out: A Sequel to Voices from the Hills*. Knoxville: University of Tennessee Press, 1995.

Hoffman, Gerhard. "Strangeness, Gaps, and the Mystery of Life: Cormac McCarthy's Southern Novels." *Amerikastudien/ American Studies* 42, no. 2 (1997): 217-38.

Holloway, David. *The Late Modernism of Cormac McCarthy*. Westport, CT: Greenwood Press, 2002.

———, ed. *Proceedings of the First European Conference on Cormac McCarthy*. Miami: Cormac McCarthy Society, 1999.

Horton, Matthew R. "'Hallucinated Recollections': Narrative as Spatialized Perception of History in *The Orchard Keeper*." In *Cormac McCarthy: New Directions*, edited by Lilley, 285-312.

James, Henry. "The Art of Fiction." In *The Norton Anthology of American Fiction. Volume C: 1865-1914*, edited by Nina Baym, 553-567. New York: Norton, 2003.

Jarrett, Robert J. *Cormac McCarthy*. New York: Twayne, 1997.

Jarvis, Brian. *Postmodern Cartographies: The Geographical Imagination in Contemporary American Culture*. New York: St. Martin's Press, 1998.

Josyph, Peter. "Suttree and the Brass Ring: Reaching for Thanksgiving in the Knoxville Gutter." *The Cormac McCarthy Journal Special Issue: Suttree* 5, no. 1 (2005): 220-235.

———. "Older Professions: The Fourth Wall of *The Stonemason*." In *Myth, Legend, Dust: Critical Responses to Cormac McCarthy*, edited by Wallach, 119-40.

Kephart, Horace. *Our Southern Highlanders: A Narrative of Adventure in the Southern Appalachians and a Study of Life Among the Mountaineers.* Knoxville: University of Tennessee Press, 2004.

King, Richard H. *A Southern Renaissance: The Cultural Awakening of the American South, 1930-1955.* Oxford: Oxford University Press, 1980.

Kolodny, Annette. *The Lay of the Land: Metaphor as Experience and History in American Life and Letters.* Chapel Hill: University of North Carolina Press, 1975.

Kristeva, Julia. *Powers of Horror: An Essay on Abjection.* Translated by Leon S. Roudiez. New York: Columbia University Press, 1982.

Lachaud, Maxime. "Carnivalesque Rituals and the Theological Grotesque in the Southern Novels of Harry Crews and Cormac McCarthy." In *Uncharted Territories/Territories Inconnus*, edited by Chollier, 61-70.

Lang, John, ed. *Appalachia and Beyond: Conversations with Writers from the Mountain South.* Knoxville: University of Tennessee Press, 2006.

———. *An Introduction to Fred Chappell.* Columbia: University of South Carolina Press, 2000.

———. "Lester Ballard: McCarthy's Challenge to the Reader's Compassion." In Hall and Wallach, 1995, 87-94.

Lefebvre, Henri. *The Production of Space.* Translated by Donald Nicholson-Smith. Oxford: Blackwell, 1991.

Lewis, Ronald L. "Beyond Isolation and Homogeneity: Diversity and the History of Appalachia." In Billings, Norman, and Ledford, 21-43.

Lilley, James D, ed. *Cormac McCarthy: New Directions.* Albuquerque: University of New Mexico Press, 2002.

———. "Introduction. 'There Was Map Enough for Men to Read:' Storytelling, the Border Trilogy and *New Directions*." In *Cormac McCarthy: New Directions*, edited by Lilley, 1-15.

Lloyd-Smith, Alan. *American Gothic Fiction: An Introduction*. London: Continuum, 2004.

Longley, John Lewis, Jr. "*Suttree* and the Metaphysics of Death." *The Southern Literary Journal* 17, no. 2 (Spring 1985): 79-90.

Lytle, Andrew. "The Hand Tit." In *I'll Take My Stand: The South and the Agrarian Tradition*, edited by Twelve Southerners. New York: Harper, 1962, 201-245.

Luce, Dianne. "The Cave of Oblivion: Platonic Mythology in *Child of God*." In *Cormac McCarthy: New Directions*, edited by Lilley, 171-98.

———. "Cormac McCarthy: A Bibliography." July 2007 Update. Accessed 20 September 2008. http://www.mid.tec.sc.us/edu/ed/eng/biblio.htm

———. "Cormac McCarthy's First Screenplay: 'The Gardener's Son.'" In *Perspectives on Cormac McCarthy*, edited by Arnold and Luce, 71-96.

———. "Beyond the Border: Cormac McCarthy in the New Millennium." In *The Road Home: Cormac McCarthy's Imaginative Return to the South*, edited by Walsh. http://www.lib.utk.edu/newfoundpress/pubs/mccarthy/dianneluceintroduction.pdf

———. "The Road and the Matrix: The World as Tale in *The Crossing*." In *Perspectives on Cormac McCarthy*, edited by Arnold and Luce, 195-219.

———. "'They aint the thing': Artifact and Hallucinated Recollection in Cormac McCarthy's Early Frame-Works." In *Myth, Legend, Dust*, edited by Wallach, 21-36.

Lukács, Georg. *The Theory of the Novel: A Historico-Philosophical*

Essay on the Forms of Epic Literature. Translated by Anna Bostock. Cambridge, Massachusetts: MIT Press, 1971.

MacArthur, William. "Knoxville History: An Interpretation." *Heart of the Valley: A History of Knoxville, Tennessee*, edited by Lucile Deaderick. Knoxville: East Tennessee Historical Society Press, 1976.

Madsen, Deborah L. *American Exceptionalism.* Jackson: University Press of Mississippi, 1998.

Malin, Irving. *New American Gothic.* Carbondale: South Illinois University Press, 1962.

Marius, Richard. "*Suttree* as Window into the Soul of Cormac McCarthy." In *Sacred Violence,* edited by Hall and Wallach, 1995, 1-15.

McDonald, Michael J., and John Muldowny. *TVA and the Dispossessed: The Resettlement of Population in the Norris Dam Area.* Knoxville: University of Tennessee Press, 1982.

McKoy, Karissa. "Whiteness and the 'Subject' of Waste: The Art of Slumming in *Suttree.*" *The Cormac McCarthy Journal Special Issue:* Suttree 5, no. 1 (2005): 85-99.

Meriwether, James, and Michael Millgate, eds. *Lion in the Garden: Interviews with William Faulkner.* New York: Random House, 1968.

Millard, Kenneth. *Contemporary American Fiction.* Oxford: Oxford University Press, 2000.

Miller, Danny L., Sharon Hatfield, and Gurney Norman, eds. *An American Vein: Critical Readings in Appalachian Literature.* Athens: Ohio University Press, 2005.

Miller, Perry. *Errand into the Wilderness.* Cambridge, Massachusetts: Harvard University Press, 1956.

Mitchell, Broadus. *William Gregg, Factory Master of the Old South.* Chapel Hill: University of North Carolina Press, 1928.

Morgan, Robert. "Cormac McCarthy: The Novel Raised from the Dead." *Cormac McCarthy Journal* 1 (Spring 2001): 12-25.

Morgan, Wesley G. "Red Callahan in *Suttree*: The Actual and the Fictitious." *The Cormac McCarthy Journal Special Issue:* Suttree 5, no. 1 (2005): 210-219.

———. "The Route and Roots of *The Road*." In *The Road Home: Cormac McCarthy's Imaginative Return to the South*, edited by Walsh. http://www.lib.utk.edu/newfoundpress/pubs/mccarthy/wesmorganarticle.pdf

———. "'A Season of Death and Epidemic Violence': Knoxville Rogues in *Suttree*." *The Cormac McCarthy Journal Special Issue: Suttree* 5, no. 1 (2005): 195-209.

Nash, Roderick Frazier. *Wilderness and the American Mind:* 4th ed. New Haven: Yale University Press, 2001.

Neely, Jack. "Excavating Knoxville Literature." In *Knoxville Bound: A Collection of Literary Works Inspired by Knoxville, Tennessee,* edited by Judy Loest and Jack Rentfro. Knoxville, Tennessee: Metropulse Publishing, 2004.

O'Gorman, Farrell. "Joyce and Contesting Priesthoods in *Suttree* and *Blood Meridian*." *The Cormac McCarthy Journal Special Issue:* Suttree 5, no. 1 (2005): 100-117.

Owens, Barclay. *Cormac McCarthy's Western Novels*. Tuscon: University of Arizona Press, 2000.

Palmer, Louis H. III. "'Encampment of the Damned': Ideology and Class in *Suttree*." *The Cormac McCarthy Journal Special Issue:* Suttree 5, no. 1 (2005): 149-170.

———. "Full Circle: *The Road* Rewrites *The Orchard Keeper*." In *The Road Home: Cormac McCarthy's Imaginative Return to the South*, edited by Walsh. http://www.lib.utk.edu/newfoundpress/pubs/mccarthy/louispalmerarticle.pdf

Parrish, Tim. "The Killer Wears the Halo: Cormac McCarthy, Flannery O'Connor, and the American Religion." In Hall and

Wallach, 1995, 25-39.

Patton, James Welch. *Unionism and Reconstruction in Tennessee, 1860-69.* Chapel Hill: University of North Carolina Press, 1934.

Peebles, Stacey. "*Suttree's* Soundscapes." *The Cormac McCarthy Journal Special Issue: Suttree* 5, no. 1 (2005): 137-148.

Phillips, Dana. "History and the Ugly Facts of *Blood Meridian.*" In *Cormac McCarthy: New Directions*, edited by Lilley, 17-46.

Polk, Noel. "A Faulknerian Looks at *Suttree.*" *The Cormac McCarthy Journal Special Issue: Suttree* 5, no. 1 (2005): 7-29.

Portrait and Biography of Parson Brownlow, The Tennessee Patriot. Indianapolis: Asher & Co., 1862.

Prather, William. "Absurd Reasoning in an Existential World: A Consideration of Cormac McCarthy's *Suttree.*" In Hall and Wallach, 1995, 103-114.

———. "The Color of This Life is Water." *The Cormac McCarthy Journal Special Issue: Suttree* 5, no. 1 (2005): 30-59.

———. "'Like Something Seen through Bad Glass': Narrative Strategies in *The Orchard Keeper.*" In *Myth, Legend, Dust: Critical Responses to Cormac McCarthy*, edited by Wallach, 37-54.

Rabinow, Paul, ed. *The Foucault Reader.* New York: Pantheon Books, 1984.

Ragan, David Paul. "Values and Structure in *The Orchard Keeper.*" In *Perspectives on Cormac McCarthy*, edited by Arnold and Luce. Jackson: University of Mississippi Press, 1999, 17-27.

Ransom, John Crowe. "Reconstructed but Unregenerate." In *I'll Take My Stand: The South and the Agrarian Tradition,* by Twelve Southerners, 1-27. Baton Rouge: Louisiana State University Press, 2006.

Reid, Ian. *The Short Story.* London: Methuen & Co, 1977.

"Resources." http://www.cormacmccarthy.com/Resources.htm. 28 August 2008.

Rosen, Elizabeth K. *Apocalyptic Transformation: Apocalypse and the Postmodern Imagination*. New York: Lexington Books, 2008.

Sanborn, Wallis R. III. *Animals in the Fiction of Cormac McCarthy*. Jefferson, NC: McFarland, 2006.

Schafer, William J. "Cormac McCarthy: The Hard Wages of Original Sin." *Appalachian Journal* 4 (Winter 1977): 105-19.

Schenkkan, Robert. *The Kentucky Cycle*. New York: Plume, 1993.

Shapiro, Henry. *Appalachia on Our Mind: The Southern Mountains and Mountaineers in the American Consciousness, 1870-1920*. Chapel Hill: University of North Carolina Press, 1978.

Simpson, Lewis P. *The Brazen Face of History: Studies in the Literary Consciousness in America*. Baton Rouge: Louisiana State University Press, 1980.

Snyder, Phillip. "Hospitality in Cormac McCarthy's *The Road*." In *The Road Home: Cormac McCarthy's Imaginative Return to the South*, edited by Walsh. http://www.lib.utk.edu/newfoundpress/pubs/mccarthy/phillipsnyderarticle.pdf

Spencer, William. "Cormac McCarthy's Unholy Trinity: Biblical Parody in *Outer Dark*." In *Sacred Violence, Volume I: Cormac McCarthy's Appalachian Works*, edited by Hall and Wallach, 2002, 69-76.

———. "The Extremities of Cormac McCarthy: The Major Character Types." Unpublished PhD diss., University of Tennessee, Knoxville, 1993.

———. "Seventh Direction, or Suttree's Vision Quest." In *Myth, Legend, Dust*, edited by Wallach, 100-07.

Sullivan, Nell. "Cormac McCarthy and the Text of Jouissance." In Hall and Wallach, 1995, 115-123.

———. "The Evolution of the Dead Girlfriend Motif in *Outer Dark* and *Child of God.*" In *Myth, Legend, Dust,* edited by Wallach, 68-77.

Sullivan, Walter. *A Requiem for the Renascence: The State of Fiction in the Modern South.* Athens: University of Georgia Press, 1976.

———. *In Praise of Blood Sports and Other Essays.* Baton Rouge: Louisiana State University Press, 1990.

Tate, Linda. "Southern Appalachia." In *A Companion to the Literature and Culture of the American South,* edited by Richard Gray and Owen Robinson, 130-147. Oxford: Blackwell, 2007.

Taylor, Peter. *In the Tennessee Country.* New York: Picador, 1994.

Traber, Daniel. "'Ruder Forms Survive,' or Slumming for Subjectivity: Self-Marginalization in *Suttree.*" *Southern Quarterly* 37, no. 2 (Winter 1999): 33-46.

Twelve Southerners. *I'll Take My Stand: The South and the Agrarian Tradition.* New York: Harper, 1962; 75th Anniversary Edition, Baton Rouge: Louisiana State University Press, 2006.

Tyburski, Susan. "'The Lingering Scent of Divinity' in Cormac McCarthy's *The Road* and *The Sunset Limited.*" In *The Road Home: Cormac McCarthy's Imaginative Return to the South,* edited by Walsh. http://www.lib.utk.edu/newfoundpress/pubs/mccarthy/susantyburskiarticle.pdf

Tytell, John. *Naked Angels: The Lives and Literature of the Beat Generation.* New York: McGraw-Hill, 1976.

Vanderheide, John. "Sighting Leviathan: Ritualism, Daemonism, and The Book of Job in McCarthy's Late Work" (privately distributed), *The Cormac McCarthy Journal* 6 (2007).

Vescio, Bryan. "Strangers in Everyland: *Suttree,* Huckleberry Finn, and Tragic Humanism." *The Cormac McCarthy Journal Special Issue: Suttree* 5, no. 1 (2005): 60-71.

Wallach, Rick. "Introduction: The McCarthy Canon Reconsidered." In Hall and Wallach, 1995, xv-xx.

———. "Prefiguring Cormac McCarthy: The Early Short Stories," In *Myth, Legend, Dust,* edited Rick Wallach, 15-20.

———, ed. *Myth, Legend, Dust: Critical Responses to Cormac McCarthy.* Manchester: Manchester University Press, 2000.

Walsh, Chris, ed. *The Road Home: Cormac McCarthy's Imaginative Return to the South* (conference proceedings, April 25-28, 2007, Knoxville). Knoxville: University of Tennessee Newfound Press, 2007. http://www.newfoundpress.utk.edu/pubs/mccarthy/program3.html

———. "'You talk like a godammned Yankee': Cormac McCarthy and East Tennessee Exceptionalism." Unpublished PhD. University of Wales, Swansea, 2004.

Warner, Alan. "The Road to Hell." Review of *The Road* by Cormac McCarthy. *The Guardian* (November 6, 2006). http://www.guardian.co.uk/books/2006/nov/04/featuresreviews.guardianreview4

Watson, Jay. "Lighting out for the Territory : *Suttree*, the Quentin Problem, and the Historical Unconscious." *The Cormac McCarthy Journal Special Issue:* Suttree 5, no. 1 (2005): 72-84.

Weaks-Baxter, Mary. *Reclaiming the American Farmer: The Reinvention of a Regional Mythology in Twentieth-Century Southern Writing.* Baton Rouge: Louisiana State University Press, 2006.

Wegner, John, ed. *The Cormac McCarthy Journal* 1, no. 1 (Spring 2001).

Weston, Ruth. *Gothic Traditions and Narrative Techniques in the Fiction of Eudora Welty.* Baton Rouge: Louisiana State University Press, 1994.

Wheeler, Bruce. *Knoxville, Tennessee: A Mountain City in the New South.* Knoxville: University of Tennessee Press, 2005.

Whitman, Jon. *Allegory: The Dynamics of an Ancient and Medieval Technique*. Boston: Harvard University Press, 1987.

Wilhelm, Randall S. "'Golden Chalice, Good to House a God': Still Life in *The Road*." In *The Road Home: Cormac McCarthy's Imaginative Return to the South*, edited by Walsh. http://www.lib.utk.edu/newfoundpress/pubs/mccarthy/randallwilhelmarticle.pdf

———. "'The Wrath of the Path': Spatial Politics and Municipal Powers in *Suttree*." *The Cormac McCarthy Journal Special Issue:* Suttree 5, no. 1 (2005): 118-136.

Winchell, Mark Royden. "Inner Dark: or, The Place of Cormac McCarthy." *The Southern Review* 26, no. 2 (April 1990): 293-309.

Witek, Terri. "'He's Hell When He's Well': Cormac McCarthy's Rhyming Dictions." In *Myth, Legend, Dust*, edited by Wallach, 78-88.

———. "Reeds and Hides: Cormac McCarthy's Domestic Spaces." *The Southern Review* 30, no. 1 (Winter 1994): 136-142.

Wood, James. *Getting to the End*. May 17 2007. http://www.powells.com/review/2007_05_17.html

Woodson, Linda. "The Road in Post-Postmodernism" (privately distributed). *The Cormac McCarthy Journal* Vol. 6 (2007).

———. "Visual Rhetoric and Cognitive Identity in *Suttree*." *The Cormac McCarthy Journal Special Issue:* Suttree 5, no. 1 (2005): 171-183.

Woodward, C. Vann. *The Burden of Southern History*. Enl. ed. Baton Rouge: Louisiana State University Press, 1970.

Woodward, Richard. "Cormac McCarthy's Venomous Fiction." *New York Times*, 19 April 1992.

Wright, Gavin. *Old South, New South: Revolutions in the Southern Economy Since the Civil War*. New York: Basic Books, 1986.

BIBLIOGRAPHY

Young, Thomas D. Jr. "The Imprisonment of Sensibility: *Suttree*," In *Perspectives on Cormac McCarthy*, edited by Arnold and Luce, 97-122.

Young, Thomas Daniel. *Tennessee Writers*. Knoxville: University of Tennessee Press, 1981.

www.ingramcontent.com/pod-product-compliance
Lightning Source LLC
Chambersburg PA
CBHW022058150426
43195CB00008B/179